THE NEW PRAETORIANS

A VOLUME IN THE SERIES
VETERANS

EDITED BY
**BRIAN MATTHEW JORDAN AND
J. ROSS DANCY**

THE NEW PRAETORIANS

AMERICAN VETERANS, SOCIETY, AND SERVICE
FROM VIETNAM TO THE FOREVER WAR

MICHAEL D. GAMBONE

UNIVERSITY OF MASSACHUSETTS PRESS
Amherst and Boston

Copyright © 2021 by University of Massachusetts Press
All rights reserved
Printed in the United States of America

ISBN 978-1-62534-611-7 (paper); 610-0 (hardcover)

Designed by Deste Roosa
Set in Adobe Caslon Pro and Bebas Neue Pro
Printed and bound by Books International, Inc.

Cover design by John Barnett, 4Eyes Design
Cover photo by Staff Sgt. Christopher S. Muncy, *Volunteers with the New York City Veteran's Alliance Hold the Ground Zero Flag during a March through Midtown Manhattan during the NYC Veteran's Day Parade November 11, 2017.* AB Forces news Collection / Alamy Stock Photo.

Library of Congress Cataloging-in-Publication Data

Names: Gambone, Michael D., 1963– author.
Title: The new praetorians : American veterans, society, and service from Vietnam to the forever war / Michael D. Gambone.
Other titles: American veterans, society, and service from Vietnam to the forever war
Description: Amherst : University of Massachusetts Press, [2021] | Series: Veterans | Includes bibliographical references and index.
Identifiers: LCCN 2021017191 (print) | LCCN 2021017192 (ebook) | ISBN 9781625346100 (hardcover) | ISBN 9781625346117 (paperback) | ISBN 9781613768860 (ebook) | ISBN 9781613768877 (ebook)
Subjects: LCSH: Veterans—United States—Social conditions. | Veterans—United States—History. | Veteran reintegration—United States. | Sociology, Military—United States.
Classification: LCC UB357 .G363 2021 (print) | LCC UB357 (ebook) | DDC 362.860973—dc23
LC record available at https://lccn.loc.gov/2021017191
LC ebook record available at https://lccn.loc.gov/2021017192

British Library Cataloguing-in-Publication Data
A catalog record for this book is available from the British Library.

THIS WORK IS DEDICATED TO:

DAVE BEOUGHER
TOM BUCCI
STEPHANIE CASADO
DAN CIRMINIELLO
DAN CURRY
JEFF DAVIS
KEKOA JUSTIN
RICH GARREN
BOBBY HOMAN
WILL JEFFERSON
ANDREW MORRIS
JOHN MUSCATEL
DEREK ORTIZ
CARISSA POKORNY GOLDEN
NORM SIGMOND
MATT STEFANCIN
LEANNE STRAUSS
NORM STRAUSS
JORDAN STOM
STEVE SULTZBACH

AND ALL THE REST.

CONTENTS

Acknowledgments
ix

INTRODUCTION
1

CHAPTER ONE
A Brief History of the American Veteran to the Vietnam War
8

CHAPTER TWO
Joining Up
16

CHAPTER THREE
The Nature of the Beast
33

CHAPTER FOUR
Coming Home
47

CHAPTER FIVE
Healing New Wounds
61

CHAPTER SIX
The Economics of the Veteran
78

CHAPTER SEVEN
Lost on Campus: Veterans and a College Education
101

CHAPTER EIGHT
The Veteran in Politics
117

CHAPTER NINE
The Women Praetorians
133

CHAPTER TEN
The Veteran in Popular Culture
146

CONCLUSIONS
160

Notes
165

Index
209

ACKNOWLEDGMENTS

I would like to thank the staff at the Kutztown University Rohrbach Library, who kept up a steady stream of books and articles despite all the new obstacles created by COVID-19.

My many thanks to Matt Becker at the University of Massachusetts Press and Dr. Brian Matthew Jordan and Dr. Jeremiah Ross Dancy, editors of the Veterans series: Matt, for his clarity and good counsel; Brian and Ross for letting me explore a research topic that unexpectedly appeared at midcareer and grew into a new vocation.

Sincere and special thanks to Nancy Raynor, who provided invaluable help with the final edits of this manuscript. On more occasions than I can count, she saved me from my own garbled syntax.

As has been the case for more than thirty years now, I am grateful for my wife Rachel's substantive and editorial help. She is a constant source of wisdom and a patient contributor.

Lastly, I want to welcome Thalia to our family. It is my hope and wish that the future brings great things.

THE NEW PRAETORIANS

INTRODUCTION

> In our pursuit of peaceful, ordinary lives, too many of us have lost touch with the horror of war. Too many have forgotten—misplaced, repressed, chosen to ignore—the anguish that once dominated our lives. . . . That's sad. We should remember.
> —Tim O'Brien, writing about Vietnam veterans, 1980

At its core, this book argues that modern veterans have developed into a distinct subculture that exercises a substantial influence on America but whose relationship with the public might best be described as "brittle and shallow."[1] There is a gap between veterans and the remainder of the country today, which comprises many complicated layers that affect the relationship between millions of people with time in uniform and those who have none. The contemporary separation between American veterans and the rest of the public is the result of both deliberate policy decisions and circumstance. Contemporary military service and the subsequent veteran's status are a matter of a choice freely made by millions of men and women since the end of the draft in 1973. But it has become a choice with accumulating, poorly understood consequences over the last fifty years. This work is dedicated to improving our understanding of the process, its component parts, and results.

PRAETORIANS

When we talk about "praetorians," the story takes us to Rome, a place that seems very far away from a history of American veterans after Vietnam. But there are some basic qualities of one era that may apply to another. Praetorians started their existence as personal bodyguards to Roman generals during its time as a republic. They were responsible for a commander's physical safety both on and off the battlefield. During the Roman Republic, praetorians generally were a small, not consistently organized, but necessary component of military affairs.

That role changed when Rome became an empire. Rome's first emperor, Caesar Augustus, refashioned his praetorians, an assemblage of reliable, experienced veterans, into something far more powerful than personal bodyguards. Rather than protect the leadership of an army comprised of citizen soldiers, the imperial praetorian guard was gradually transformed into the gatekeepers of absolute power. As the Roman

Empire evolved, the praetorians' distance from the citizenry grew, as did their power. They became more of a political than a military entity, assassinating opponents of the empire and, ultimately, intervening against individual emperors.[2]

Historians and students of history know these features well, but the key question is, How do they apply to this manuscript's narrative? The most important quality Roman praetorians illustrate is the separation between citizens and soldiers. When Rome was young, military service and citizenship were closely intertwined as the republic grew and prospered. Unfortunately, as Rome evolved over time into an empire, this linkage began to atrophy. The collective sacrifice that formed the foundation of the system gave way to imperial power increasingly disconnected from society as a whole. Therein lies our underlying question: Did the same gap between the military and its parent society appear after the Vietnam War?

THE NEW PRAETORIANS

Like Rome, American veterans persist into the twilight of empire. As American power declines on the international stage, its wars continue regardless. Modern U.S. conflicts have far less structure or clarity than did World War II. The clash of conventional forces commanded by national governments and governed by strategic milestones, such as "island hopping" to Japan or the Normandy invasion and the opening of a second front in Europe, are absent today. As abstract as Cold War "containment" might have been, it had borders–the 38th parallel, the 17th parallel—and antagonists headquartered in political capitals like Moscow or Beijing. There was a certain geographic certainty to nearly fifty years of animosity between the free world and the Communist bloc.

Twenty-first-century war has none of these features. The enemy is a constantly shifting combination of "fighters," "militants," and terrorists grouped around the Taliban, al-Qaeda, ISIS/ISIL, and all of their attendant factions. We are not even sure what to call our conflicts. Definitions commonly conflate doctrine and strategy with labels and acronyms such as "Rapid Decisive Operations" (RDO), the "Global War on Terrorism," "overseas contingency operations," "fourth-generation warfare" (4GW), and so forth. America's forever war comes with many names, but little agreement.[3]

The lack of clarity evident in current American conflicts is only one necessary prerequisite to understanding the civil-military gap today. As our definition of war becomes more opaque, direct experience is increasingly rare. Contemporary Americans generally value former members of the military as heroes, even as fewer and fewer people comprehend the virtue of this service. Bolstered by the World War II participation of the Greatest Generation, the U.S. veterans' population peaked at 28 million in 1980.[4] The following year, one-third of men eighteen to fifty-nine were veterans.[5] Over time, old age eventually took these men and women, and even with high levels of Cold War mobilization, overall participation in the military declined.[6] By the new century, the proportion of Americans in uniform was dramatically lower: According to the Pew Research Center, in the twelve years following the September 11 attacks, only 0.5 percent of the American public served in the active duty military.[7] An even smaller percentage have seen combat. In the meantime, this same public lavishes praise on military service. "Support the troops" and "Thank you for your service" have become ubiquitous parts of the twenty-first-century American lexicon. We regularly celebrate the military's sacrifice on official holidays, during sporting events, and through traditional parades and commemorations.

At the center of this book are two basic questions: First, what defines military service and its impact on veterans? Some of the qualities that inform the process are timeless: youth, confidence in risk taking, patriotism, and tradition. Americans leaving the military in our contemporary wars share many of the same motives as their grandparents had when they went to Vietnam. Moreover, much like their predecessors, death, shared suffering, and the unique bonding that occurs in war reinforces these timeless tendencies to the point where they become permanent, embedded traits in later life.

Second, how much true understanding informs the relationship between American society and its veterans? We place a higher degree of recognition and trust in military service than virtually any other institution in the country.[8] Yet the number of Americans with direct military experience wanes with each passing year. As the number declines, so too does an internalized, full understanding of the virtue of military service.

Vietnam is a useful starting point to examine the many facets of this topic. The end of the draft in 1973 was the most important personnel policy change of the Vietnam War. In broad terms, it triggered a significant shift in the entire social practice linking citizenship with military service. The great sociologist Morris Janowitz noted the potentialities of an all-volunteer military after Vietnam when "its linkages with civilian society become attenuated and tied to special segments of the social structure." Today, we live with the results Janowitz identified all those years ago. Veterans persist, but they might be best described in the title of Sebastian Junger's short, but powerful book *Tribe* (2016). What authors like Janowitz and Junger identify are the important elements of a very large subculture inside the civilian world.⁹

The complex status and interaction of veterans within American society is a topic ripe for historical study. With the exception of a few notable examples, it is a field in need of much more work. James Wright's *Those Who Have Borne the Battle: A History of America's Wars and Those Who Fought Them* (2012) and Andrew J. Huebner's *The Warrior Image: Soldiers in American Culture from the Second World War to the Vietnam Era* (2008) offer a long-term view of the topic, addressing American wars since the Revolutionary War and subsequent public treatment of veterans. While these histories provide excellent exposition on the nature of each conflict and reveal the social and political complexities affecting veterans, the main protagonist in the narrative is the larger public that defined the value of service rather than veterans themselves.

As they approach veterans in greater detail, most histories tend to compartmentalize the topic either by time period or issue. Robert J. Topmiller's *Binding Their Wounds: America's Assault on Its Veterans* (2011) takes on the host of modern medical problems experienced by U.S. veterans—from radiation injuries during nuclear testing in the fifties to Agent Orange and Gulf War syndrome—as well as public policy decisions that have compounded their difficulties rather than alleviate them. The GI Bill continues to be an historical topic of great interest, combining a discourse on public policy, education, health care, and veterans' lobbying efforts. Stephen R. Ortiz, *Beyond the Bonus March and the G.I. Bill* (2010), Suzanne Mettler, *Soldiers to Citizens: The G.I. Bill and the Making of the Greatest Generation* (2005), Kathleen J. Frydl, *The G.I. Bill* (2009), Milton Greenberg, *The GI Bill: The Law That Changed America* (1997), Raymond B. Lech, *Broken Soldiers* (2000), Michael J. Bennett, *When Dreams Come True: The GI Bill and the Making of Modern America* (1996), and Keith W. Olson, *The GI Bill, Veterans, and Colleges* (1974) have addressed these issues.

This book will feature veterans as the primary protagonist in the modern American historical narrative. This approach is long overdue, especially considering the tens of millions who have belonged to a distinct group present in American society since World War II. A careful analysis also invites attention to detail. John Lewis Gaddis referred to the choice of historical approaches as a dichotomy between "lumping" versus "splitting."¹⁰ This work will follow the latter path, incorporating a series of issues—social, economic, political, institutional, cultural—that may help our understanding of these critical actors in American history. It is not meant to offer a final word but rather to contribute to an ongoing conversation.

Chapter One, "A Brief History of the American Veteran to the Vietnam War," is intended to set the scene. Veterans have been present in America since the first colonial settlement and, over the ensuing centuries, have become ingrained parts of culture, politics, and public policy. Understanding the historical context of this process and some of the general emerging trends is important to the post-Vietnam narrative.

Chapter Two, "Joining Up," will start at the literal beginning of the veteran's story by examining the reasons Americans entered service and the changing composition of the military after Vietnam. The all-volunteer military defined late twentieth-century veterans. So too did the larger public consensus on service, which fluctuated between hostility and adulation as it evolved after Vietnam, from the latter years of the Cold War to our current overseas contingency operations.

Chapter Three, "The Nature of the Beast," examines the factors that shape civilians once they put on the uniform. The American military establishment possesses something Russell Weigley called the "American way of war."[11] This chapter will examine a variety of specific characteristics—from being "logistically excellent" to a focus on firepower—that shape military service and leave a definitive stamp on veterans. The variations on the type of military service from the broad range of logistical specialties to the diverse nature of combat experience are important to understand before examining veterans as a group or individually.

Chapter Four, "Coming Home," addresses the social structure that veterans leave behind and what awaits their return. Home is both a lifeline and a potential prerequisite for disillusionment. The public composition of the home front is a yardstick for the value placed on service and social perceptions shaping a veteran's status. It is also an important element to our understanding of the gap that sometimes appeared between veterans and society in the years after Vietnam.

Chapter Five, "Healing New Wounds," speaks to the millions of physical and mental casualties incurred by American veterans, from the effects of Agent Orange and Gulf War syndrome to traumatic brain injury and post-traumatic stress disorder (PTSD). Thanks to breakthroughs in medicine and body armor, modern veterans are more likely to survive their wounds, which has contributed to the growing demand for long-term care. Although the Department of Veterans Affairs is primarily responsible for veterans' medical care, its recent record has been at best inconsistent. Contemporary veterans continue to struggle with maladies unique to their times, such as opioid addiction or the recent increase in suicide rates, and, tragically in the case of military sexual trauma, to their service.

Chapter Six, "The Economics of the Veteran," covers two primary aspects of the story. The first regards the job market and training opportunities that usher men and women from uniform back into the general economy. The second aspect is more abstract and potentially more interesting: How does the economy treat the veteran as a commodity? In the aftermath of September 11, schools, businesses, sports organizations (e.g., the National Football League), and a host of institutions around the country began advertising themselves as "military friendly" so as to attract both veterans as consumers and cultivate pro-military sentiments for the sake of market advantage. This trend, while not entirely new, has transformed the literal and figurative value of military service in ways that are now deeply embedded in our culture.

Chapter Seven, "Lost on Campus: Veterans and Education," looks at the proposition that education is a key vehicle for veterans' assimilation back into civilian life. The original 1944 Serviceman's Readjustment Act (otherwise known as the GI Bill) and its successors introduced millions to the potentialities of higher education and advanced vocational training. As their presence in the classroom grew, veterans clearly affected curriculum, pedagogy, and campus culture in general. Just how far did they become integrated into this slice of American society, particularly in the wake of the Vietnam War, when colleges became literal battlegrounds? Does this cleavage persist in contemporary higher learning?

Chapter Eight, "The Veteran in Politics," begins with the premise that military service can be the ultimate filter for aspirants to public office. In modern politics, it provides a vivid definition of nationalism, patriotism, and citizenship. Combat veterans, particularly those wounded in war, like John McCain or Tammy Duckworth, represent the apex of this status. Although veterans filled out a significant percentage of legislatures and executive offices after World War II, their number and influence declined after Vietnam but began to recover in the new century. Veterans clearly have neither escaped the personal and political acrimony defining our times nor produced a consensus on domestic or foreign policy. What, then, has been their value to American politics in the last fifty years?

Chapter Nine, "The Women Praetorians," covers an important and growing constituency within the ranks of American veterans. Women have always served in American wars, yet their service has been affected by persistent blind spots within the military, institutions subsequently tasked with their care, and society as a whole. The rising proportion of women in the military continuously challenges these ingrained habits and is slowly changing the way we recognize service. This chapter will address the evolution of women's service and the measures taken to gain well-earned support and recognition.

Chapter Ten, "The Veteran in Popular Culture," looks at war and military service as a featured part of American film, theater, television, poetry, and other genres. Representations of the veteran's experience illustrates the personal and often terrible consequences of war. This chapter will consider evolving representations of the veteran in various art forms after Vietnam. The time period started with characterizations—*Taxi Driver* (1976) or *Rambo: First Blood* (1982)—of the veteran as a damaged, rootless returnee. Contemporary depictions—*Jack Reacher* (2012) and *American Sniper* (2014), among them—transform the veteran into a hero with a special kind of agency, one that recognizes hardship but also idealizes the protagonist. During the course of this transition, it will be important to understand the evolving nature of both the artistic topic as well as its audience.

To go back to Gaddis's analogy about lumping and splitting, this work presents many opportunities to indulge in the former approach as well. There are obvious points where veterans' culture intersects with politics and marketing. Similarly, the changing nature of women's service is a new element in both popular culture and American politics. These interactions are rich with opportunities to add breadth as well as depth to the veterans' narrative. Finally, as mentioned earlier, this book will hopefully provide a foundation for further "splitting" of its topics into even smaller parts–regarding gender, race, ethnicity, and identity—that clearly deserve greater attention and analysis as our understanding of veterans evolves.

CHAPTER ONE

A Brief History of the American Veteran to the Vietnam War

> In the usual contests of Empire and Ambition, the conscience of a soldier has so little to share that he may very properly insist upon his claims of Rank, and extend his pretensions even to Punctilio; but in such a cause as this, where the Object is neither Glory nor extent of territory, but a defense of all that is dear and valuable in Life, surely every post ought to be deemed honorable in which a Man can serve his Country.
> —*George Washington, 1775*

Veterans are a permanent, often overlooked part of American society. Long before the United States existed, they constituted a critical body of experience necessary for basic survival among settlements scattered along the Eastern Seaboard. At the start of the seventeenth century, veterans formed town "trainbands" and militia companies who regularly mustered against Native Americans and enemies of the Crown.[1] Colonial veterans fought and died close to home in brief skirmishes and sometimes far away as part of the global wars that reached America from Europe. Their sacrifices embodied both the value and virtue of military service at the beginning of our nation's history.[2]

When Americans moved west, they took their veterans with them. They fought in bloody clashes between Virginians and the Powhatans in the 1620s and during the vicious fighting that erupted between the scattered settlements in New England and an alliance of Native American tribes fifty years later during King Philip's War (1675–78). As generations of veterans accumulated, they contributed to a body of knowledge regarding a particular "American way of war" and its practitioners' standing in society as a whole.[3]

Not all veterans were equally virtuous. Colonial American militias were notoriously reluctant to conform with conventional line and column formations on the battlefield. They lacked the fortitude of professional soldiers when faced with concentrated musket volleys and the bayonet.

Although some of the older militia units tried to maintain their readiness, most began to decline after the frontier shifted further west and the proximity to danger moved with it. Without the presence of an imminent threat, it became difficult at best to convince local forces to deploy far from home. This reluctance became an embedded part of American military service.

Absent an imminent threat, American veterans had other uses. For colonists growing ever restive under the mantle of British rule, the local militia veteran shielded local sovereignty against the threat of a standing professional army. As the eighteenth century dawned and the grasp and reach of empire advanced further into American life, the article of faith that a well-equipped militia might someday protect the public against the coercive power of the state grew ever stronger.

Veterans were a core element of society before the American Revolution. The monthly muster might start with military training, but it did not end there. Armories were key social gathering points in America, where like-minded men and their families could pursue fund-raising for charity, business partnerships, and personal friendships. Once the mundane task of drilling was complete, it was normal for wives, children, and soldiers to gather to drink, gossip, and enjoy one another's company.[4]

Veteran status rather quickly became an American litmus test for political as well as military leadership. George Washington's experience at the conclusion of the war against England set a precedent for what would become a continuous thread in American history. The general said goodbye to his assembled senior officers in December 1783, but he could not escape the crowds that thronged along the route to Whitehall Ferry. For years after the war, he had to consistently reassure some Americans that he would not use his military connections to transform the Republic into a dictatorship. However, Washington's credibility as president rested in part on a reputation for leadership formed during the war. His coolness under fire, an almost foolhardy bravery, and strategic vision shaped his path to the presidency in 1789.

Veterans' credentials have provided agency for American leadership ever since. When victory over the British at New Orleans in 1815 thrust Andrew Jackson into national prominence, many a lawmaker grumbled at this virtue. Henry Clay famously lamented, "I cannot believe that killing 2,500 Englishman in New Orleans qualifies for the various, difficult and complicated duties of the Chief Magistracy."[5] Yet, for many Americans, it did and would continue to do so. After the Civil War, a meeting at the Soldiers' and Sailors' Convention in Chicago officially nominated Ulysses S. Grant as the Republican Party candidate for president. Veterans who formed the Grand Army of the Republic organized torchlight parades to campaign for their former general.[6] When Theodore Roosevelt departed for the invasion of Cuba a generation later, he brought his own cameras to capture the moment for his political posterity. On the campaign trail only a few weeks after the war, Colonel Teddy Roosevelt was introduced by his old Rough Rider bugler Emil Cassi and spoke to cheering crowds flanked by old veterans of the 1st New York Volunteer Cavalry Regiment.[7] Many modern-day presidents and public leaders have followed a similar path. Some, like John F. Kennedy and George H. W. Bush, were legitimate war heroes. Others, such as Nixon, Carter, Ford, and Reagan, enjoyed nondescript periods in uniform.

From the very beginning of the story, public policy evolved as a mechanism to recognize both the value and virtue of being a veteran. In 1636, the Plymouth Colony decided that any soldier who was disabled as a result of his service should be maintained by the colony for the rest of his life. In 1718, Rhode Island enacted a law that included medical care and an annual pension drawn from the colony's treasury.[8] Once the Revolution began, American leaders promised bounty lands to the west and pensions for veterans. The federal government created rudimentary programs for disabled veterans at the end of hostilities. In 1782, Congress agreed to provide a pension of five dollars a month to sickened soldiers for the rest of their lives.[9]

After the Revolution, the discourse regarding veterans' benefits gravitated between moments of great generosity and fits of remorse over excessive costs. One senator noted during a debate over an 1818 expansion of veterans' pensions: "I consider this bill as a branch of a great system, calculated and intended to create a permanent change upon the Treasury, with a view to delay the payment of the public debt, and to postpone, indefinitely, the claims of the people for reduction in taxes, when the dead shall finally be extinguished."[10]

Veterans' benefits took a major step forward after the Civil War. Congress began significant revisions of existing policy in the spring of 1862, a matter that gained momentum as the Union army approached and surpassed one million men under arms. New law provided for extensive increases in pensions for disabilities and disease. The definition of family dependents also changed significantly. Widows and children under sixteen qualified for benefits after the death of a veteran head of the household. Mothers and orphan sisters, previously excluded by federal law, could also receive the pensions of their sons and brothers. All in all, the General Pension Act of 1862 committed the federal government to an enormous and costly benefits program that would extend far past the lives of the original veteran beneficiaries. The already rapidly rising costs of this program mirrored its commitments. Although the Congress estimated that the 1862 law would cost the Treasury $7 million per year, by 1883 it had ballooned to an incredible $158.1 million annually.[11]

Gaps remained despite the growing expenditures for veterans. Benefits did not include hospitalization or rehabilitation for former soldiers and sailors, causing most veterans to rely on their families or charity for long-term care. By the end of the nineteenth century, the American Red Cross and the National Home for Disabled Volunteer Soldiers organized to meet the demands of veterans who were sick or disabled.[12]

In an era when millions immigrated to the United States, military service became a pathway to citizenship. Almost a quarter million new arrivals joined American forces in World War I, contributing to the polyglot of languages and cultures within the U.S. military.[13] During World War II, over a hundred thousand men joined up, many taking advantage of the Nationality Act (1940) that allowed military commanders to expedite the citizenship process.[14]

New policies dedicated to veterans' benefits did not appear until after World War I. The "war to end all wars" ushered more than four million Americans into uniform, of whom 116,516 died and 204,002 were wounded.[15] How the country honored this sacrifice became bound up in the national mobilization for the war. As David Kennedy observes in *Over Here: The First World War and American Society*, the Wilson administration's wartime propaganda campaigns cultivated prowar sentiment that carried into many corners of American society and politics. Concentrated as these campaigns were on the virtue of military service, they left little room for debate as to how the nation might recognize its veterans.[16] Public policy followed suit. The War Risk Insurance Act of 1917 provided rehabilitation for the war injured and approximately 675,000 veterans of the Great War applied for benefits through this one law. Under the Rehabilitation Law of 1919, disabled veterans received tuition, books, and a subsistence allowance of between $90 and $145 per month.[17]

However, for millions of veterans seeking work, homes, and a means to reassimilate after the war, demobilization proved abrupt and unrewarding. Most discharged soldiers received a separation payment of only sixty dollars and a railroad ticket home.[18] Beyond that, individuals were left to their own devices with respect to a sharp economic recession that lasted until 1921, the Red Scare, the outbreak of the great influenza epidemic, and a public consensus that emerged around "normalcy" under the incoming Harding administration.

The federal government belatedly attempted to address some of these problems by consolidating the existing benefits system into the Veterans Bureau in 1921. Unfortunately, consistent with Republican administrations of the era, corruption soon overwhelmed the new agency. The bureau's first director, Lieutenant Colonel Charles R. Forbes, was charged with fraud while arranging sweetheart deals for the construction of veterans' hospitals. The former Harding campaign worker accepted bribes for bids on contracts and kickbacks of up to a third of the profit made on each separate project. Forbes was eventually convicted and sentenced to two years in prison.[19]

To fill the vacuum created by public indifference and official corruption, veterans organized as their own advocates. The American Legion (est. 1919) joined the Veterans of Foreign Wars (VFW) as the second major national institution designed to protect and promote the interests of former service members. In many important respects, the legion and VFW represented a traditional need among veterans for community and camaraderie. Local chapters served those functions but also become outreach centers dedicated to public causes. The VFW and the American Legion became synonymous with community activities, charity fundraisers, youth sports, educational contests, and a host of other activities.

After World War I, veterans emerged as highly organized, powerful members of American society. Drawing on war chests created by the membership dues of hundreds of thousands of veterans, the legion and the VFW maintained lobbyists in state capitals and Washington, DC. By 1932, the year of the disastrous Bonus March in Washington, 12.8 percent of the total federal budget was dedicated to veterans.[20]

World War II altered the course of veterans' history in ways that few Americans understood at the time. Wartime mobilization produced the largest military in American history. After Japan formally surrendered in September 1945, more than sixteen million veterans began the process of returning home. They did so eagerly and impatiently, not full well knowing what the future might bring. Back home, the country debated the prospect of a second Great Depression after millions of newly returned service members flooded a job market that was not prepared for their return. Some Americans, perhaps prompted by Willard Waller's dystopian *The Veteran Comes Back* (1944), worried about the prospects of fascism and violence born by a gigantic cohort of men trained for combat and no longer rooted in political and social norms.[21]

One key piece of legislation awaited their return. The Serviceman's Readjustment Act of 1944 represented a national commitment to help veterans reintegrate into society. Guided by veterans' organizations, especially the American Legion, the GI Bill, as it was popularly known, was designed to facilitate veterans' access to education, homeownership, and small business loans. Millions took advantage of these benefits in the postwar period, a process that sparked a prolonged economic boom and explicitly endorsed a broad inclusion of federal welfare policy into American life. However, although the GI Bill was officially race and gender blind, in practice a million African American and other minority veterans too often struggled to receive equal benefits. Ongoing segregation of minority veterans both highlighted and motivated the post-1945 civil rights movement.

Accompanying the GI Bill was a major reform and expansion of the Veterans Administration (VA). The Truman administration recalled Omar N. Bradley from command of the 12th Army Group in Europe to replace Frank T. Hines as VA administrator. What Bradley found was "the huge load of World War II on a chassis built for World War I."[22] The general took to his task with a passion, bolstered by a cohort of officers cherry-picked from his personal staff. Bradley successfully argued for civil service reform and pay raises, introducing a new generation of doctors and nurses to the VA health care system. He oversaw the construction of dozens of new medical facilities, the creation of hundreds of new VA field offices, and administrative staff hires that more than doubled the size of the organization by 1946, all the while shrewdly cultivating public support for reform.[23] In just two years, he rebuilt an institution with an aptitude that future generations would be hard-pressed to replicate.

In the postwar years, veterans entered into every corner of American life. Reflecting the traditional acceptance of former military members in political life, they poured into local, state, and federal government. When the 80th Congress convened in 1947, ninety veterans of World War II were present. They included Richard M. Nixon and Joseph P. McCarthy, as well as Senator John Sherman Cooper, a Democrat from Kentucky who enlisted as a private at the age of forty-one and served in Patton's Third Army.[24] Taking into account all of America's previous conflicts, some stretching back to the western frontier in the case of Texas representative Joseph J. Mansfield, veterans were a dominant contingent in American government in the forties.

Veterans also occupied an important place in American life. A continuous peacetime draft to support a substantially larger Cold War force structure normalized military service. It became a milestone in the life course for millions of American men. Both average people and celebrities contributed their time and effort. Jimmy Stewart, the American everyman in Hollywood, flew twenty bombing missions in World War II and remained in the Air Force reserves until his retirement as a brigadier general in 1968. The Boston Red Sox player Ted Williams earned his pilot wings as a Marine in World War II and was later recalled to active duty during the Korean War, flying thirty-seven combat missions.

Even as veterans became ubiquitous, public policy for them was inconsistent at best. Korea and Vietnam saw a similar, if diminishing commitment to the next generation of American veterans. The Veterans' Readjustment Assistance Act (1952) did nothing to keep pace with either college costs or basic inflation, offering single veterans only $110 a month for tuition and living expenses.[25] Veterans lost more ground under the Veterans' Readjustment Benefits Act of 1966, otherwise known as the Cold War GI Bill, which reduced monthly allotments to only $100. Congressional parsimony, as historian Mark Boulton points out, was the result of many legislators, primarily centered around World War II veteran Olin E. Teague (D-TX), who simply did not believe that Cold War service members deserved the same recognition as his generation.[26]

Debate over legislation was just one of the many cleavages opening up between American veterans after World War II. The American Veterans Committee (AVC), founded at the end of 1944, challenged the primacy of the American Legion and VFW. Bill Mauldin, who won fame as a cartoonist for *Stars and Stripes* and later led the AVC, characterized speeches made by legion leaders as "a mixture of National Association of Manufacturing advertising and a Hearst editorial page." Young veterans like Mauldin chafed at the prospect of joining veterans' organizations that wanted their membership dues but not their ideas. A senior delegate to the American Legion 1946 national convention in San Francisco encapsulated the friction between the two generations: "This is a billion-dollar corporation. You don't turn something like that over to a bunch of inexperienced kids."[27]

A small but vocal and well-organized minority of veterans joined the AVC and built working relationships with other contemporary progressive organizations such as the National Conference of Christians and Jews, B'nai B'rith, and the National Association for the Advancement of Colored People.[28] The AVC consistently lent their veterans' status to provide agency for civil rights issues. As early as December 1945, AVC legal staff assisted veterans attending city colleges in New York who were protesting tuition and fees that violated state law. In 1946, the Hollywood chapter of the AVC joined in an American Federation of Labor strike against seven movie studios.[29] A Minnesota AVC chapter picketed the Minneapolis Real Estate Board when it banned a nisei veteran from purchasing a home. In 1947, the AVC unsuccessfully attempted to add race to a Minnesota law that banned restrictive covenants on property purchases and rentals.[30]

During the Vietnam War, the split between generations of veterans deepened and widened in much the same manner as the rest of the country. The sixties saw bitter contests between tiny, albeit vocal and increasingly media-savvy veterans' groups and mainstream institutions such as the American Legion and VFW, which generally aligned themselves with the establishment on domestic and foreign policy issues. African American veterans organized the Deacons for Defense and Justice in 1964 as a response to violence against civil rights workers in the South.[31] Their early advocacy of armed self-defense was controversial even within the civil rights movement. The Vietnam Veterans Against the War (VVAW) formed in 1967 and joined an increasingly militant antiwar movement, culminating in the 1971 Winter Soldier Investigation of alleged war crimes and the Operation Dewey Canyon III protests held later that same year.[32]

Both the Deacons and the VVAW attracted official attention and retaliation. Vice President Spiro Agnew repeatedly denounced veteran activists and attempted to drive a wedge between protestors and the "loyal" majority of veterans in mainstream society.[33] The FBI's COINTELPRO (Counterintelligence Program) categorized the Deacons as "extremely militant" and maintained constant surveillance on the group.[34] The same was true with respect to the VVAW. Declassified files indicate years of constant FBI surveillance as well as attempts to infiltrate the organization to collect intelligence and provoke illegal actions. The bureau also reported the possibility of communist infiltration of a number of VVAW chapters.[35] Meantime, the Justice Department started a series of legal actions designed to waste VVAW time and funding.[36]

Vietnam was the crucible for the modern American veteran. The war marked a divisive, bitter, and public debate about the virtue and overall purpose of military service. It resulted, as promised by the incoming Nixon administration, with the end to a hugely unpopular draft. Yet, the end of the draft in 1973 marked not just the finalization of a particular public policy but also a new era in which the Pentagon and the public alike confronted a historically wide disagreement over the value of military service. Standing astride this gap was a generation of veterans attempting to find a path home.

CHAPTER TWO

Joining Up

> War must rely on the young, for only they have the two things fighting requires: physical stamina and innocence about their own mortality.
> —*Paul Fussell,* Wartime

INTRODUCTION

The first step a person takes into the military does not seem rational on its face. What would possess someone to leave behind family, friends, and relationships? Why, in the prime of young adulthood, would a person risk life and limb and possibly carry scars, both mental and physical, forever? Why would anyone challenge taboos formed by a life of religious training and moral nurturing, shedding elements of mercy and tolerance at the foundation of civil society? Why would a young member of that same society forfeit the Golden Rule? In other words, why learn to kill by choice?

Young men, and not a few women, have wrestled with these questions for millennia as they contemplated crossing over from civilian life into the military. The choice to put on a uniform is a reality check in an early stage of life, for many one of the first serious ones. It tests long-standing convictions, understood in principle, with hard, unavoidable reality. And it is with these first few steps that the embryonic qualities of a veteran begin.

Some aspects of this transition are timeless. They come from naive, romantic assumptions about military service. When he enlisted, a fifteen-year-old David Hackworth was attracted to the glamorous image of an airborne constabulary soldier on duty in occupied Berlin. The image of an elite uniform with "a very jazzy yellow scarf around his neck . . . the whole look made complete by two beautiful blonde fräuleins the guy had perched on his knees" captured the young Hackworth's imagination.[1] This must be what it was like to be a soldier.

The pull of service could also come from youthful impatience. As was the case since time immemorial, young men worry that peace might come too soon and they would lose out on the experience, somehow losing a step on life if they were not participating in the dangerous enterprise of war. In his memoir, *With the Old Breed*, Eugene Sledge recalled "a deep feeling of uneasiness that the war might end before I could get into combat" when he enlisted in 1942.²

Media representations of war are another long-standing factor that influenced the decision to join up. It is fairly common to hear Vietnam-era veterans such as Ron Kovic and Philip Caputo recall the impact of movies like *Sands of Iwo Jima* (1949) and actors like John Wayne on their understanding of what war meant.³ They remembered heroism and a clear-cut cause. For a generation of men, Wayne came to symbolize not just honorable sacrifice but also the best qualities of postwar patriotism.

For the post-Vietnam generation, war movies could mean something else entirely. In *Jarhead* (2003), Anthony Swofford articulated what they meant to him as a young Marine about to deploy to Saudi Arabia as part of Operation Desert Shield: "We concentrate on the Vietnam films because it's the most recent war, and the successes and failures of that war helped write our training manuals. We rewind and review famous scenes, such as Robert Duvall and his helicopter gunships during *Apocalypse Now*, and in the same film Martin Sheen floating up the fake Vietnamese Congo; we watch Willem Dafoe get shot by a friendly and left on the battlefield in Platoon; and we listen closely as Matthew Modine talks trash to a streetwalker in Full Metal Jacket. We watch again the ragged, tired, burnt-out fighters walking through the villes and the pretty native women smiling because if they don't smile, the fighters might kill their pigs or burn their cache of rice." The Marines watching these movies, relished the "various visions of carnage and violence and deceit, the raping and killing and pillaging." As Swofford notes, they didn't care about carefully crafted political or moral messages. Instead, "Corporal Johnson at Camp Pendleton and Sergeant Johnson at Travis Air Force Base and Seaman Johnson at Coronado Naval Station and Spec 4 Johnson at Fort Bragg and Lance Corporal Swofford at Twentynine Palms Marine Corps Base watch the same films and are excited by them, because the magic brutality of the films celebrates the terrible and despicable beauty of their fighting skills. Fight, rape, war, pillage, burn. Filmic images of death and carnage are pornography for the military man."⁴

In his stunningly honest appraisal of what went on in a military mind circa 1990, Swofford also pointed out just how demystified war and military service had become. The Marines deploying to fight the First Gulf War no doubt were motivated by patriotism as Eugene Sledge had been, but there was a motive for service at work that simultaneously was more visceral and candid.

Part of this honesty might have been a legacy of Vietnam veterans to their sons, daughters, and grandchildren. In some respects, they resemble the veterans of World War I passing along their jaundiced view of conflict to the next generation who stood on the brink of another world war in 1939.[5] However, what the children of Vietnam veterans lacked was a unifying event, a Pearl Harbor or Bataan Death March, that provided clear-cut forces of good and evil or a remedy to the tragedy. In fact, the generation who joined up after Vietnam seemed to follow in the opposite direction. Phil Klay, who deployed to Iraq in 2007, recounted one of the first things his father shared with him about his two tours in Vietnam: "My dad only told me about Vietnam when I was going over to Iraq. He sat me down in the den and took out a bottle of Jim Beam and a few cans of Bud and started drinking. He'd take long pulls of the whiskey and small sips of the beer, and in between sips, he'd tell me things. The sweatbox humidity in the summers, the jungle rot in the monsoons, and the uselessness of the M16 in any seasons. And then, when he was really drunk, he told me about the whores."[6]

It seems at first glance that military service after Vietnam had lost the mythology employed by the World War II generation. But what other factors contributed to the understanding of service and the first steps toward joining the military and becoming a veteran? This chapter will examine some of these, starting with the end of the draft in 1973, when Selective Service ended and real, personally selected service began in an all-volunteer military. Absent a draft, recruiters reentered competition with the civilian marketplace for the first time in more than thirty years. As they did so, the literal face of their target audience began to change as significant numbers of minorities and women joined up. Understanding a host of interrelated and evolving circumstances following the Vietnam War—economic, social, political, and international—will help us understand the foundation underlying the contemporary veteran.

JUST ANOTHER JOB

When he campaigned for president in 1968, Richard Nixon pledged to end the Vietnam War. Explicit in that promise was an end to the highly unpopular draft. In October 1968, only a few weeks before Americans went to the polls, he said: "Today all across our country we face a crisis of confidence. Nowhere is it more acute than among our young people. They recognize the draft as an infringement on their liberty, which it is. To them, it represents a government insensitive to their rights, a government callous to their status as free men. They ask for justice, and they deserve it."[7]

Once Nixon entered the White House, he intended to make good on his promise. The question was how. For an answer, the new president looked, as he often did, to the private sector. Nixon believed that the free market offered opportunities to make policy better in ways that the public sector could not. He applied this basic assumption to issues as diverse as welfare reform and the Alliance for Progress in Latin America.[8] The same premise applied to fixing the draft.

The administration formed the President's Commission on an All-Volunteer Armed Force to examine the issue in late 1969. The commission included such notables as Roy Wilkins, executive director of the National Association for the Advancement of Colored People.[9] Otherwise known as the Gates Commission after its chairman, the former secretary of defense Thomas Gates, it actively emphasized a free market solution to the selective service imbroglio. As Beth Bailey points out, three members of the commission, Milton Friedman, Alan Greenspan, and W. Allen Wallis, all free market economists, had a significant influence on basic assumptions and subsequent plans for the all-volunteer military that would follow selective service.[10]

Essentially, the Gates Commission assumed the position that the modern volunteer military needed to compete for quality employees in an open labor market. To attract talented volunteers, it had to offer competitive wages, benefits, and working conditions as would any other business.[11] Friedman and his academic cohort made this argument against the expressed objections of Pentagon leadership, who believed that monetizing recruitment demeaned the fundamental nature of military service.[12]

In point of fact, the controversies surrounding the Vietnam War had already created this erosion. The early seventies were a decidedly hostile market for military service. A survey of young men in 1971 indicated that 88 percent "probably" or "definitely" would not consider military service.[13] It was obvious that any marketing strategy had to overcome the initial reluctance of these new self-selecting soldiers. The Pentagon's approach to rebranding resembled that of Hasbro, the company famous for its G.I. Joe action figure, a toy that graced millions of baby boomer houses in the sixties. However, rather than have four versions of the toy, one for each branch of the military, Hasbro made its product line more palatable to parents by introducing the G.I. Joe Adventure Team in 1970. Instead of wielding weapons stored in an olive drab footlocker, Adventure Joe was a scuba diver and parachutist clad in bright civilian colors.

Military recruiting campaigns followed the same approach, emphasizing a compatibility with civilian life. In 1976, Bates Advertising created the slogan, "Navy. It's Not Just a Job, It's an Adventure." Campaigns of this type focused on excitement, travel, and exploration.[14] Modified grooming standards reflected this new approach. Longer hair was common throughout the military during the seventies. Although the Marine Corps hung onto its traditional expectations, the Navy allowed beards and longer hair starting in 1970.[15]

In keeping with the original thrust of the Gates Commission, military recruiters adopted the mantra that service translated into applicable civilian job skills. This was particularly true of technical training sought out by employers that would give recruits an edge after they left the military. When designing the 1981 "Be All That You Can Be" campaign for the Army, market research conducted by the N. W. Ayer advertising agency discovered that young people in the recruiting demographic responded well to an emphasis on high-tech training and equipment.[16]

The end result of this recruiting strategy was a transformation of military service in the seventies. Although Cold War–era recruiting increased its emphasis on benefits, in part to accommodate the growing number of military families as well as to compete with civilian employers in some high-skill sectors, the post-Vietnam free market approach pushed this idea much further.[17] All military service came under a basic premise that it was transactional and temporary, at best an interruption in a career path rather than a commitment to an abstract idea, more in tune with personal adventurism than collective patriotism.

There certainly were many young men and women who still joined out of a sense of duty and altruism, but it seemed as if the narrative regarding service had shifted and they were becoming the exception rather than the rule. There was a cost to this that Friedman and the architects of the all-volunteer force perhaps refused to recognize: volunteer service was not always a rational cost-benefit decision. Beth Bailey explained the moment this way: "These, however, were not days of measured rationality in American society. And the market, in 1970s America, was not simply a realm of rational economic choice. It was a site of consumer desire; it was a volatile space of inchoate needs, hopes, and fears."[18]

Although the military did initially increase its investment in making service more competitive—personnel costs rose from 48 percent to 60 percent of the defense budget from 1964 to 1975—the volunteer military did not overcome the intangible factors affecting enlistment that Bailey points out.[19] The stigma attached to service remained, dissuading untold millions from even considering enlistment. Many who did enlist found the opportunity for travel and adventure circumscribed by the mundane realities of military life. Still other recruits, primarily minorities, who saw the military as a way to better their lives, had to find a way to overcome obstacles rooted in systemic racism and their own socioeconomic disenfranchisement.

The literal face of the military changed in the seventies, particularly its racial composition. Recruitment strategy focused on the armed services as race neutral. "All Marines Are Green" and "One Navy" were common slogans at the time. In fact, the United States Navy actually contracted the National Urban League to assist with recruiting in the city of Philadelphia.[20] By 1974, almost a third of new recruits were African American. Low standardized tests scores relegated a large proportion to combat arms.[21] Regardless, the overall number of African Americans significantly increased in all branches. In 1964, they were 9.7 percent of the enlisted ranks in the military. By 1974 this had grown to 15.7 percent.[22] In 1973, African Americans were most prevalent in the Army (19.9%) and Marine Corps (17.7%).[23]

The all-volunteer military also included a far higher percentage of women. For two decades following World War II, the Women's Armed Services Integration Act (1948) restricted women to 2 percent of enlisted personnel.[24] However, as the military ramped up the all-volunteer force, the services branches prepared plans to at least double this number.[25] When the all-volunteer military began, one-third of Army occupational specialties were open to women. As time progressed, opportunities slowly increased, although the combat arms remained closed and women in support units were considered nondeployable well into the eighties. By 1979, 7.6 percent of all enlisted personnel were female.[26]

The officer corps also changed in the seventies, and not for the better. In the years after World War II, the increasing complexity of weapons systems, logistics, and technology in general placed a premium on education, some of which was available only in U.S. colleges and universities. A four-year bachelor's degree increasingly became a requirement for career officers. Consequently, the number of officers with college diplomas increased from 55 percent in 1956 to 73 percent in 1967.[27]

The Reserve Officers' Training Corps (ROTC) was one of the institutions that kept this system alive. However, as the Vietnam War wound down, the ROTC saw enrollments substantially decrease. Without the draft to motivate men to enter the program for its deferment, the number of cadets in basic ROTC military science courses declined by two-thirds between 1961 and 1971.[28] The military academies proved inadequate to sustain the need for junior officers. A particular dilemma for the all-volunteer military was how to arrest the loss of talent and training.

The struggle to find trained officers pointed to a far more systemic problem of quality within the new military. Colin Powell reflected on the times in his autobiography: "We were in transition from the draft to the all-volunteer force. As we dragged ourselves home from Vietnam, the nation turned its back on the military. Many of our troops, in Army shorthand, were 'Cat Four,' Category IV, soldiers possessing meager skills in reading, writing, and math. They were life's dropouts, one step above Category V, those who were considered unfit for Army service. Today [1995], about 4 percent of the Army is Cat Four, while in those days the figure was closer to 50 percent." Yet the military, faced with an annual need for three hundred thousand new recruits in the seventies, had to find a way to fill its ranks.[29]

Educational standards clearly suffered in the early years of the all-volunteer force. Morris Janowitz noted that in 1961, 18 percent of enlistees had some college training. By 1973, fewer than 3 percent of new personnel could claim the same credential. Such declining numbers of high school graduates in the Army and the Marine Corps were becoming worrisome. When selective service ceased in 1973, only 54 percent of recruits in these two branches held diplomas.[30] Over time, poor educational quality became a chronic problem and constant source of public embarrassment. The Army in particular struggled to acquire recruits with four years of high school. Halfway through FY 1980, only 38 percent of its recruits achieved this goal.[31]

As bad as this situation was, it worsened in 1980 when the Pentagon discovered errors in its new version of the Armed Forces Qualification Test (AFQT), which indicated that 46 percent of Army recruits were CAT IV, the lowest allowable category for military service. A subsequent investigation found that 350,000 individuals entered the military between 1976 and 1980 who would have normally not scored high enough for enlistment.[32]

Systemic problems followed from that root source. According to an internal study of Army training standards conducted in 1977 and 1978, a sense of resignation had settled into active duty units. Complacency was running rampant. The report noted that there was "little perceived change in the training environment since 1971. The environment is still seen as hostile to the conduct of good training." At Fort Benning, a 1976 review of literacy rates among recruits revealed that 53 percent of incoming soldiers had a reading level of fifth grade or lower.[33] Further investigation revealed that these rather appalling standards were not limited to the Army. Approximately one-quarter of Navy enlistees fell into Category IV between 1978 and 1982.[34]

It became increasingly obvious to policymakers that in day-to-day work, troops simply did not know how to do their jobs. A 1979 report on the results of Army Skill Qualification Tests revealed that 90 percent of nuclear weapons maintenance specialists, 98 percent of tank turret and artillery repairmen, and 91 percent of aviation maintenance personnel failed to meet minimum proficiency requirements. Overall, of the 370 military occupation specialties, 179 experienced a failure rate of 40 percent or higher.[35]

Poor job performance also correlated with alarmingly low retention rates throughout the military. Only 64 percent of all Navy enlistees completed their initial enlistment contracts between 1978 and 1982. In practice, the retention rate could be as low as 50 percent, particularly for recruits without a high school diploma.[36]

Although the all-volunteer military began with a sense of optimism based on a rational assessment of market efficiencies and celebration that the draft was finally over, the seventies ended on a sour note. The new volunteers were diverse and, at least for a few years, paid at least as well as their civilian counterparts. For the first time, significant numbers of women were putting on the uniform. As had been the case during much of the post-1945 period, military service offered training and the prospect of advancement to disenfranchised peoples of U.S. society. However, deep systemic problems overshadowed progress. The volunteer military was an institution besieged by disciplinary problems, low quality, and a general sense of malaise. The U.S. military forces were beginning to resemble what General Edward C. Meyer described as a "hollow army" in testimony before Congress in 1980.[37] On balance, it seemed that the military was just another job, and not a particularly good one at that.

THE EIGHTIES RENAISSANCE

In just a few short years, better times returned to the United States military and its recruits. Many period histories give credit to Ronald Reagan, who resurrected unapologetic patriotism and bolstered the country with his sunny optimism. Portions of this trope applied to military recruiting were partly true and will be discussed below. However, much of the eighties renaissance was the product of improving circumstances and deliberate efforts to reconstruct American defense, a process that started with the men and women who joined up.

Demographics and basic economics provided reformers with a good foundation. The 1980s was the last decade to enjoy the baby boom and its concurrent pool of eighteen- to twenty-five-year-old recruiting prospects. Unlike their grandparents, these young men and women were better fed, better educated, and in better health than the volunteers and draftees who fought in World War II and Korea. They were also motivated to enlist by a steep recession that was savaging the country at the start of the decade. At a time when industry and manufacturing concerns were shutting their doors and unemployment reached almost 11 percent in 1982, the military looked like a good choice.³⁸

To facilitate this decision, Reagan had to address military compensation, which was a national embarrassment by the end of the seventies. Although the Nixon administration bolstered pay and benefits at the start of the all-volunteer military, attention to these items had diminished over time. By 1979, a junior noncommissioned officer (NCO; E-4) with a family earned a salary that actually placed him below the poverty line.³⁹ Consequently, one of the most important line items in Reagan's first defense budgets was concurrent pay increases of 11.1 percent in 1981 and 14.3 percent in 1982.⁴⁰

While improvements in pay was a key incentive for enlistees, resurrected educational benefits had an even greater impact. By the time Ronald Reagan entered the White House, the last legislative vestiges of the Vietnam-era GI Bill had lapsed and been replaced by much more limited aid for veterans.⁴¹ Interestingly, when a much-improved version of educational assistance was narrowly voted out of the House Armed Services Committee in 1982, the proposal faced stiff opposition from the White House and Defense Department, which argued that it would be too expensive and unnecessary.⁴²

Military officials changed their tune once the Montgomery GI Bill became official policy and transformed recruiting in the eighties. According to a 1986 report, 85 percent of new entries into the Army cited it as a key reason for enlistment. Despite earlier concerns regarding expense, the Army estimated that new benefits would cost approximately $400 million by 1993. In comparison, the Pell Grant program cost $3.9 billion at the time.⁴³

Advertising for military recruitment also underwent a dramatic shift during the Reagan years. In a nod to the president's former career in Hollywood, the Pentagon commenced an active relationship with the U.S. film industry, something that benefited both the box office and the military's image at the time. The Defense Department provided locations, equipment, and technical support for pro-military films such as Clint Eastwood's *Heartbreak Ridge* (1986). However, the hugely popular *Top Gun* (1986) was perhaps the best example of the relationship between art and national defense. A *Time* magazine article noted that "the truly impressive stars of the film are its sleek, roaring fighter jets." Featured throughout *Top Gun* are a variety of Navy aircraft, ships, and bases, none of which was an accident. Paramount paid the Department of Defense $1.8 million dollars for their use, which included up to $7,000 an hour for flying time for a variety of aircraft used in the film, especially the F-14 Tomcat.⁴⁴

Defense Department support also came with one additional string attached: approval of the movie's final script. Military authorities removed one scene where two planes collided, killing a pilot, opting instead to illustrate the death as the result of a freak accident.

When *Top Gun* premiered in May 1986, the Navy set up a number of recruiting stations in the lobbies of theaters featuring the film.[45] During an interview with the *Los Angeles Times*, one recruiter noted: "Two groups I can identify (as having increased interest) are individuals who have applied in the past and were turned down or dropped out of Aviation Officers Training School, and individuals who are approaching the maximum age limit (to apply). . . . On the other end of the spectrum, we've seen a general increase in interest in young men who don't yet qualify for the program, and I have to attribute that to 'Top Gun' also."[46] In many respects, the movie was a perfect platform for the military. It showcased modern technological improvements to U.S. forces, a proven commodity identified by focus groups during the "Be All That You Can Be" campaign. *Top Gun* also perfectly captured the image of youth and adventure in the star power of newcomer Tom Cruise. While Oliver Stone's *Platoon* (released the same year) belonged to the oldest part of the Baby Boom generation, *Top Gun* became an iconic moment for its youngest.

Taken as a whole, the combination of better pay and benefits, a new GI Bill, and an improving image all led to a better crop of recruits in the eighties, which in turn improved the U.S. military as a whole. As early as 1985, 93 percent of enlistees had high school diplomas as compared with 68 percent in 1980 and 75 percent of the general youth population at the time.[47] Retention rates also improved during the Reagan years. By 1989, the Army had exceeded all of its recruiting goals.[48]

There were problems on the horizon, however. The latter years of the Reagan administration were encompassed by vehement debates regarding the exploding federal deficit, which effectively tripled to almost $3 trillion (1989 dollars) in just eight years.[49] Budget hawks began reasserting themselves, particularly on the subject of defense spending. As the Pentagon and lawmakers began to cast about for ways to address these concerns, personnel costs emerged as an obvious target. Consequently, many of the gains in pay made at the start of the decade began to erode.

A GLOBAL FORCE FOR PEACE

The abrupt collapse of the Soviet Union in 1991 signaled an end to the Cold War and forced a basic reassessment of U.S. military priorities. It was a time of dramatic changes, one that juxtaposed the success of Operation Desert Storm against a congressional debate arguing for cuts in the defense budget, even as troops deployed to Saudi Arabia at the end of 1990.⁵⁰

A few lawmakers attempted to stem the clamor for large-scale defense cuts. John McCain warned in 1993: "Time and again, we have learned that our readiness measures are unrealistic or fail to anticipate real-world demands.... The Gulf War, for example, demonstrated all of these problems. In spite of the highest readiness funding in our history, we were not ready to fight when we deployed. We took months to adjust the organization, training, and support structures of our active combat forces, we experienced major problems with some aspects of the call up and training of our reserves, and we literally had to make thousands of modifications to our combat equipment, munitions, support equipment, and battle management and communications systems. Without the months Saddam Hussein gave us, these readiness problems might well have cost us thousands of lives."⁵¹

McCain's warnings largely went unheeded as the country stampeded toward the "peace dividend" and dramatic reductions to the military establishment. Budget cuts and a drastic drawdown in personnel became the new normal. Many career officers and enlisted discovered that they had been "RIF'd," becoming part of a mandatory reduction in force. Between 1990 and 2000, the U.S. military shed almost a third of its total active duty force, dropping to just over 1.3 million people, a level lower than just prior to the Korean War.⁵²

The military ebb tide had a corresponding impact on recruiting in the nineties. For a time, all of the service branches enjoyed the benefit of drawing from a pool of involuntarily separated veterans who wanted to return to service. Having thousands of eager volunteers made the job of selling enlistment much easier, producing a safety net for recruiters. The process also made recruiting somewhat incestuous, reinforcing service within a self-selecting group rather than a broader pool of talent.⁵³

The easy days for military recruiters did not last. The booming economy, which saw the stock market quadruple in value, witnessed structural changes that siphoned off talent and interest from the armed services. Software and hardware development in the Sun Belt, as well as the information economy in general, offered a plethora of job opportunities, particularly for people with technical skills.⁵⁴ Equally important was the fact that high school graduates in the critical eighteen- to twenty-five-year-old demographic were opting out of both work or military service. In 1998, 67 percent were going to college in hopes of increasing their economic viability.⁵⁵

Diverging civil-military relations also worked against recruiters. For all the attention spent on Bill Clinton's avoidance of the draft in the sixties, there were deeper, more complex conflicts within American society with respect to military service. A 2000 study pointed out a substantial separation between civilian and military elites regarding religion, gay rights, and the role of women in uniform.[56] There seemed to be greater agreement between the military and the public as a whole on these issues, although the study's authors admitted that the declining number of veterans in the general population was producing a "brittle and shallow" relationship. According to contemporary research, more people admired the military in principle, but fewer wanted to belong to it.[57] The "Cold War drawdown," as one article described it, took away the visibility and sense of urgency that accompanied military service. This contributed to a decline in overall youth "propensity to serve," from 33.7 percent in 1989 to 28.6 percent ten years later. In 1999, interest in military service was highest among Hispanic males (46.1%) and lowest among white females (9.1%).[58] Among African American youth, a significant part of the all-volunteer recruiting base, interest in the military sharply declined during the nineties. In 1983, more than half of the Black high school students surveyed considered serving, a rate twice that of their white peers. However, in less than ten years, that number dropped by more than twenty points.[59]

Some of the reasons for declining interest may have been tangible and simple. The pay gap, partially addressed by the 1981 and the 1982 military salary increases, had languished afterward. During the nineties, the difference was 13 percent in favor of the civilian sector. For most of the remainder of the decade, military pay failed to keep pace with the consumer price index and did not catch up until after the September 11 attacks.[60]

The end result was a military notable for its increasing isolation and declining quality. On the brink of the new millennium, there was notable drop in recruit education levels. Incoming "high quality" recruits—individuals with both a high school diploma and a score in Categories I–IIIA of the Armed Forces Qualification Test—were much less prevalent. This trend was most pronounced in the Army, where such enlistees dropped from 78 percent in 1991 to 52 percent by 2000.[61]

VOLUNTEERING FOR THE FOREVER WAR

The September 11 attacks wrenched the United States from peace to war. Simultaneous strikes in New York, Virginia, and Pennsylvania translated terrorism from an abstract, post–Cold War concept to an imminent reality within U.S. borders. The event also altered America's understanding of military service. In addition to a reduced active duty military, hundreds of thousands of National Guard reservists fought the Global War on

Terrorism. All told, it was a mobilization that went beyond the scope and scale of the Korean War.

The post-2001 military was distinct from its predecessors in many respects. It was definitely younger: 49 percent of the active duty force was seventeen to twenty-four years old, compared with 15 percent of the civilian workforce. More service members were married: 49 percent of active enlisted military and 68 percent of officers. It was a well-educated force. In 2005, 92 percent of recruits had high school diplomas. Racially, the military was more diverse in some respects, but less so in others. African Americans were slightly overrepresented (16% of military, 14% of the population) but served in smaller numbers than past versions of the all-volunteer military. Latinx tended to be underrepresented at 16 percent of population but only 11 percent of the military.[62]

As they unfolded, overseas contingency operations placed an enormous strain on the military. The burden fell most heavily on the Army and Marine Corps, which contributed the bulk of ground forces to the invasions of Afghanistan and Iraq. Between 2001 and 2014, 815,000 reservists were called up, separating them for months, if not years, from their civilian jobs.[63] By 2005, fifteen of the Army National Guard's combat brigades had deployed for a variety of missions ranging from securing key infrastructure and bases to active counterinsurgency operations.[64]

A massive nationwide mobilization of people and resources did not follow the September 11 attacks. Selective service remained on the shelf. Instead, the Pentagon largely relied on forces in place and approved only modest increases to the Army and Marine Corps. To close the gap between rapidly growing operational needs and standing forces, the Bush administration fell back on various options. The number of private contractors employed by the U.S. government grew explosively to the point where they actually outnumbered the U.S. military occupying Iraq in 2007.[65] The military also adopted a number of highly unpopular policies to maintain its forces. The Pentagon resurrected the stop-loss policy that involuntarily extended service obligations for both the reserves and active duty military. Although it was technically a legal part of enlistment contracts and had affected seventy thousand people by 2007, the nature of the policy reeked of bad faith and adversely affected morale throughout the ranks.[66] For their own part, reservists discovered that tours of duty could last for as long as sixteen months. Many individuals in key specialties such as civil affairs, military police, intelligence, or transportation were subject to multiple deployments over very short periods of time. The Maryland National Guard's 115th Military Police Battalion was called up three times in a two-year period, for example.[67]

The overall operational tempo of the Global War on Terrorism very effectively ground down active duty, reserve, and National Guard personnel alike. Public support for the war also suffered in the wake of a consistent stream of casualties, the slow drip of scandals involving civilian deaths and "enhanced interrogation" in such facilities as Abu Ghraib, as well as a growing impatience with progress against the al-Qaeda and Taliban insurgents.[68]

Recruitment accordingly suffered within a shrinking youth demographic. Members of Generation X (born between approximately 1961 and 1981) offered a smaller (65 million) and less interested pool of talent.[69] The percentage of young people who said they would "probably or "definitely" join the military hovered around 20 percent in 2005, down from a brief surge immediately after September 11. Also on the decline was support from adult "influencers"–parents, coaches, counselors—who recruiters recognized as critical to the enlistment process.[70] Consequently, the Army failed to make its recruiting goal in 2005 by almost eight thousand personnel, or 8 percent. The Army National Guard similarly missed its own recruiting targets each year between 2003 and 2005 by 13 percent.[71] The Air Force and Navy were relatively unaffected and were actually reducing their ranks by the end of the first decade of the twenty-first century.[72]

The military developed a number of measures to compensate for these lean years. New recruiting offices opened throughout the country. A new media campaign built around the slogan "Army of One" replaced the venerable "Be All That You Can Be" in 2001. Military recruiters introduced a first-person shooter game *America's Army* in 2002 in an effort to tap into youth culture through popular entertainment.[73] Perhaps most important, the Defense Department funded a massive increase in enlistment bonuses. Incentives for critical skills grew from $112.6 million in 2001 to $505.6 million in 2005. In the Army National Guard, the budget for regular enlistment bonuses increased from $60.4 million (2001) to $138.6 million (2005).[74]

At the same time, the Army compromised on incoming recruit quality. The time period after September 11 saw a slow decline of "highly qualified" recruits, from 73 percent in 2003 to 67 percent in 2005. The Army was the only branch between 2000 and 2005 to miss the 90 percent high school diploma threshold.[75] Although they represented a small percentage of enlistments overall, the number of CAT IV recruits increased 400 percent between 2003 and 2005.[76] To broaden the recruiting pool, the Army also raised its maximum enlistment age from thirty-five to forty-two.[77]

Other systemic compromises accompanied these changes. There was a marked increase in medical and conduct waivers. Exceptions for prior drug use became more common, both before enlistment and while in uniform. In fiscal year 2018, 2,410 Marines tested positive for drugs, but only half were separated from the service. In his 2019 annual report, the Marine Corps commandant made note of the problem: "I remain troubled by the extent to which drug abuse is a characteristic of new recruits, and the fact the vast majority of recruits require drug waivers for enlistment. I am equally troubled by the fact that we do not specifically monitor personnel for continued substance abuse while in-service."[78] Similar waivers followed for recruits with criminal backgrounds. Between 2003 and 2005, the Army granted 4,230 "moral waivers" to convicted felons.[79] In 2007, nearly 12 percent of Army recruits received a "moral waiver" for criminal records, twice as many as in 2003. Offenses ranged from vandalism to burglary and aggravated assault. Army officials acknowledged the increase was the result of difficulties in meeting minimum quotas.[80] One possible consequence of this policy was a surge in gang incidents within the armed forces reported by both the FBI and the Army Criminal Investigation Division. Between 2003 and 2007, a total of 183 appeared in official records, with seventy-nine gang incidents in the Army in 2007 alone.[81]

In the recent past, the military has addressed some recurrent challenges as well as a number unique to contemporary twenty-first-century America. One of these was the return to good economic times, a period that lasted from retrenchment after the Great Recession of December 2007–June 2009 to the 2020 COVID-19 pandemic. As was the case in past economic booms, it became increasingly more difficult for the military to compete with a civilian economic sector that offered better opportunities and fewer risks, despite increases to military pay after 2003 that finally created parity with the private marketplace.

Education remains a concern for military recruiting, albeit with a relatively recent twist. The penchant for standardized testing facilitated by federal No Child Left Behind policy (2002) and its successors has proven to be problematic for military enlistees. "Teaching to the test," in this case the ACT or SAT, has not translated well for young men and women with military aspirations. A 2015 Congressional Research Service study noted that the individual service branches generally were able to sustain two metrics of recruit quality: 90 percent possessing a high school diploma, and 60 percent scoring above average (Category I through IIIA) on the AFQT. However, these statistics were undercut by the reality that only 70 percent of enlistees with high school diplomas could pass the AFQT.[82]

Various emerging social factors present in contemporary American society also affected retention rates for incoming military recruits. A

2010 study of the all-volunteer force noted a higher rate of enlistments from single-parent homes. Overall, research revealed a "lack of social stability, personal control, and reliable social ties."[83] Health problems have reemerged as a serious problem among potential recruits. However, where malnutrition and its consequences disqualified millions from service in World War II and Korea, the modern military now confronts chronic obesity prevalent in the United States. According to a 2018 *Army Times* report, 30 percent of eighteen- to twenty-four-year-olds were automatically disqualified from service because of their weight.[84] Taken as a whole, 71 percent of potential recruits did not qualify for military service because of poor health, education, or criminal records in 2019.[85]

One last potential element of future recruiting deserves some attention. In 2013, the Naval Postgraduate School in Monterey, California, conducted a survey of community college students drawn from among "millennials" (people born between 1981 and 1996) who form one of the two cohorts comprising the recruiting base for the United States military.[86] As many authors have pointed out, from Robert D. Putnam in *Bowling Alone* to more recent work done by the Pew Research Center, millennials are distinct from their great-grandparents.[87] They have different goals and expectations on a host of political, social, and economic issues. The same is true for military careers, where respondents to the Naval Postgraduate School survey expressed a desire for "more flexibility/ more personal freedom" and choice of assignments.[88] Such sentiments have caused the military to seriously reexamine its Permanent Change of Station (PCS) policies with greater attention to stability for the sake of service members and their dependents.[89]

CONCLUSIONS

Although the all-volunteer military started with a plan to leverage marketplace efficiencies for competitiveness and quality, it has evolved into an increasingly insular institution whose members take some pride in their separation from mainstream society. Evan Wright's *Generation Kill* (2004) offers an ironic counterpoint to the original logic of the all-volunteer military: "What unites them is an almost reckless desire to test themselves in the most extreme circumstances. In many respects the life they have chosen is a complete rejection of the hyped, consumerist American dream as it is dished out in reality TV shows and pop-song lyrics. They've chosen asceticism over consumption. Instead of celebrating their individualism, they've subjugated theirs to the collective will of an institution. Their highest aspiration is self-sacrifice and self-preservation."[90]

The Gates Commission assumed that personal choice could be the driving engine for military recruitment. It was a bold approach, one that directly challenged the existing ethic regarding service. Historically, serving voluntarily or by complying with a draft was a reflection of traditional civic duty. At its worst, service was a necessary evil that balanced temporary personal risk against a threat to national security. These two boundaries encompassed much of military service throughout U.S. history.

That narrative began to change with the post-Vietnam all-volunteer military. Morris Janowitz pointed out in 1975 his belief that voluntary service would lead to the "civilianization" of the military.[91] This observation was certainly true with respect to demographics. The increasing number of women in uniform was more representative of the United States as a whole even if it did not reach the same proportions as civilian society. The opposite was true with respect to race. The rapid rise in Latinx and African American participation in the military beyond their proportion in the U.S. populace redefined the issue of integration barely a generation after it became official policy.

However, in another, more profound sense, the premium placed on personal choice set in motion a military institution and culture that became more self-selecting and insular, shaped by what Janowitz called the "special segments of the social structure." To put it another way, the military came to rely on the disadvantaged, a status defined by economic hard times as well as racial or gender bias.[92] That the military could offer opportunities to these groups is as much a testament to its strengths as it is to American society's weaknesses. What this process shaped was a divergence between the uniformed armed services and the rest of the country.

The return to mass wartime mobilization in 2001 changed the nature of service yet again and arguably widened the divide between soldier and civilian. Unlike World War II, the Global War on Terrorism did not result in a collective commitment to national survival. The draft remained an unpopular, politically impossible option. In the meantime, a small contingent of Americans bore the brunt of repeated deployments for years and, now, two decades. Over time, these deployments refined the crucible that created and maintained military insularity, becoming a key reason why civil-military relations were so "brittle and shallow" in contemporary America.

CHAPTER THREE

The Nature of the Beast

> The young recruit is silly—'e
> thinks o' suicide;
> 'E's lost 'is gutter-devil; 'e asin't
> got 'is pride;
> But day by day they kicks 'im,
> which 'elps 'im on a bit,
> Till 'e finds 'isself one mornin'
> with a full an' proper kit.
> *Gettin' clear o' dirtiness, gettin'*
> *done with mess,*
> *Gettin' shut o' doin' things*
> *rather-more-or-less.*
> —Rudyard Kipling, "The 'Eathen," 1895

INTRODUCTION: THE AMERICAN WAY OF WAR

Military service defines the veteran. It is a simple proposition, but one that invites a number of intricacies. What type of service: Combat or support? What type of unit: Elite or run-of-the-mill? At what rank? It is a common mistake to assume the military is a homogeneous organism. There are currents and eddies within the armed forces where unique features exist and define the military experience. Fort Lewis, Washington, and Fort Indiantown Gap, Pennsylvania, may belong to the same branch, but they occupy separate planets within the Army. Every veteran leaves the service with the stamp of these plural military cultures on them.

To understand the veteran, it is necessary to understand their military as a culture and an institution. Luckily, there is scholarship that offers a perfect starting point. Russell Weigley's *American Way of War* was published in 1973 at the end of both the Vietnam War and the draft. Weigley wanted to understand, to use his rather elegant phrase, the military's "habits of mind."[1] He primarily applied this lens to strategic thinking, inviting the reader to consider the evolving historical complexities of American strategic goals as well as the means to achieve them. In doing so, he opened up the field of military history to arenas reaching far beyond leadership studies or great battles. Weigley proved to be as influential as Samuel P. Huntington, who asked questions about military culture and civil-military relations that are still being discussed and debated. A generation of scholars followed both, looking beyond the standard menu of strategy, doctrine, and tactics to the features of a distinct American military culture.[2]

Colin S. Gray was part a generation of military historians who kept faith with Weigley and built on his work. When he revisited the "American way of war" in a 2005 essay, Gray leaned into potential variations of culture influencing American military practices. He sought out more complexities than "attrition" or "annihilation," the benchmark concepts of the "American way" originally posited by Weigley thirty years earlier. However, while Gray sought out a model with greater facets, he understood its limits. "Culture is a vague concept," Gray notes. "Its presence is as certain as its relative influence is uncertain."[3]

Yet culture is useful as a starting point to understand both the military and the veteran. For his purposes, Gray constructed twelve specific cultural features of the "American way of war." Some clearly overlap in fascinating ways. The American military employs technologically enhanced firepower to mitigate casualties. Similarly, impatience often leads the U.S. military to be culturally ignorant (table 1).

TABLE 1. CHARACTERISTICS OF THE AMERICAN WAY OF WAR

1. Apolitical	7. Firepower focused
2. Astrategic	8. Large-scale
3. Ahistorical	9. Profoundly regular
4. Problem-solving, optimistic	10. Impatient
5. Culturally ignorant	11. Logistically excellent
6. Technologically dependent	12. Sensitive to casualties

Source: Colin S. Gray, "The American Way of War: Critique and Implications," in *Rethinking the Principles of War*, ed. Anthony D. McIvor (Annapolis, MD: Naval Institute Press, 2005), 27. Reprinted by permission.

Gray's list is not intended to be exhaustive, but portions of it are useful to understand military service and the modern veteran. These characteristics are a broad brush applied to the topic, one that can draw out some of the important aspects of service and the military experience. However, some of his points exercise a greater influence than do others and are worth additional attention.

"LOGISTICALLY EXCELLENT"

Most of the men and women who serve in the contemporary U.S. military do not fight. Instead, they provide a vast array of services necessary to maintain a complex and technologically dependent institution. The passage of time and the constant incorporation of more complicated weapons systems, vehicles, aircraft, and logistics constantly adds to the inventory of expertise necessary to make a modern armed force function.

The military calls this the "tooth-to-tail ratio"—the number of combat troops to support personnel—and it is easy to measure over the course of American conflicts. A Civil War infantry regiment was almost entirely composed of riflemen. With the exception of a camp desk and a handful of officers, noncommissioned officers, and enlisted in the headquarters staff, most men fought. Mechanization changed that experience. One study of the U.S. Army in World War II found that 60 percent of personnel were in the combat arms in 1944.[4] During the next two wars, but particularly in Vietnam, the number of warriors diminished as the military institution became more complex and more dependent on logistics. By 1968, only 29 percent of personnel were assigned to the combat arms.[5] A detailed investigation of Army forces deployed to Iraq in 2005 indicated that a mere 25 percent of the personnel in country were actually in combat units.[6]

There are thousands of military occupational specialties (MOSs) in the armed forces. A review of the catalog of these positions opens up the dizzying complexity of the American military. Some include traditional jobs in medicine, communications, maintenance, and administration. Some are more recent products of the times. Air Force MOSs include unmanned vehicle pilots and cyberspace operations.[7]

The logistical tail has been a traditional subject of derision in the military. Vietnam saw the term "REMF," or "rear-echelon motherfucker," uttered with the same contempt as "POG" (person other than a grunt) or "fobbit" (referring to someone who never left a forward operations base in Iraq or Afghanistan) would have been for subsequent generations of soldiers. In the not-too-distant past, this distinction has taken on a sharper edge given the extravagant creature comforts enjoyed by support personnel on U.S. military bases in combat zones: air-conditioned housing units, all-you-can-eat dining facilities, morale support centers.

The "logistically excellent" armed forces place a premium on educated personnel, essentially creating a separate class of service within the military. Each branch, but particularly the Air Force and the Navy, husbands these technicians because they are critical for the routine upkeep of increasingly complex combat and logistical operations. Since Vietnam, these individuals have been segregated by occupational specialties. They live and work in daily contrast to the sizable number of personnel with grade school reading levels who rely on simplified World War II–vintage modular training techniques and the comic book *PS, The Preventative Maintenance Monthly* to keep the rest of the military running.

Peacekeeping and peace enforcement missions in the nineties narrowed the distance between the logistical and combat military. The risks of being commingled with civilians, military forces, and nongovernmental organizations in high-threat environments such as the Balkans, Africa, or Kurdistan was a significant departure from the Cold War status quo. After the 2003 coalition invasion of Iraq, all military forces were equally vulnerable to indirect rocket and mortar fire and improvised explosive devices (IEDs). This point was driven home when a maintenance company was ambushed near Nasiriyah on March 23, 2003, resulting in eleven killed and five captured. One of its members, Jessica Lynch, became briefly famous after she was rescued by U.S. special operations forces.[8]

Veterans of the logistical military remain segregated from combat veterans when they leave the service. The former more often finds better rewards in a modern information economy that places a premium on high-tech skills; the latter, usually not. It is a common trope in the infantry to talk about how much one's training prepared the way for a civilian career as a janitor. One online discussion thread put it this way: "Lack of relevant transferable skills is another important factor. Once you decide or are forced to leave the military, not many other jobs in the civilian world are looking for *'can live like a homeless bum'* as a skill set."[9] Denials to the contrary, the combat veteran resents this.

The combat veteran also remembers the disproportionate cost of his risks, something that can be measured in hard facts. For Army units deployed to Iraq and Afghanistan between 2003 and 2011, combat units suffered significantly higher numbers of killed and wounded than did logistical units. In 2003, the casualty rate for combat troops was more than double that of combat support and combat service support. By 2011, when the fighting had largely shifted to Afghanistan, it was four times higher.[10] At the heart of these differences, separate military cultures grow.

THE MAGIC BULLET

Most of the men and women who served between the end of the Vietnam War and today never fired a shot in anger. The rest apply the basic practice, whenever possible, of spending firepower instead of American lives. Their military conventional wisdom follows the axiom, to quote Colin Gray: "The exploitation of machinery is the American way of war."[11]

A number of basic reasons exist for this belief. One is a natural abhorrence of casualties. Americans may memorialize their war dead and wounded each year, but we try to avoid the human cost of war at every opportunity. This was true in the case of our traditional conventional wars. Finding a way to prevent casualties took on a new importance as American conflicts evolved after World War II, adopting more abstract goals like "containment" or the "global war on terrorism" without finite deadlines or milestones.[12]

Americans are also drawn to the proverbial "magic bullet" because our culture is fascinated with complex solutions for seemingly intractable problems. We glory in the moon landing not only for that reason but also because it added one more element to the process: the triumph of *American* know-how over what seemed to be impossible. The military applications of this concept offer the possibility of combining both ideas, while effectively doubling down on our own ethnocentrism. Modern military weapons systems are a chance to demonstrate our ability to innovate while saving *American* lives.

Although various forms of the "magic bullet" have been present throughout military history—the adoption of the Minié ball comes to mind—it was the Industrial Revolution that offered startling ways to augment military firepower. Breechloading, rapid-fire weapons, steam, and improved metallurgy revolutionized war at sea and on land.[13] After World War II, American defense research rapidly expanded our catalog of military tools, from composites and communications infrastructure to targeting and surveillance systems. The U.S. military-industrial complex became extremely adept at producing cutting-edge weaponry.[14]

The last fifty years are populated with instances of incredible American military lethality. The First Gulf War introduced Global Positioning System (GPS) navigation systems en masse that wiped away much of the "fog of war" on the modern battlefield. Thermal imagining and high-velocity munitions made armored warfare exponentially more lethal for Iraqi units, as proved by clashes at Medina Ridge and 73 Easting.[15] In 1997, then colonel David Petraeus contributed to a jointly authored article for the *Field Artillery* journal that spoke to the new era with the subtitle, "Never Send a Man When You Can Send a Bullet."[16] The Second Gulf War simply built on the foundation established in 1991. The widespread use of Joint Direct Attack Munitions (JDAMs), first in Afghanistan and later Iraq, ushered in what the U.S. military establishment declared to be a "revolution in military affairs."[17]

Standoff weapons were the response of choice in escalating battles against terrorism even before September 11. Al-Qaeda attacks on two U.S. embassies in Africa in 1998 resulted in more than five thousand casualties (mostly African). In a show of decisive force, the Clinton administration authorized Operation Infinite Reach, which relied entirely on cruise missile strikes against al-Qaeda targets in Afghanistan and Sudan.[18]

It seemed that the United States was on the cusp of one of the primary goals of the "American way of war," that is, conflict with almost no casualties. Improved firepower offered the prospect of overwhelming an enemy with precise force. It was an appealing proposition for a country, all claims to the contrary, where the ghosts of Vietnam remained deeply embedded in society.

The nature of post-September 11 conflict illustrated the limits of American technology. This happened very early in the Global War on Terrorism, specifically during the latter stages of Operation Enduring Freedom. As American and Afghan forces closed in on the last Taliban refuge in the Tora Bora mountains, they had unchallenged air superiority. This allowed ground commanders unfettered use of virtually the entire catalog of U.S. weapons, from modern air- and sea-launched precision guided munitions to "dumb" bombs dropped from ancient B-52 Stratofortresses.[19] None of these advantages proved decisive. Taliban forces, Osama bin Laden among then, escaped and lived to fight on. The war continues today.

In practice, much of the Global War on Terrorism was extremely ugly, whether the culprit was al-Qaeda, the Taliban, or ISIS.[20] While the United States and coalition forces attempted to restrain civilian casualties, mistakes were not uncommon. Caught between the contending sides, tens of thousands of civilians have been killed and wounded.

Faced with this new and dangerous reality, American technology turned inward toward self-defense. The military deployed the Warlock system to jam frequencies used for remote IEDs. The Defense Department spent billions upgrading individual body armor that added extra layers of protection at the cost of an almost absurd amount of weight. The most elaborate version, with upper arm and groin protection, weighed slightly more than thirty pounds.[21] After years of service members suffering casualties from increasingly sophisticated roadside bombs, the Pentagon introduced a new generation of Mine Resistant Ambush Protected (MRAP) vehicles.

American doctrine also turned away from traditional approaches to combat. General Petraeus, who had earlier endorsed the primacy of firepower, spoke in 2008 of the Iraqi people as the "decisive terrain" in the war. To secure their loyalty, he emphasized a constructive, "nonkinetic" (noncombat) methodology designed to preserve reconciliation and civil stability. Essentially, Petraeus was asking the military to embrace a doctrine that combined contradictory practices with its basic mission. American forces simultaneously were tasked to "pursue the enemy relentlessly" while, at the same time, building support within the civilian community.[22]

What followed were increasingly stringent rules of engagement (ROE) for air and ground operations. These made sense to policymakers interested in avoiding civilian casualties while employing the best practices of counterinsurgency. For the average rifleman clashing with al-Qaeda or Taliban forces on a regular basis, the ROE bore little resemblance to the snap decisions necessary under combat stress. In an email to General Stanley McChrystal, an Army staff sergeant stationed in Afghanistan expressed a concern held by many American combatants: "I also understand your restraint tactic. But if you look at the light infantry soldiers of today [we] have no place here. We have lost many soldiers in this area and don't want to lose any more. With the new R.O.E. it is telling the men that they should not shoot even when they are threatened with death. Sir, it may not be the way you intended it to be, but that is how all the soldiers here took it."[23]

One simple fact that persists in war is its dependence on the ugly work of the infantry. As much as today's military establishment tries to cocoon the combat soldier in body armor, move around in MRAPs, and fill the airwaves with jamming, it needs people to kick in doors and pull triggers. Every time planners start believing that push-button war and the magic bullet are on the brink of taking over, events prove them wrong. This was true at the dawn of the nuclear age when the Korean War erupted, and it was just as true when Donald Rumsfeld pronounced "shock and awe" had prevailed in Afghanistan.[24]

Despite this fact, there remains a great deal of public ambivalence about combat and the combat veteran. Times have changed. T. Grady Gallant, a Marine who served on Guadalcanal, was characteristically blunt about what combat meant to him and his generation: "They did not look upon war as dying. War is killing. Seeking out the enemy and killing. Killing without mercy. Killing for God and country."[25] That type of clarity and candor still exists in the combat arms today, but it is far more difficult to express openly in contemporary society.

Sebastian Junger found the pulse of the combatant in his book *War*, conveying the ugly, raunchy, merciless, and timeless soul of the infantry.

One passage drew the difference between garrison soldiers and combat soldiers: "I used to score three hundreds on my PT tests shit-canned . . . just drunk as fuck, O'Bryne told me. That's how you get sober for the rest of the day. I never got in trouble, but Bobby beat up a few MPs, threatened them with a fire extinguisher, pissed on their boots. But what do you expect from the infantry, you know? I know all the guys that were bad in garrison were perfect fucking soldiers in combat. They're troublemakers and they like to fight. That's a bad garrison trait but a good combat trait—right?"[26]

Modern combat is trapped in a paradox. The military wants "warriors" and applies that label liberally in its doctrine and public relations literature. In 2003, the U.S. Army went so far as to revise the traditional Soldier's Creed, augmenting it with the Warrior Ethos. Its purpose, was to close the gap between combatant and noncombatant. A study commissioned by the Army Research Institute for the Behavioral and Social Sciences put it this way: "The Warrior Ethos helps ensure that all Soldiers, regardless of rank, branch or military occupational specialty, are prepared to engage the enemy in close combat, while serving as a part of a team of flexible, adaptable, well-trained and well-equipped Soldiers."[27] At the same time, the military wants sanitized warriors, individuals who are deadly in combat according to exacting standards of behavior that will stand up to public scrutiny in an age of Twitter, Instagram, Facebook, and twenty-four-hour cable news. The Warrior Ethos rejects the garrison soldier–combat soldier dichotomy. Individuals who step outside these guardrails do so at their own risk.

Accompanying the new warrior model were concurrent policies that altered and expanded the definition of combat service. Since World War II, the Combat Infantry Badge (CIB) and Combat Medical Badge (CMB) have been the standard for recognition in the Army. The Navy and Marine Corps award the Combat Action Ribbon (CAR) as well as a number of other citations acknowledging air and ground service.[28] Recipients treat these badges as a rare rite of passage, an entry into a special fraternity. It was not uncommon for soldiers in World War II to wear their CIBs exclusively without any other service awards or ribbons.[29] The Army officially changed its policy in 2005 with the creation of the Combat Action Badge (CAB), which was open to all Army branches and specialties. The official regulation for the award defined a qualifying individual in these terms: "A Soldier must be personally present and under hostile fire while performing satisfactorily in accordance with the prescribed rules of engagement, in an area where hostile fire pay or imminent danger pay is authorized."[30]

Although the Combat Action Badge may have granted overdue recognition for participation in combat, such awards did not pass without some criticism from within the military and the veterans' community. Many complained that the CAB and other similar awards set a low standard that diminished their value and diluted overall standards for recognizing combat service. One veteran complained about the proposed Expert Action Badge, launched in 2019 to recognize noncombat soldiers: "Just name it the PPA. The POG Participation Award. They can bust it out, and show it off to the grandchildren when they tell them the story about walking back from salsa night at the MWR [Morale, Welfare, and Recreation Center], when they heard a mortar go off that one fateful night."[31] The Marine Corps did not escape the debate. When Sergeant Major Ronald Green was appointed the branch's senior enlisted man in 2015, comments about his lack of combat experience popped up immediately on the *Marine Corps Times* Facebook page: "No CAR . . . not the right guy for the job," one poster simply noted.[32]

Military operations abroad have tested the new warrior model and exposed the limits of its ethos. In January 2012, a YouTube video revealed three Marines urinating on Taliban dead in violation of the rules of engagement. Cable news readers were shocked and issued viewer advisories. Secretary of Defense Leon Panetta called it "deplorable" and launched an investigation, which resulted in guilty pleas from all three Marines for a variety of charges. The Marines involved were defiant. One interviewed by ABC News simply said: "These were the same guys that were killing our family, killing our brothers, but do I regret doing it? Hell no."[33]

*

There are three important features at work in the discourse on the combat experience. The first involves proximity. Since the advent of projectile weapons, military thinkers have been fascinated with the prospect of combat at a distance. That fascination multiplied with the advent of the airplane and today lives on with unmanned aerial vehicles. This hope for warfare at a distance has coexisted with the realization that the bloody tip of the spear remains essentially the same today as it had in antiquity: close combat is an unavoidable reality of war. A Marine engaged in bitter room-to-room fighting in Fallujah is a different combat veteran by definition than a person piloting a drone above the embattled city.

The second feature involves risk. Simply put, combat involves calculated risk. Tactics and doctrine are designed for the efficient application of military force while mitigating risk. However, as any combat veteran will attest, the best plans are vulnerable to circumstances, accidents, or just plain bad luck. For obvious reasons, proximity to conflict affects the risk to individuals and whole units. The same is true for the duration of exposure to military action, which is largely why military institutions to this day invoke rotation policies and service limits for combat forces.

A third feature involves policy designed to conflate, manipulate, or sanitize the objective importance of proximity and risk to combat. Not all "warriors" are equal despite the best official efforts to recognize them, rightly or not. Nor can combat always be contained within neat, legal parameters despite the obvious, objective need for restraint in many cases. The law and codes of moral behavior may demand mercy in war, but it is not always a choice for the infantry in the heat of battle.

These are general categories designed to capture some of the complex elements that comprise a combat veteran. Their experiences are composites—matters of degree varying broadly across a wide spectrum. Some veterans are marked by selfless acts of bravery. They are the one-percenters of the military. Most simply endure terrible, prolonged danger. Others perform "satisfactorily in accordance with the prescribed rules of engagement." Some of these experiences are objectively riskier and more dangerous than others. As much as the twenty-first century American military might attempt to become more inclusive, there are important gradations of combatants and, subsequently, types of combat veterans.

STOLEN VALOR

Wartime can create a social bandwagon effect. It is a time to rally for good reasons, as an expression of genuine patriotism. Other motives are more pragmatic. War can be an existential threat to national survival. Whether real or perceived, the threat is a powerful reason for a public to reach a consensus.

In 2001, American society seemed an unlikely body for any bandwagon. The presidential election that set the stage for the new century was the most divisive in living memory. The times indulged hyperbole. Writing about the U.S. Supreme Court decision that allowed George W. Bush's victory, Vincent Bugliosi did not disappoint: "The stark reality . . . is that the institution Americans trust the most to protect its freedoms and principles committed one of the biggest and most serious crimes this nation has ever seen—pure and simple, the theft of the presidency. And by definition, the perpetrators of this crime *have* to be denominated criminals."[34]

September 11 changed that. It transformed Bush from a chief executive derided by half the country into a wartime president. Bush's approval ratings jumped from a (then) dismal 51 percent on September 7 to 90 percent just two weeks later. Generations of politicians have and still understand the value of a crisis to a public consensus.[35]

Individuals understand this as well, albeit for different reasons. When the military is popular and celebrated, it creates an impetus for other types of hangers-on. Many succumb to the desire to be celebrated or cunningly craft ways to manipulate the status of a hero for personal gain. Much of this behavior is relatively benign; exaggerations about service are as common as fishing stories told on Friday nights at the local American Legion.

There was fertile ground for this type of behavior after September 11 as the public showered praise on police, first responders, and the military. For almost twenty years, the military has maintained a higher approval rating than almost any other institution in the country. According to a 2020 Gallup poll, 72 percent of respondents said they had a "great deal" or "quite of lot" of confidence in the armed forces. Soldiers enjoyed far more support than the Supreme Court (40%), organized religion (42%), unions (31%), or Congress (13%).[36]

Unfortunately, as the public consensus on the military solidified, there was a corresponding increase in bad behavior by both veterans and nonveterans that ranged from self-aggrandizement to felonies. Many of these acts fall under the rubric of "stolen valor," a term that began to appear with increasing frequency after September 11. A 2010 *Stars and Stripes* article summed up its meaning rather well: "'Stolen Valor' is a term applied to the phenomenon of people falsely claiming military awards or badges they did not earn, service they did not perform, Prisoner of War experiences that never happened, and other tales of military derring-do that exist only in their minds."[37]

Some practitioners are easy to spot and relatively harmless. They tended toward improperly displayed medals, tabs, and badges that festooned dress uniforms. Debunking them was sometimes as simple as comparing their age to the claimed heroic act and war. The internet proved invaluable for this purpose. Websites such as Ancestry.com allowed access to military records. Freedom of Information Act (FOIA) filings, requests under various state "sunshine" laws, and other publicly available sources covered much of the rest.[38]

Other actors went from crafting bragging rights to outright fraud. Army veteran Gregg Ramsdell, who obtained a 70 percent disability from the Veterans Administration for post-traumatic stress disorder (PTSD) incurred while serving in Afghanistan, was found to have faked his claim.[39] Michael J. Parker, the owner of a construction company in

Missouri, claimed a military injury to qualify for the Service-Disabled Veteran-Owned Small Business Program. He eventually received $7.4 million from the Department of Veterans Affairs and Department of Defense before being caught and sentenced to fifty-one months in federal prison.[40] William G. Hillar portrayed himself as an Army Special Forces colonel with experience in Afghanistan and Colombia. Hillar parlayed his claim into lucrative speaking fees and payment as an instructor for dozens of police and fire departments. He was caught when a member of the special forces community questioned his credentials on an online forum.[41]

Rooting out individuals like this has become cottage industry in recent years. Individual veterans began to investigate some of more flagrant abusers and share their findings through professional organizations and, later, a variety of "stolen valor" groups that began to appear on Facebook and other websites.[42] This led to public pressure for legal reform. Given the high-profile nature of veteran community and the millions of dollars involved in some crimes, Congress passed the Stolen Valor Act in 2005. After the Supreme Court ruled six to three that the law unconstitutionally limited free speech, it was amended in 2013, making it a crime for individuals to fraudulently represent themselves with the "intent to obtain money, property, or other tangible benefit."[43] The law made such actions a misdemeanor punishable with fines or imprisonment up to one year.

MILITARY CONTRACTORS: MEN WITH GUNS AND OTHERS

In 2007, as U.S. Central Command began ramping up operations for the "surge" in Iraq, there were 190,000 contractors of all types in country in comparison to 160,000 U.S. military forces.[44] This proportion reflected the fact that modern military operations cannot occur without an enormous number of individuals who are technically not in the conventional military but essential to military operations. Many of them are veterans and are hired because of their past military credentials. Most cover logistics, although a small percentage are actively involved in such tasks as site security, convoy escort, or bodyguard duties.[45] Such a large contingent exists in plain sight and is frequently ignored by both policymakers and students of veterans' history.

Contractors are a fixture in American history. A careful read of the U.S. constitution, Article 1, Section 8, reveals the term "letters of marque and reprisal," which allows the government to hire "privateers" in times of war, codifying a practice that other countries had used for centuries. Contractors took on a new value during the industrial age as the federal government adopted increasingly complex weapons systems that mandated a partnership with American corporations. As mentioned above, two world wars and the Cold War solidified this ongoing relationship.[46]

By the eighties, federal officials were ready to apply free market philosophy as well as its utility. A generation of Democrat and Republican administrations argued for introducing private sector efficiencies into the Defense Department. These officials made the case that outsourcing military logistical functions would enhance time and energy spent on combat forces. Such private military contractors (PMCs) as Kellogg Brown & Root (KBR) subsequently earned billions adopting previous military responsibilities like housing, food service, power generation, vehicle maintenance, and other mission-critical support functions.[47]

After September 11, the number of military contractors rapidly expanded, first as force deployments to Afghanistan and Iraq began and, later, as occupation settled in for the long haul. Private military contractors provided the "logistically excellent" foundation for coalition forces. Their other added bonus was that although hundreds of contractors were killed and wounded, they drew minimal media coverage, obscuring a significant human cost to the so-called Global War on Terrorism.

Also lost in the narrative was the fact that most of these people were not American. While every PMC had an assortment of U.S. citizens and expatriate Europeans and South Africans, most of their work fell to local nationals drawn from host nations like Iraq and Afghanistan and "third-country nationals," low-paid employees from the Philippines, Fiji, Uganda, and numerous other poor countries.

The proliferation of PMCs has essentially created a new category of veteran. The PMC industry highly values and rewards expertise as well as up-to-date security clearances. Contractors are well paid in terms of salary but individually responsible for their long-term medical care, pensions, and any disabilities incurred while under contract.[48] Government regulation is minimal and guided by a series of antique laws that predate World War II. For the most part, they are on their own once they return home. Still, American contractors enjoy far better treatment than local and third-country employees, who receive very little beyond cash or wire transfer payment for monthly salaries. The difficulties faced by U.S. military interpreters seeking sanctuary and citizenship is a well-documented and shameful example of their treatment.[49]

Private military contractors are commingled with conventional forces fighting around the world. In many cases, they are a new version of the Korean War–era "retread." Former Gurkhas, South African Defence Forces, and Kurdish *pershmerga* may all share the same battlefield today in

Afghanistan or Syria. Collectively, they further muddy our contemporary understanding of what constitutes a "veteran." They fight for nations that will never recognize their sacrifice or construct monuments to their service. They are wounded and largely have to count on themselves for healing. Their numbers are significant and may enjoin consequences that few policymakers care to contemplate and fewer still may remember.

CONCLUSIONS

Much of the contemporary U.S. military brings to mind the pre–World War I institution that Max Boot examined in *The Savage Wars of Peace*. It is a small, specialized and insular military that spends much of its time as an expeditionary force far from home.[50] More than geography separates the military from its parent society. Cleavages appear with respect to basic values dictating a spectrum of behavior from civil discourse to treatment of the dead.

Complicating military culture is the fact that there is no single class of military service. Those who serve in the logistical "tail" are likely the closest to resembling civilian corporate cultures just as much as the combat arms on the bleeding edge are not. Within these two divisions, or "tooth" and "tail," are further shades of participation and commitment, of proximity and risk, that further complicate this mosaic.

Veterans follow in close parallel to these complexities. They are the products of both logistical complexity and the ongoing struggle with both avoiding and embracing the violence of war. Each retains the natural pride that comes with professional accomplishments over brief stints in uniform or long careers. But they are not all the same.

CHAPTER FOUR

Coming Home

> Cheryl said, "How are you?" which meant, How was it?
> Are you crazy now?
> —*Phil Klay,* Redeployment

INTRODUCTION

In 2005, when I started writing about veterans' history, my first chapter began with: "Home is what they all dreamed about."[1] In that first sentence, I was trying to impart the value of home to a deployed soldier and the sometimes unrealistic expectations that grew up around it. It is not uncommon even today for people in the military to bring tokens of home with them to war. Pictures stuffed into a pouch or pocket. "Graduation pictures. Baby pictures. Standing with their family. Pictures of them with their cars," as one soldier assigned to Mortuary Affairs in Baghdad recounted.[2] Sonograms. Letters. Until the advent of satellite phones, mail call was one of the most time-honored rituals in the military, a link in the chain going back home.

Home is an ideal, an anchor point for a anyone caught in a war. It is a conglomeration of wants and needs, sometimes as simple as clean sheets and that special meal, sometimes as profound as a place where they know love and mercy still exist. When they come back, home is something veterans want to shield from the war left behind. At points, that might mean protecting their homes and loved ones from themselves.

Home has a real value when the veteran of war comes back. It sets a tone for their recovery and reassimilation. Home is at the core of what sociologists call the "life course theory." It asserts that social context is a key means to mitigate individual trauma, that is, if the public accepts a war as honorable, its endorsement will ease the psychological damage caused to the warrior.[3] What defined the "post-military experience," or determined whether a veteran was a hero or a villain, was public perception.[4] When home can construct and support a positive trajectory, it serves the veteran best. When it is littered with obstacles or tainted by hostility, it can help break a veteran.

THE SCORNED VETERAN

Treatment of Vietnam veterans upon their return home has occupied academics and journalists for more than fifty years. Most writers illustrate a country that treated returning soldiers within a spectrum that ranged from ambivalence to open confrontation. They often draw a direct contrast between that landscape and the parades and accolades that greeted returning World War II veterans a generation earlier.

In 1998, sociologist Jerry Lembcke challenged this narrative when he published *The Spitting Image: Myth, Memory, and the Legacy of Vietnam*.[5] Lembcke's thesis was that the spat-on returning Vietnam veteran was basically an urban myth. His research failed to find evidence that any incident like this ever happened during the war. In work that predated Lembcke's, historian Eric Dean offered his own take on the nature of the Vietnam veteran: "The Vietvet was seen as *unique* amongst veterans of all American wars in receiving this ungrateful, if not outright hostile treatment. As a result, the Vietnam veteran has acquired an almost mythic stature, where he is seen as the 'survivor-as-hero,' who fought under insane conditions in Vietnam and then rebuilt his life in ungrateful America; some critics even see the Vietnam veteran—because he lost the most, because he did it seemingly for nothing—as the most romanticized war hero in American history."[6] Two obvious sets of questions flow from this analysis. Was the whole idea of the "spat-on veteran" a mistake? Was it a version of the Mandela effect, a widely held false memory, applied to veterans' history? Or was it simply a matter of exaggeration?

An enormous amount of anecdotal evidence exists about the mistreatment of Vietnam veterans. One soldier recalled an incident in 1970 when a Seattle policeman intervened to stop an altercation with two drunken businessmen offended by his Army uniform. Another veteran talked about the need to hide his military haircut with a wig when he went out in public. A 1968 edition of *The Nation* depicted a Navy veteran who was referred to as "the resident fascist pig" of his Harvard dormitory. A 1972 American Veterans Committee report noted the "indifference, even hostility, of a society weary of the war" that increased the "sense of isolation" felt by men returning from Vietnam.[7]

Obviously, anecdotes can go only so far. Polling data provides a broader and more complex picture of public sentiments regarding Vietnam and its veterans. Analysis of public opinion from the initial deployment of American regular forces in 1965 to the Tet Offensive indicates a creeping sense of frustration over a military stalemate that undercut support for the war. Throughout, it is clear that people disliked the use of ground forces but did not abandon support for American airpower. Lyndon Johnson clearly understood the value of the "magic bullet" and the positive correlation between air strikes and his poll numbers. The president's approval rating increased by 14 percent after U.S. retaliation for the Gulf of Tonkin incident. In 1966, 61 percent of Americans favored escalating the air campaign against North Vietnam if the bombing halt failed to obtain concessions. A year later, despite its apparent lack of decisive success, 67 percent of the public still supported Operation Rolling Thunder.[8]

The encroaching cost of Vietnam and the absence of a clear path to victory seriously eroded public support. When the Johnson administration imposed a 10 percent surcharge on corporate and personal income taxes in August 1967, the portion of Americans who considered Vietnam a "mistake" (46%) outnumbered those who did not (44%) for the first time.[9] The Tet Offensive that followed only a few months later juxtapositioned rapidly escalating U.S. casualties against what the average American could see was a military stalemate.[10]

Public disclosure of direct U.S. involvement in atrocities, particularly reports about the Mỹ Lai massacre by Seymour M. Hersh, represented a breaking point over not only the war but also public perception about veterans.[11] In some cases, evidence of horrifying war crimes came from veterans in the antiwar movement. The Winter Soldier Investigation, held in Detroit at the start 1971, featured more than a hundred veterans who offered testimony on a litany of murder, rape, and torture committed against the Viet Cong and innocent South Vietnamese civilians.[12] Although journalists like Neil Sheehan of the *New York Times* would uncover a clear pattern of inaccurate and uncorroborated information, the event, and others like it, left a mark.[13] As the conflict wound down, people began to see Vietnam veterans not as "victims of a cruel war," as historian James E. Wright explains, but as "perpetrators of a cruel war."[14]

In many respects, Vietnam veterans were trapped by circumstances and the actions of a tiny minority of soldiers who belonged in jail for crimes against humanity. The war itself was a case study that academics would use to study the reasons for the gradual erosion of public support: the absence of tangible goals beyond Cold War "containment," the lack of a reasonable timeline, and the lack of consistent elite support among opinion makers and political leaders.[15] Moreover, although William L. Calley Jr. and the soldiers responsible for Mỹ Lai deserved severe punishment, they represented a small fraction of the 29 percent of U.S. forces actually assigned to combat in the Vietnam War.[16]

For its own part, the public did not separate the conduct of the war from the conduct of its veterans, regardless of their actual role. According to a 1971 Harris poll, most Americans characterized Vietnam veterans as "suckers, having to risk their lives in the wrong war, in the wrong place, at the wrong time."[17] What they assigned was collective guilt, and they did so with an extremely broad brush.

Jan Barry, a cofounder of the Vietnam Veterans Against the War, turned the whole issue of guilt on its head in a 1971 *New York Times* editorial: "One cannot participate in the Vietnam war without being at least in complicity in committing war crimes." Barry concluded that the sin extended to the entire baby boom generation: "America's Vietnam generation isn't up against the wall: it's bricked in. Going to Vietnam is a war crime, refusing to go is a domestic crime and just sitting still, somewhere or somehow in exile or limbo, is a moral crime. It is a terrible time today to be American and young. In fact, it apparently is a crime."[18]

THE QUIET RETURN OF THE COLD WARRIOR

When peace returned and the all-volunteer military gained traction, a degree of normalcy returned to military homecomings. The end of the draft took away the controversy surrounding military service. Protests died down well before the fall of Saigon in 1975. Departures and returns from service became routine, individual experiences. Military families attended graduation ceremonies from boot camp, advanced training, and specialty schools. Fort Benning recognized military tradition by allowing parents of successful Jump School candidates to pin their old airborne wings on their sons and daughters. There was a distinctly insular quality to such exercises. The real, personal connections and recognition came from within only a small part of the country.

In the meantime, it seemed as if the American public was experiencing a fit of remorse regarding the treatment of Vietnam veterans. A 1985 CBS/*New York Times* poll indicated that 84 percent of respondents thought that Vietnam veterans did not receive the same respect as World War II veterans, but 94 percent believed they deserved it.[19] As one *Time* article put it, "Those who stayed home, or even fought in the streets to keep from going, now feel guilty about those who fought and never came home. Most of those who sent the soldiers to Viet Nam are still pained by what they did, and they usually cannot—or will not try to—explain it. Veterans speak most bitterly about those who sent them half a world away to die and then retreated into silence when the war went bad."[20] Trailing in the wake of these sentiments, and perhaps bolstered by them, public support for the military recovered and grew.

By the mideighties, the country acted on these changing convictions. In May 1985, twenty-five thousand Vietnam veterans received a ticker tape parade in New York City before thousands of cheering spectators. Watching from the sidelines, D. Keith Mano wrote: "Good God, how old they look. Hair defoliated. Reflex-shot. Many hip-thick and slow as professional house-sitters." There was a normalcy to them, their ranks comprised of "police, fire, sanitation, court; thousands, apparently went from one uniform to another." In subsequent years, even larger celebrations followed in Chicago and Houston, where hundreds of thousands cheered on almost equal numbers of veterans.[21]

Contemporary veterans also benefited from a renaissance in public approval for the American military. In 1981, a Gallup poll recorded a country evenly split at 50 percent regarding confidence in the military as an institution. By 1986, however, support had grown to 63 percent, where it remained for the rest of the eighties.[22] Honoring peacetime service ran concurrent with emerging accolades for Vietnam veterans. Increasing numbers of people, perhaps encouraged by Reagan's unapologetic nationalism, began to embrace the idea of military service again. The move almost certainly resonated with the veterans, who peaked at 28 million in 1980, the year he was elected president.[23]

Actual military deployments tested this faith. Two days after the disastrous truck bomb attack on the U.S. Marine barracks in Beirut, which resulted in the death of 241 U.S. personnel and 128 wounded, the normally bellicose Reagan went to great pains to avoid the idea of escalating military conflict and casualties in Lebanon. "But, you see, what that entails, and that is the difficult thing, we would then be engaged in the combat. We would be the combat force. We would be fighting against the Arab states. And this is not the road to peace. We're still thinking in terms of that long-range peace."[24]

Reagan understood his audience. Although people generally believed it was proper to honor military service and heal the old wounds of Vietnam with that recognition, Vietnam's legacy continued to shape the value of types of service. The country was ambivalent at best regarding the prospect of a ground war. Only 48 percent of respondents approved of sending Marines to Lebanon as peacekeepers.[25] That number plummeted when the prospective mission changed to conventional war. When the country contemplated an invasion of Nicaragua, people who supported overthrowing the Sandinista government increased from an anemic 23 percent in 1983 to just 32 percent in 1985.[26]

Americans did not abandon combat service, but they placed significant qualifications on it. In an echo of support for Operation Rolling Thunder, the public overwhelmingly backed airstrikes against Libya in 1986. When the Air Force bombed targets in Tripoli, 77 percent of Americans approved of the action.²⁷ People also supported short-term, decisive ground operations. Operation Urgent Fury, the U.S. invasion of Grenada in October 1983, was a classic example of a lopsided David versus Goliath contest that resulted in a decisive outcome that garnered majority support.

When the troops came home from the Caribbean, celebrations followed, but they were local and largely limited to military bases and their surrounding communities. Ten years after the Vietnam War, the country was ready to recognize military service again, but with preconditions. Americans consistently supported military spending increases, a new GI Bill in 1984, and the idea of service in general. But for all this, they also paradoxically wanted the Cold War and the emerging conflict over terrorism kept distant, limited in nature, and quiet.²⁸ This grassroots consensus would be the foundation for basic policies such as the Weinberger Doctrine, which placed distinct limits on the use of military power.²⁹ Meanwhile, new veterans added their names to the roster of service, their families saw them off, and the military honored them as best as it could. It became a muted process that drew further away from the public as a whole, even as country's esteem for the military grew.

YELLOW RIBBONS

The First Gulf War saw a seismic shift in how the country treated war and military service. The August 1990 Iraqi invasion of Kuwait was a shock, as was the rapid deployment of the 82nd Airborne Division to Saudi Arabia. Throughout the fall, while Operation Desert Shield proceeded and hundreds of thousands of military personnel streamed to the Middle East, the country debated the possibility of war and its cost. In editorial columns, public forums, and cable news, the issue of casualties returned again and again. At the time, military experts considered the prospect of untested American forces pushing the fourth largest army in the world out of Kuwait to be extremely risky.³⁰ American casualty estimates ranged from twenty thousand to as high as one hundred thousand in a prospective clash with Iraq.³¹

Enormous relief followed the "hundred-hour war" against Iraq. Initial U.S. casualties were stunningly low: 382 dead and 467 wounded.³² On this basis alone, Operation Desert Storm seemed to be a complete repudiation of Vietnam. Commentary following the war went to great length to explain the United States had decisively dealt with the "ghosts" or "specter" of Vietnam. Others treated the "Vietnam syndrome" as if it were a national pathology for which the liberation of Kuwait was a cure. Some writers favored overt religious terms. "Schwarzkopf Exorcised the Demon of Vietnam," one headline exulted.³³

Whether motivated by relief or vindication, the country celebrated on a massive scale not seen since World War II, and deliberately so. In the spring of 1991, more than fifteen thousand sailors and Marines descended on Manhattan in time for its traditional Fleet Week, held alongside Operation Welcome Home celebrations planned by the city. Following close behind were twenty-four thousand soldiers redeploying from the Persian Gulf.[34] Organizers took great pains for replicate all the hallmarks of past public spectacles: troops marching in formation, military aircraft flyovers, public dignitaries, and tons of ticker tape. The June 1991 National Victory Celebration in Washington, DC, and similar massive parades in Chicago and Dallas followed the same format.

Smaller celebrations appeared in hundreds of towns and cities around the country, many welcoming reserve and National Guard units returning home from the Persian Gulf. Motivated by what one historian described as "a combination of pride, guilt, and relief," people caught up in the moment emptied shelves of flags and patriotic bric-a-brac or anything featuring red, white, and blue ornamentation.[35] One store owner quipped: "All of a sudden, everyone is becoming an American."[36]

Yellow ribbons appeared everywhere alongside American flags in these celebrations. Author Cynthia Enloe wryly noted that they "were sprouting in my neighborhood like daffodils in spring."[37] The ribbon was a throwback, first popularized when Iranian hostages returned from their captivity in January 1981. A decade later, the yellow ribbon became one of the most enduring symbols of the First Gulf War. A veritable cottage industry of t-shirts, refrigerator magnets, coffee cups, and bumper stickers soon followed in the wake of the nation's patriotic buying spree.

On its face, the yellow ribbon seemed very simple. Displayed individually, it was a cumulative national recognition of the sacrifices made for the war in Kuwait and the prevailing sense of relief that the troops were coming home. But there were powerful undercurrents affecting so simple a symbol. Journalist Tom Wicker spoke to the complexities of the national mindset just as combat operations were winding down in February 1991: "Instead of the long national agony over the 'morality' of the war in Vietnam, Americans saw themselves this time in their chosen role—waging a crusade for the right, against a devil figure who tortured captured U.S. pilots and blighted the Persian Gulf with oil. Instead of stalemate and defeat in the jungle, television brought them an American technological triumph of smart bombs, Patriot missiles and magnificent flying machines. Instead of ever-lengthening rows of body bags arriving from Indochina, casualties in the gulf were light and largely unseen."[38] For many Americans like Wicker, the Gulf War was a moment of unearned clarity that ignored pressing domestic problems—drugs, crime, economic decline—in favor of a brief moment in the international sun. For this part of the country, the clash with Iraq had exorcised nothing regarding problems at home or abroad. The discourse regarding the precise reasons for Desert Shield/Desert Storm, that is, oil, the Kuwaiti monarchy, the international status quo, lingered on.[39]

The yellow ribbon subsequently became part of a broadening debate about war and recognition, a discourse that intensified after a new conflict broke out in 2001. Roger Stahl described one portion of this discourse in terms of "deflection," or an overt effort to split combatants away from their war. Following this approach, it is possible to support the individual for his or her heroism or victimhood without embracing any larger political or strategic objective or the more generalized concept of whether a war was "just" or not.[40] Antiwar protestor Trish Shuh offered an opinion in 1991 that foreshadowed the post-September 11 era when she said, "You can oppose the policy but still support the troops."[41]

Yellow ribbon debates also invite the concept of what constitutes good citizenship, not so much in terms of directly participating in war but supporting those to whom society delegates the responsibility. As Stahl notes, this tack "drives a wedge between the deliberating citizen and the soldier." Support for or against a conflict is reduced to a matter of loyalty to an abstract individual. It is a common device in modern propaganda campaigns and what David Flores characterized in a 2017 issue of *Armed Forces & Society* as the "discourse of betrayal."[42]

The transition of the fighting man (or woman) from a tangible to an abstract participant in the discussion began much earlier than Desert Storm. Andrew J. Bacevich argues that this change was occurring during the Reagan years, when White House rhetoric "was establishing support for the troops—as opposed to actual service with them—as the new standard of civic responsibility."[43] It is likely that this shift predated the eighties, when selective service gave way to an all-volunteer military. After 1973, more and more citizens saw the yellow ribbon as a means to vicariously "serve" with the troops, as the idea of service became increasingly less tangible to them.

This lack of a real connection with military service was apparent in the immediate aftermath of the First Gulf War, when George H. W. Bush discovered just how tentative an issue the war was during his 1992 reelection campaign. The triumph of Desert Storm waned and was replaced by concerns about rising unemployment and a recession. As much as Bush tried to rally the country around his wartime leadership, voters worried about their pocketbooks. When then governor Bill Clinton took up the mantra of "It's the economy, stupid," people listened.[44] So did Congress, which saw opportunities to spend the new "peace dividend" once the Soviet Union ceased to exist barely ten months after the fighting stopped in Kuwait.

In hindsight, the optimism that graced the start of the nineties is heartbreaking, particularly as it evolved around military affairs and veterans. Desert Storm proved to be a poor precedent for America's renewed global policing role. As much as the Pentagon was enamored of airpower and decisive conventional engagements, suffering from what one officer described as "victory disease," post–Cold War conflicts made Vietnam seem almost simple in comparison.[45]

Mogadishu characterized George H. W. Bush's "New World Order," whether he or the American military establishment comprehended it at the time. American forces participating in peacekeeping and "peace enforcement" missions entered a dangerous vortex of racial, ethnic, and religious conflict where nation states had once been. Faced with the prospect of casualties in a new round of open-ended war, the country balked. The troops came home. When they did deploy, it was under elaborate rules of engagement designed to limit risk and U.S. casualties.

The 1st Armored Division's deployment to the Balkans in 1995 was a case in point. Under the general heading of "peace enforcement operations," Task Force Eagle's portfolio during its first six months in Bosnia included the surrender of heavy weapons, mine removal, monitoring of police equipment and vehicles, and prisoner release. However, the number one priority issued by its headquarters was "force protection," a function that stressed the safety of U.S. personnel stationed in Bosnia above all other missions.[46]

In an interesting planning document entitled "Beyond D+120: Tasks We Don't Want, May Get," Task Force Eagle contemplated involvement in securing mass grave sites, controlling black market activities, the apprehension of war criminals, providing civilian medical care, and security operations during elections.[47] The Defense Department made rudimentary efforts to prepare deploying troops that demonstrated a greater degree of sophistication than Operation Restore Hope had in 1992. A sixteen-page pocket guide was issued to American personnel prior to their departure that offered a brief synopsis of Bosnian history, politics, and key phrases with pronunciation keys. Under the section "Religion and Sensitivities," it recommended: "Remember, these people are the product of more than 1,000 years of history and culture. They can be easily insulted when they perceive any disrespect of them or their culture. Simply act in a respectful and considerate manner at all times."[48] Clearly, the U.S. military had traveled a long way from Operation Desert Storm in just four years.

Although it never returned to its February 1991 heyday, public confidence in the military remained consistently higher in the nineties than through the Reagan era. In 1993, 67 percent of respondents said they had a "great deal" or "quite a lot" of faith in the military. In 1999, it was 68 percent.[49] Accompanying that sentiment, however, was the tacit assumption that the United States would steer clear of war and focus on domestic affairs such as social security and taxes. In the run-up to the 2000 election, candidates George W. Bush and Al Gore avoided the issue of national security with the understanding that military affairs usually ranked last as a national priority in the polls.[50] It was a careful balancing act that turned out to have a very short half-life.

FOR THE TROOPS, BUT AGAINST THE WAR

War came in 2001, first in Afghanistan and, two years later, Iraq. Active duty forces deployed abroad in numbers not seen since the peak of the Vietnam War. And, for the first time since Korea, active duty personnel were joined by hundreds of thousands of National Guard and reservists. Despite the scope and scale of the newly named Global War on Terrorism, there was no mass mobilization of the home front. Selective service stayed in mothballs. By 2006, a total of approximately 1.3 million U.S. service members had participated in Operation Enduring Freedom (OEF) in Afghanistan or Operation Iraqi Freedom (OIF). Measured in terms of simple demographics, veterans of these wars comprised less than 0.5 percent of Americans. Discounting combat veterans, the actual proportion was even lower.[51]

Additional differences also stand out. Unlike Vietnam or Korea, many men and women served multiple deployments. In 2006, as many as one-third of Army personnel served at least two tours, while almost two-thirds served in both Iraq and Afghanistan.[52] Specialties in high demand—military police, civil affairs, transportation, aviation, and intelligence, among others—also mandated additional time spent overseas. Unlike Vietnam and Korea, average deployments for individuals and whole units lasted longer than a year. This was especially true for the reserves, which required months of additional training to prepare for the rigors of a combat deployment.[53]

Veterans of the Global War on Terrorism were also distinct for other reasons. By 2005, nearly fifty-six hundred military personnel in Iraq and Afghanistan were fifty or older. Most of these were in National Guard or reserves, where slightly more than one-fifth were over forty years old. In comparison, only 6 percent of the regular military that went to war was in the same demographic.[54]

In keeping with trends established by the all-volunteer military, veterans were a racially diverse group, with African Americans serving at a rate that was more than twice as high as their proportion of civilian society. The number of women in uniform was also distinctly higher than in past conflicts. By 2010, 14.4 percent of the active forces were female.[55] Although Defense Department policy officially excluded them from combat units until 2013, the nature of conflict regularly exposed them to improvised explosive devices (IEDs), small arms, and indirect fire.

All veterans of U.S. contingency operations in Iraq and Afghanistan experienced the vicissitudes of public opinion. Initial support was strong. A CNN/USA Today/Gallup poll in March 2003 found that 72 percent of Americans were in favor of a war against Iraq.[56] Five years later, after almost four thousand military deaths and little stability to show for the cost, the stance was completely reversed. A March 2008 poll by the *Washington Post* and ABC News reported that 63 percent of respondents believed that the war in Iraq was not worth fighting.[57]

In contrast, U.S. public support for the individuals in the military followed a different dynamic. A September 2006 Gallup poll recorded a 72 percent favorable rating for military personnel, double that which supported military operations in Iraq.[58] The survey reflected an important dichotomy between service and the object of that service. Millions of Americans sincerely offered support to the contemporary military and were mindful of the long discourse regarding treatment of Vietnam veterans. They were motivated by patriotism and a desire to avoid the mistakes of the past.

However, this support turned out to be fragile for a number of reasons. Most telling was the outright public rejection of a military draft. A 2004 *Newsweek* poll of eighteen- to twenty-nine-year-old voters found that 36 percent said they would not serve if drafted for the war.[59] As late as October 2007, two-thirds of Americans polled completely dismissed the idea.[60] As the war progressed it also became bound up in a national debate regarding civil liberties and national security. The Guantanamo Bay military prison and the use of torture in interrogating "enemy combatants" in U.S. custody became an ongoing cautionary story about the abuse of power and the rule of law.[61] Equally damaging to military credibility were alleged reports of abuse of civilians during the course of military operations in Iraq. Civilian deaths in Haditha in November 2005 initiated a full-scale investigation of misconduct. As later revelations regarding the nature of civilian casualties at the hands of U.S. military forces becomes more common, the callousness of the American service members increasingly defined the public debate, stripping away the gloss that had protected the military throughout much of the war.[62] By June 2006, a majority of Americans (57%) asked by the Opinion Research Corporation believed that American troops had committed atrocities in Iraq.[63]

CHAPTER FOUR

Veterans coming home today are caught in the fickle tides of public support and are disconnected from American society to a degree that is, in many cases, more profound than during the Vietnam era. Media access to the battlefield is unprecedented, dwarfing coverage of Southeast Asia forty years earlier. It has, as one writer observed, "dissolved" the distinction "between the spectator on the couch and the soldier in the field."[64] Beyond the traditional television outlets are a host of internet blogs, websites, and YouTube channels.[65] None of this unprecedented exposure has translated into public cognizance of either the costs or the risks of military service. It is difficult if not impossible to inculcate the viewer with the sense of fear, fatigue, or danger depicted on a screen. What currently exists is an understanding more akin to a first-person shooter video game than the real war.[66] Where broader public participation in the military might have bridged that gap in the sixties during Vietnam, when the mass of World War II veterans populated America, that link has grown increasingly tentative. The end result, as journalist Sara Corbett observed in 2004, is that veterans "must live with the confounding mix of anonymity and exposure wrought by surviving the war."[67]

The sincere, disjointed, and ultimately repellent disparity between civilian and military is brilliantly captured by Ben Fountain in *Billy Lynn's Long Halftime Walk*:

> There was one man in particular who attached himself to Billy, a pale, spongy Twinkie of a human being crammed into starched blue jeans and fancy cowboy boots. "Was never in the military myself," the man confided, swaying, gesturing with his giant Starbucks, "but my granddaddy was at Pearl, he told me all the stories," and the man embarked on a rambling speech about war and God and country as Billy let go, let the words whirl and tumble around his brain

                    terrRist

                                   freedom

   evil

                                   nina leven

    troops

                               currj

                   support

               sacrifice

                             Bush

     Values

God[68]

It is in this context that the uniform, reflexive support for the troops rings hollow for returning veterans. Many have turned their backs on peacetime society because they lack the faith in ever reestablishing a connection with it. The systemic difficulties discussed in following chapters—in medical care, employment, and other fundamental areas—have only reinforced this point. One veteran spoke for many when he commented that "I realized that whatever friends I had made before the Army no longer really existed. The only friends that I now have are the ones I made while I was in."[69]

CONCLUSIONS

The home front has been and will continue to be essential to the reassimilation of veterans. If the past is any guide, it is interesting to see how quickly the iconic generals placed in charge of veterans' programs after World War II recognized the importance of local communities as the final arbiters of multibillion-dollar government programs. Both Omar Bradley at the Veterans Administration and Graves B. Erskine, a Marine Corps division commander briefly placed in charge of the Retraining and Reemployment Administration, were fully prepared to delegate recovery efforts down to the grassroots level.[70]

At the same time, it is equally important to understand the dynamic qualities of the home front. Support for any war effort is analogous to capturing and keeping lightning in a bottle. Public passions cool. Casualties inevitably accumulate, and the wounded become a daily reminder of what belligerent rhetoric means. In conflicts lacking goals with tangible objectives or distinct time lines, the prospect of maintaining public support is problematic at best. Adam J. Berinsky's *In Time of War: Understanding American Public Opinion from World War II to Iraq* offers a master class in understanding the forces at work on the modern home front. Clarity was a rare commodity in conflicts after 1973. Vietnam, the Cold War, the peace enforcement missions of the nineties, and much of the Global War on Terrorism were open-ended exercises in the use of power for contested objectives. The First Gulf War in 1990–91 seems to be the one exception.

Veterans were caught in these crosscurrents of events and public opinion. The treatment of Vietnam veterans stands out for its crassness, if not its widespread practice. Whether the spat-on Vietnam veteran is an urban legend or not is immaterial to polling data and an accumulation of personal experiences that speak to the degree of hostility present in America. Subsequent public recognition from the mideighties to the present day made amends for some of this ugly history, but it has served only to paper over the old schisms.

Even when it is focused, positive, and supportive, there are distinct limits to what the "folks back home" can comprehend or empathize with when it comes to the veteran's experience. Since 1980, both the number of veterans in American society and the overall percentage in uniform have been declining. Veterans live in this gap. When Paul Fussell wrote of post–World War II wounded, he easily could have been describing them today: "Among friends, the veteran is not self-conscious about his wounds; he is willing to talk or write about his last battle and his hospital ordeals. To cope with life, whatever comes, he had a preparation deep in his youth. Did we not choose him for his health, both mental and physical?"[71] While Fussell understood the value of home, the source of real resiliency was "among friends," from veterans.

CHAPTER FIVE

Healing New Wounds

> They had crossed a strange line; they had become wounded men;
> and everybody realized, including themselves, dimly,
> that they were now different.
> —*James Jones,* The Thin Red Line

INTRODUCTION

Every war requires time and resources for healing. The purposes of this process vary. During a conflict, the main objective is immediate, following the Army Medical Department motto "to conserve the fighting strength." Whether the casualty is mental or physical, returning a soldier to duty as soon as possible is a necessary and pragmatic goal.[1] Modern militaries have developed this practice into an art form. The overall initial incidence of combat-related psychological casualties in Vietnam was far lower than the two previous wars. Whereas mental breakdowns accounted for one hundred casualties per thousand soldiers per year in World War II and forty casualties per thousand troops per year in Korea, they amounted to only twelve per thousand per year in Vietnam.[2]

Long-term healing comes later if at all. On that count, U.S. institutional support for veterans' medical treatment might be charitably described as inconsistent. Care for veterans tends to wax and wane, enjoying public attention at war's end, which slowly drifts away as time passes. The cycle usually involves a scandal followed by outrage, recrimination, reforms, and backsliding. Such was the case at the end of World War II, when the Veterans Administration (VA) being run by Frank Hines was bombarded by media accounts of massive backlogs of disability claims, inept administration, and antiquated treatment protocols. When Omar Bradley took over the VA between 1945 and 1947, he initiated a sea change in medical care that succeeded in expanding and modernizing the veterans' health care system. However, almost as soon as Bradley returned to the Army, budget cuts followed, and atrophy again set in.[3]

The cycle reappeared during the Vietnam War and again in the midst of our current wars abroad. As Vietnam began to wind down, a series of exposés, in major publications such as *New York Times,* illustrated a Veterans Administration that neglected the basic needs of young veterans housed in decrepit, understaffed hospitals. *Life* magazine likened the VA system to a "medical slum." Doctors who worked in the system described conditions as "medieval."[4] Congressional investigations followed, and Veterans Administration hospitals became part of the regular 1972 campaign circuit.[5] Thirty years later the *Washington Post* broke an almost identical story about the dysfunctional system at Walter Reed Army Medical Center, until then a facility considered to be the "crown jewel" of military medicine. It read in part: "Life beyond the hospital bed is a frustrating mountain of paperwork. The typical soldier is required to file 22 documents with eight different commands—most of them off-post—to enter and exit the medical processing world, according to government investigators. Sixteen different information systems are used to process the forms, but few of them can communicate with one another. The Army's three personnel databases cannot read each other's files and can't interact with the separate pay system or the medical recordkeeping databases."[6]

Despite the apparent cyclical history of veterans' health care, there are some important and consistent features that require additional attention. One of the most obvious is the consistent improvement of technology and combat evacuation, which has dramatically increased survivability rates but has also increased the number of veterans in need of intensive, long-term care. A second is the accumulation of millions of veterans in the VA medical system and the resulting age gap between older veterans with non-service-related conditions and newer waves of combat casualties. The two constituencies have been in an almost constant competition for funding, bed space, and staff since the Vietnam War.

There are also a few new medical challenges that regularly appear after each American war. For a period of time, veterans of the Vietnam War who experienced acute mental distress were described as having "post-Vietnam Syndrome" before post-traumatic stress disorder (PTSD) was properly identified by the medical community.[7] Attempts to garner official recognition of problems caused by Agent Orange took even longer. After the first clash with Iraq in 1991, veterans began to complain of symptoms caused by what would be labeled Gulf War syndrome. America's ongoing contemporary wars have produced a host of new medical problems, from respiratory illnesses and rashes caused by military burn pits to traumatic brain injuries (TBI) incurred by improvised explosive devices to military sexual trauma, opioid addiction, and escalating suicide rates.[8]

The subsequent story of veterans and their healing process is one of many layers. It is made up of well-meaning but too often neglected institutions responsible for veterans' care. It is defined by ongoing legacies of old wars and the undertow they create for budgets, lawmakers, and priorities. In another sense, the history of veterans' health is influenced by the gaps that exist between new and unique types of wounds created by war and their official recognition. In some cases, the process of comprehension and action can span years if not decades.

THE GENERATION GAP AND VETERANS MEDICAL CARE

Although the main focus of this book is the era after Vietnam, it is impossible to ignore the impact of the enormous number of World War II and Korea veterans on the health care system. Concerns about this massive cohort emerged long before the Vietnam War began in earnest.

In 1955, Dwight Eisenhower asked Omar Bradley to again address problems within the Veterans Administration. This time, however, the challenge was not a lack of resources or expertise, but the future costs of rising expectations. When the Bradley Commission convened, the World War II and Korea GI Bills covered approximately 22 million individuals. Eisenhower balked at the idea of a full retirement pension or medical coverage for all veterans regardless of their service in peace or war. Administration budget analysts estimated the new costs for the former alone would be $762 billion.[9] Eisenhower's 1956 budget message pointedly identified veterans' benefits as an ongoing and increasing expense that needed "constructive reconsideration."[10]

Bradley's task in 1955 was not reform but retrenchment. He advocated prioritization, drawing a distinction between "programs which take care of the needs arising directly out of military service" and other normal problems of aging and infirmity. The commission recommended a division of labor between the two. The VA could take care of service-related medical needs, and the existing social welfare system would take charge of the rest.[11]

It seemed like a reasonable proposition made by a respected public figure. And it utterly failed. Veterans groups responded early, often, and negatively to the Bradley Commission report when it came out in 1956. The strongest reply came from the American Legion, which attacked the commission's report as "filled with cliches [sic], self-contradictions, inaccuracies, looseness of expression, non-sequitors [sic], statistical monstrosities." The Veterans of Foreign Wars characterized commission recommendations as "impractical, contrary to national tradition and replete with distortions and exaggerations" and an "attempt to reverse the traditional national policy of the United States with respect to those who have served in the Armed Forces."[12]

Collectively, the individuals and veterans' groups who opposed the Bradley Commission created a stalemate with the Eisenhower administration in an election year. As the fifties proceeded, the Veterans Administration witnessed small cuts to educational funding and VA bed space, but overall, the 1957–64 period saw consistent spending increases, from $4.8 billion in 1957 to $5.3 billion in 1960 and $6.0 billion in 1964.[13]

As the sixties progressed, World War II and Korean War veterans often found themselves at odds with the new generation coming out of Vietnam. The 1966 Veteran's Readjustment Benefits Act (PL 89–358) kept many older provisions from the original GI Bill, such as veterans' preference for federal employment as well as home and farm loans. However, it essentially froze educational assistance at Korean War–era levels, allotting only $100 a month for school tuition, fees, and "subsistence" for a full-time student with no dependents. Veterans attending classes with two or more dependents received a monthly stipend of $150.[14]

Both the Johnson and the Nixon administrations openly contemplated cuts to veterans' health care just as the war in Vietnam was escalating. Johnson originally proposed reductions in the number of VA medical facilities for the sake of "modernization" in 1965 but eventually reversed himself two years later.[15] The Nixon administration took a different approach. The president resisted increases to the budget for veterans care in October 1969, noting: "It is not easy to criticize the pending bill for it promises some appealing benefits to a most deserving group. But our veterans have long known that they must be champions of responsible government. They know the basic truth that a veterans' program not good for the nation as a whole cannot ultimately be of benefit to veterans themselves."[16] A year later, Nixon vetoed a $105 million appropriation for VA hospitals. However, in a nod to the older veterans' community and power lobbying groups like the American Legion and Veterans of Foreign Wars, he signed PL 88–450, which lifted a six-month limit on nursing home care for veterans.[17]

Within this atmosphere of fiscal austerity, generational priorities drove VA medical spending. A study published by Ralph Nader in 1973 found that only 15 percent of the $12.2 billion VA budget was going to Vietnam veterans. In contrast, 40 percent was spent on non-service-connected programs for older patients whose average age was 51.6 years.[18] These same trends remained two decades later. A 1994 study of VA hospital use indicated increasing demands on facilities by veterans over the age of sixty-five, particularly for physical rehabilitation. These individuals directly competed with veterans under the age of forty-five who were beginning to demand increasing help with a host of problems that also include rehabilitation and general medical treatment along with psychiatric care. In fact, younger veterans recorded the largest increase (59%) among all age groups for mental health treatment.[19]

As the veterans' population aged, their demands on the VA medical system not surprisingly grew. According to Veterans Affairs, by 2020, the average age of a veteran using VA medical care was sixty-four. Overall, although there were fewer veterans in the new century, the number declining from 23.3 million in 2008 to 20 million in 2017, benefits usage increased, specifically medical benefits.[20] Among this group, World War II (74.1%) and Korean War (69.6%) veterans recorded the highest demand on medical services.[21]

At the same time, the number of beds maintained by the VA medical system dramatically declined in the decades following Vietnam. In 1970, there were 98,956 total (medical, surgical, psychiatric) beds in Veterans Administration facilities around the country. By 1998, as a result of years of systemic budget cuts, there were 45,303.[22] Interestingly, the shift to full-scale combat deployments did not arrest this trend. Four years into the Global War on Terrorism, in 2005, there were actually fewer beds (41,731) in the VA system and more than a third (15,109) were designated for long-term nursing home care.[23]

New arrivals crowded into these diminished facilities. By 2015, Operation Enduring Freedom (OEF) and Operation Iraqi Freedom (OIF) had produced 1.9 million veterans, and as a result of repeated deployments, these individuals accumulated additional wounds and injuries over time. Of the 1.9 million OEF/OIF veterans, 1.2 million, or 63 percent, availed themselves of VA health care. While most relied on outpatient treatment, 8 percent (97,252) required some type of inpatient treatment.[24]

There is a lot of bad math in these numbers, which partially explains what led to the Walter Reed Army Medical Center tragedy. The data illustrates many of the same prerequisites that shaped military medicine in 1970: age and priority. In both cases, the veterans' health care system reflected a constant tug-of-war between an older, more powerful cohort, in this case a combination of World War II, Korea, and aging Vietnam veterans, that asserted its privilege over newer arrivals. In the zero-sum climate of assigning federal budget priorities, the maladies of old age competed with the new needs of combat wounded streaming in from Iraq and Afghanistan. The system did not break, but it certainly buckled under old and new demands. Thousands of men and women began to slip into the emerging cracks in this system.

INDIVIDUALS WARS AND THEIR WOUNDS

Some wounds are specific to the wars fought. They are often the product of modernization, of new technologies and subsequent transformative doctrines. History is littered with examples: the machine gun, the tank, nerve gas, and depleted uranium munitions. They alter war and bequeath their own unique legacies to the people who fight and the institutions later charged with veterans' care. However, although the military places a premium on innovation for the purpose of war, applying the same principle for the sake of addressing its consequences is a much more problematic enterprise.

In many respects, the history of the herbicide Agent Orange is an ideal illustration of the human impact of the U.S. "magic bullet" in modern conflict. At the start of the Vietnam War, U.S. military planners saw a value in reducing enemy cover and destroying food crops through aerial spraying and did just that between 1962 and 1971 under Operation Ranch Hand. Both the Pentagon and the White House ignored North Vietnamese claims that herbicides poisoned more than 1.5 million people during this period. Unknown by most at the time was a finding by the National Cancer Institute that 2,4,5-Trichlorophenoxyacetic acid, one of the active ingredients of Agent Orange, caused tumors in lab animals.[25]

It proved to be years before the United States officially acknowledged any human consequences of Ranch Hand or any other use of herbicides in Vietnam, a policy position that included veterans. Individuals who either directly participated in aerial spraying or served in areas affected by it began to suffer a long list of health problems that included everything from skin lesions and cysts to immune disorders and cancer.[26] More ominous was an upsurge in birth defects experienced by veterans' children.

What ensued was twenty years of escalating veterans' claims, official obstruction, and litigation against both the federal government and Dow Chemical, the maker of Agent Orange. One class action lawsuit filed in 1979 claimed that 2.4 million personnel who served in Vietnam were affected by the spraying program.[27] Unfortunately, both the Reagan and the George H. W. Bush administrations actively resisted recognizing the problem, a position highlighted in 1990 when Admiral Elmo Zumwalt Jr. testified before Congress about "a discernible pattern, if not collaboration," within the federal government to deny Agent Orange disability benefits. Litigation resulted in an out-of-court settlement and the creation of a $180 million Agent Orange Settlement Fund in 1984.[28] Congress did not effectively address the matter of disability compensation until 1991, when it passed the Agent Orange Act. More than a decade later, federal policy addressed some of the birth defects experienced by children of veterans.[29] As of this writing, lawmakers and veterans continue to debate a growing list of physical ailments related to the herbicide.[30]

Vietnam's other medical legacy involved mental health, what doctors in the sixties initially characterized as "post-Vietnam syndrome." By the time U.S. military forces deployed to Vietnam, military medicine had developed an effective system to identify combat stress, treat it close to the fighting, and return soldiers to duty. The system failed, however, when it came to veterans' mental health. In practice, the medical community lacked even basic protocols to identify wartime trauma or treat it. As one scholar observed in 1990: "Mental health professionals across the country assessed disturbed Vietnam veterans using a diagnostic nomenclature that contained no specific entries for war-related trauma. The DSM-II nomenclature, used by hospitals, insurance companies, and the courts provided official diagnoses for sickness. VA physicians typically did not collect military histories as part of the diagnostic workup. Many thought that Vietnam veterans who were agitated by their war experiences, or who talked repeatedly about them, suffered from a neurosis or psychosis whose origin and dynamics lay outside the realm of combat."[31]

Ultimately, the combination of public controversy over veterans' mental health and considerable internal professional debate culminated in 1980 with the creation of the category of "post-traumatic stress disorder."[32] According to the *DSM-III: Diagnostic and Statistical Manual of Mental Disorders*, PTSD was the result of a "psychologically traumatic event that is generally outside the range of usual human experience."[33] The manual offered a laundry list of such "events," from "bereavement, chronic illness, business losses" to rape or assault, natural disasters, and military combat. More important than the causes of trauma were its long-term effects. According to the manual, individuals who experienced a "traumatic event" could suffer a number of chronic problems such as survivor's guilt, depression, or anxiety. More severe ailments could include "dissociative-like states" in which "components of the event are relived and the individual behaves as though experiencing the event at that moment." Such states could last minutes or days.[34] One 1992 study speculated that as many as 470,000 Vietnam veterans (15% of those who served) suffered from some form of post-traumatic stress.[35] Another speculated that the number might be as high as 1.5 million.[36]

Although initially applied to Vietnam veterans, the concept of PTSD became a valuable tool for veterans of other wars. As additional research integrated data from veterans of World War II, Korea, and Vietnam, a number of similarities emerged. According to work done by Kathryn H. Andersen and Jean M. Mitchell, veterans of all three wars experienced the same rate (27%) of alcohol abuse. Korean War and Vietnam veterans reported depression at the same rate (4%), while World War II veterans' rates were somewhat lower (2%).[37]

Assessment techniques grew increasingly more sophisticated with the passage of time. They incorporated a variety of variables that fleshed out the basic DSM-III protocols to include race, gender, age, type of combat exposure, and its duration.[38] Improved diagnostic techniques seemed to reap some benefits, particularly during the First Gulf War, where psychiatric casualties represented only 6.5 percent of all medical evaluations during Operations Desert Shield and Desert Storm. In the years that followed, initial research indicated an 8 percent PTSD rate among active duty veterans and 9.5 percent among veterans who were reservists.[39]

The First Gulf War saw hundreds and, later, thousands of its veterans complain of a range of problems that included joint pain, difficulty focusing, insomnia, and depression. Within a span of fifteen years, the list also featured "chronic fatigue syndrome, multiple chemical sensitivities, and fibromyalgia" and other difficulties affecting one hundred thousand veterans.[40] These symptoms collectively become known as "Gulf War syndrome."

The cause was unclear, although the syndrome seemed related to a toxic soup of medical, environmental, and military factors. Some studies correlated symptoms with hastily approved and implemented medical vaccinations. The experimental drug pyridostigmine bromide was administered to four hundred thousand American troops as a preventative treatment for nerve gas without the warning that it could cause neurological damage if combined with other chemicals contained in common insect repellent.[41] Other research indicates that exposure to low levels of nerve agents and other chemical weapons was to blame. During the invasion of Kuwait, coalition forces destroyed or damaged thirty-four nuclear, chemical, and biological sites.[42] Still other research highlighted radioactivity produced by depleted uranium munitions used by the U.S. military and prolonged exposure to tainted air from Kuwaiti oil fires lighted by retreating Iraqi forces in 1991.[43]

The Pentagon initially attributed some Gulf War syndrome complaints to post-traumatic stress. In may have been an odd example of good intentions gone awry. When the Defense Department surveyed troops after the war, approximately the same number tested positive for PTSD as for Gulf War syndrome. Some officials assumed a newly recognized disability explained the range of new symptoms and that the core problem was psychological and not physical.[44]

It was not. By 1995, 29,000 veterans were on the VA Gulf War Registry, a list that was growing by 1,000 people a month. By 2003, it comprised 70,000 veterans.[45] And, in an echo of Agent Orange, Gulf War veterans were affected by health problems that extended to their spouses and children. A Mississippi National Guard unit reported that of fifteen children born to its members after redeployment from Desert Storm, thirteen had birth defects.[46] Additional medical research reinforced the body of evidence indicating serious health risks for exposed troops. A study published in 2005 by the Institute of Medicine reported a death rate for brain cancer that was double for troops in the vicinity of Khamisiyah, Iraq, where personnel were exposed to chemical munitions after their demolition by coalition forces.[47]

The U.S. government actively avoided the issue for years after the First Gulf War. The Department of Veterans Affairs deliberately slow-walked research of low-level chemical agent exposure.[48] The Pentagon revealed that Central Command combat diaries containing key evidence of Iraqi chemical stockpiles were "missing" from its official records. The same was true for 75 percent of the chemical weapons logs kept during the war.[49] In 1997, following in the wake of these revelations, Deputy Secretary of Defense John P. White finally announced that he would increase the number of Department of Defense investigators assigned to the issue from 12 to 110.[50] That same year, department officials began a systematic survey of Gulf War veterans. Follow-up work in 2000 contributed to a more reliable Gulf War syndrome database.[51]

Once the federal government recognized the legitimacy of Gulf War syndrome, it created a process for disability benefits in the same manner as with Agent Orange. The VA extended the deadline for applicants five times between 1994 and 2016, with one addition period offered until 2021.[52] The long window of time for applications did not translate into easily obtained benefits. Between 2010 and 2015, the VA approved only 18,000 of 102,000 applications (17.6%).[53]

HEALING THE WOUNDS OF THE FOREVER WAR

When the United States began overseas military operations in 2001, the effort produced a steady stream of sick and injured, not anywhere near the volume experienced during the Vietnam War, but in numbers not witnessed in fifty years. By June 2020, United States military forces had suffered 6,955 killed and 53,241 wounded, a total that did not include contractors or local nationals in U.S. service.[54]

The ongoing Global War on Terrorism was also notable for the extremely high quality of U.S. equipment and combat medicine. The combination of improved vehicle and body armor, the widespread use of basic emergency equipment such as tourniquets and blood coagulants, ample access to air medical evacuation, and sophisticated frontline medical technology translated into a 90.7 percent survival rate in 2007. Troops who would have died in past wars from traumatic amputations, blast overpressure, infection, or diseases returned home in unprecedented numbers.[55]

Although clearly a boon to the individual wounded and their families, the better rate of survival placed new burdens on the VA and agencies tasked with long-term care. Between 2001 and 2016, approximately two million veterans filed disability claims with the Department of Veterans Affairs. Between 2002 and 2015, the total number of outpatient visits to VA health care facilities almost doubled. Inpatient demand grew by almost 20 percent.[56] Under the sheer volume of this new demand, the VA system began to buckle.

The types of patients varied according to official VA categories. There are eight of these, each defined by military service history, disability, income, and other factors. Individuals under "Priority group 1," for example, have a 50 percent disability or a disability that prevents them from working. The number of veterans in this category increased from 482,448 in 2001 to in 2,005,689 in 2017.[57] There was a more than fourfold increase in veterans with 70–100 percent disability, from 352,082 in 2001 to 1,575,952 in 2016.[58] Overall, according to a 2016 Veterans Affairs report, the disability rate for post-9/11 veterans was 35.9 percent compared with 18.6 percent for all other veterans.[59]

TABLE 2. SELECTED VETERANS HEALTH CHARACTERISTICS, FY 2002-FY 2015

	Total enrolled in VA health care system (millions)	VA Outpatient visits (millions)	VA Inpatient residents (thousands)
2002	6.8	46.5	564.7
2003	7.1	49.8	567.3
2004	7.3	54.0	589.8
2005	7.7	57.5	585.8
2006	7.9	59.1	568.9
2007	7.8	62.3	589.0
2008	7.8	67.7	641.4
2009	8.1	74.9	662.0
2010	8.3	80.2	682.3
2011	8.6	79.8	692.1
2012	8.8	83.6	703.5
2013	8.9	86.4	694.7
2014	9.1	92.4	707.4
2015	9.0	95.2	699.1

Source: Department of Veterans Affairs, National Center for Veterans Analysis and Statistics, *Selected Veterans Health Administration Characteristics, FY 2002 to FY 2015*, https://www.va.gov/vetdata/Utilization.asp.

Many of these men and women suffered from physical disabilities. Between 2001 and 2015, 1,645 service members experienced "major limb amputations" as a result of combat. Unfortunately, these numbers pale in comparison to traumatic brain injury, an affliction caused by the blast and shockwave of mortars, rockets, and improvised explosive devices. Although Kevlar and armor plating could offer some physical protection, internal organs remained vulnerable. Between 2001 and 2015, a total of 327,399 military personnel were diagnosed with varying degrees of TBI.[60]

However, a significantly large number claimed disabilities from PTSD. There is no agreement from official sources regarding the extent of this problem. According to the Congressional Research Service, 177,461 personnel reported some degree of post-traumatic stress between 2002 and 2015.[61] More recent VA estimates are higher but imprecise. The National Center for PTSD put the number between 11 percent and 20 percent of post-9/11 veterans. Taking into account only individuals who started their military careers after September 2001 (2.8 million), this would mean at least 308,000 to 560,000 veterans suffered from PTSD.[62]

Recent research also indicates disturbing correlation between race and PTSD/TBI. With the exception of the Marine Corps, Hispanics were underrepresented in the military in 2008. However, Hispanic veterans experienced a higher rate of TBI and were three times as likely to experience "major depression" and PTSD than any other racial group. A 2014 study indicated that the greater incidence of problems may be rooted in the larger proportion of Hispanic participation in the combat arms, which increases their overall exposure to trauma.[63]

There are a few explanations for the confusion of numbers. One is the often-blurred line between physical and mental trauma. Some specific types of wounds illustrate the problem. Veterans affected by TBI have commingled neurological and psychological damage that requires concurrent treatment. As noted earlier, individuals wounded in Iraq and Afghanistan had a substantially higher survival rate than did those who fought in earlier wars, defying the sheer magnitude of their injuries. The recovery process comes at the physical and mental price of multiple surgeries and years of rehabilitation. The process is, by definition, a "traumatic event" and, as more recent research indicates, is a trigger for the long-term onset of PTSD.[64]

A second factor involves the lack of agreement within the medical community regarding the causes and proper diagnosis of PTSD, which is rooted in a disparity over Vietnam PTSD rates that emerged between a 1988 Centers for Disease Control (CDC) study and a survey conducted by the National Vietnam Veterans Readjustment Study (NVVRS) two years later. The CDC estimated that 14.7 percent of Vietnam veterans developed PTSD symptoms immediately after leaving the military, but by the time of its report, that number had declined to only 2.2 percent. The NVVRS produced significantly different conclusions. The study noted that at least 30.9 percent of male Vietnam veterans were affected by PTSD and 15.2 percent still suffered from it in 1990.[65]

Debate centered on the definition of "post-traumatic stress" that had been determined in the 1980 *DSM-III: Diagnostic and Statistical Manual of Mental Disorders*. Critics argued that the diagnostic criteria for post-traumatic stress, intended in part to address the Vietnam War, was too broadly applied to patients. It often interpreted symptoms of depression, anxiety, or problems involving social reintegration as PTSD. This debate remained largely unresolved when war returned in 2001. One Harvard University psychologist noted in 2009 that "PTSD is a real thing, without a doubt, but as a diagnosis, PTSD has become so flabby and overstretched, so much a part of the culture, that we are almost certainly mistaking other problems for PTSD and thus mistreating them."[66]

Treatment is often complicated by racial and cultural differences. Minority veterans who were recently surveyed about VA health care frequently mention perceived racism as a major obstacle to medical care. Some issues, such the shortage of Spanish language translators within the VA and its subsequent impact on medical assessment, require relatively simple solutions.[67] Other factors will require more study and effort. More contemporary scholarship notes the importance of "familialism"—the intrinsic value of immediate family—to mental health care treatment for Hispanic veterans.[68] The challenge for the VA system will be to find constructive ways to incorporate these actors into existing therapy regimes.[69]

The VA further complicated physical and mental treatment by horribly mismanaging the use of prescription drugs, particularly opioids. Department of Veterans Affairs doctors, encouraged by companies like Purdue Pharma, began issuing painkillers for both physical injuries as well as PTSD and actively assisted the Defense Department and the VA in developing opioid use guidelines that claimed the medication "rarely" caused addiction.[70] Subsequent opioid prescriptions by VA doctors increased by 270 percent between 2001 and 2013. According to a 2012 study published in the *Journal of the American Medical Association*, veterans with PTSD were three times more likely to be prescribed opiates for pain than other veterans.[71] In too many instances, VA physicians prescribed opiates with depressants that dramatically increased health risks for their patients. When former Marine Jason Simcakoski died of an overdose in

2014, he was taking fourteen different VA-prescribed drugs, including opioids, tranquilizers, and antipsychotics.[72]

Whether it can be correlated with misdiagnosed PTSD or poorly managed drug prescriptions, veterans' suicide rates emerged as another sobering tragedy produced by overseas military contingency operations. At first glance, the statistics do not seem particularly alarming. According to the VA's 2019 *National Veteran Suicide Prevention Annual Report*, the total number of suicides increased by 6.1 percent between 2005 and 2017.[73] However, taking into account the decline in veterans' population, as well as age and sex, veterans' suicide rates increased by almost 50 percent during this period. During a May 2019 hearing, the House Committee on Oversight and Reform noted that veterans were committing suicide at a rate that was 1.5 times higher than civilians in 2016.[74]

Faced with these terrible realities, the VA reversed course on opioid use and attempted to reform its mental health care system. Between 2012 and 2017, there was a 56 percent decrease in VA patients receiving opioids.[75] Senator John McCain introduced the Veterans Overmedication Prevention Act in 2017, which would require the VA to "to review the deaths of all covered veterans who died by suicide during the last five years, regardless of whether information relating to such deaths has been reported by the Centers for Disease Control and Prevention."[76] Veterans Affairs revised its outreach programs to include more timely support for suicide prevention, and its health services hired five thousand counselors who maintained a twenty-four-hour suicide hotline. Between 2007 and 2016, it fielded approximately two million calls.[77] To fund these initiatives, Congress authorized more than a billion dollars for suicide prevention between 2013 and 2019.

Another response to ongoing problems in the Department of Veterans Affairs has been calls for privatization.[78] The logic followed previous arguments that free market efficiencies would solve the many apparent problems plaguing veterans' care at the time.[79] Despite some initial resistance from the George W. Bush administration, the VA began experimenting with outsourcing functions soon after the September 11 attacks.[80] The Department of Veterans Affairs in Philadelphia moved prostate cancer treatment to the University of Pennsylvania between 2002 to 2008. Of 114 patients in the program, 92 received either too much or too little radiation therapy. A subsequent 2008 investigation by the VA inspector general also discovered billing problems in 37 percent of $3.2 billion spent on outsourced care around the country.[81]

Regardless of these obvious problems, calls for reform through privatization picked up additional momentum in 2014, when national attention gravitated to prolonged delays in veterans' treatment and corrupt practices at a VA hospital in Phoenix. According to press reports, the average wait time for a doctor's appointment was 115 days, on an order of magnitude worse than the official policy mandating a maximum wait of two weeks. According to the *New York Times*, VA management actively threatened doctors, nurses, and staff if they did not produce positive official statistics.[82] Although initial attention focused on Phoenix, further investigation revealed systemic manipulation of VA record keeping on a national scale. The American Legion published details on similar problems in dozens of VA facilities in Wyoming, Colorado, West Virginia, Florida, South Carolina, Texas, Missouri, and Illinois.[83]

The scandal revealed chronic underfunding and staff shortages throughout the VA health care system. Joe Violante of Disabled America Veterans testified before Congress in 2014 that legislators had underfunded the VA by 5.5 billion dollars over the preceding decade. One result was chronic staff shortages, which included four hundred primary care physicians that year.[84]

Rapid federal action followed the revelations. Pressured by both Democrat and Republican lawmakers, the Obama administration demanded the resignation of Department of Veterans Affairs head Eric Shinseki. In August 2014, Obama signed the Veterans' Access to Care through Choice, Accountability, and Transparency Act. The president hailed the measure as a means to ensure "stronger management and leadership and oversight" as well "a critical culture of accountability."[85]

The "VA Choice Program," as it came to be known, also included a three-year pilot program that allowed veterans who could not get a VA doctor within 30 days to seek outside private treatment.[86] Conservative groups, specifically the nonprofit Concerned Veterans for America, commended the decision as a long-overdue reform that would sidestep the VA bureaucracy in favor of better medical care.[87] It was a narrative that Donald Trump quickly adopted as one of his campaign's primary talking points, stating simply: "Under a Trump administration, no veteran will die waiting for service."[88]

The VA Choice Program continued and expanded once Trump became president. By 2018, one-third of the sixty million appointments made within the VA were outsourced to private doctors. Projected spending for 2019 was $14 billion, almost doubling the amount spent on the program in its first three years.[89] It appeared that VA privatization was firmly ensconced as a viable policy option.

Veterans groups, which included the Veterans of Foreign Wars and American Legion, as well as smaller organizations like American Veterans

(AMVETS) and the Paralyzed Veterans of America, were uniformly against the change. Sherman Gillums Jr., AMVETS representative, noted: "The word 'choice' has become a dog whistle for urging veterans to seek care outside of the VA. The demand for healthcare would then become profitable for corporations and organizations that provide healthcare, essentially commoditizing veterans' healthcare, with no competition from a government system."[90] Other advocates pointed to the potential negative impact to veterans' treatment. A 2018 RAND study noted that private medical practitioners lacked specific experience with military health problems—ranging from PTSD to respiratory conditions caused by burn pits—and could not be relied on to render appropriate treatment.[91]

Regardless of these concerns, the Trump administration proceeded with plans to expand privatization of VA health services. At the start of 2019, officials referred to the possibility of a new program that might resemble the military Tricare system, which offered a combination of government treatment and private options for health care.[92] When the White House offered its 2020 VA budget request to Congress, it set aside 18 percent of VA medical funding for private providers.[93]

As privatization efforts continue, so too did problems within the VA health care system. National Nurses United, the largest professional union in the country, reported in June 2019 a total of forty-three thousand total unfilled vacancies among VA health workers.[94] At the same time, a senior VA manager came forward as a whistle-blower regarding the old issue of wait times for medical treatment. According to Jereme P. Whiteman, the VA's director of clinic practice management, the official count of veterans in line for help was nearly three times larger than stated in publicly available data.[95]

THE "COMMUNITY OF SUFFERERS"

Institutional responses to the plight of war wounded are important to understanding the healing process, but there are other intangible elements likely at work. Various studies have considered the correlation between training standards and susceptibility to PTSD, arguing that elite units tend to withstand the mental pressures of war better than their less prepared counterparts, which explains why airborne, special forces, and Marine Corps forces generally retained their cohesiveness in wartime despite significant casualty rates.[96] In World War II, Easy Company of the 506th Parachute Infantry Regiment, featured in Stephen E. Ambrose's *Band of Brothers*, underwent a highly selective and grueling training process for two years before deploying to Europe.[97] Shared adversity before and during the war proved to be a key component of its persistence as a unit.

What supported cohesiveness among a "community of sufferers," as Sebastian Junger put it, also defined their separation from civilian society and the difficulties of recovery once home. Junger makes the interesting point that contemporary veterans enjoy broad public support, very much unlike Vietnam veterans, but paradoxically are three times more likely to suffer from PTSD. Why? What seems to be missing is a "shared public meaning" of military service and its consequences.[98] When Omar Bradley began rebuilding the Veterans Administration in 1945, he pointed to the absolute necessity of an involved public: "While we can assist with benefits and offer guidance, it is the community that must do the grass-roots work. For it is in his daily association with neighbors that the veteran rubs shoulders with so many troublesome problems Washington cannot hope to solve."[99]

In other words, although Vietnam may have been the more unpopular war, peacetime selective service at least spread the military experience far more broadly through society than it exists today. Junger's point is that public support is more vicarious today and prone to delegate PTSD to the medical community, which treats it as an isolated disease rather than a holistic community problem.

Lacking this community support, veterans seek out relief in other forms. One of these is monetary compensation, where a disability payment becomes both a means of financial support and some larger indication of social recognition. Abuse of this system has become an open secret in recent years as stories of veterans abusing the VA's largess have become more frequent.[100] There is some evidence of veterans abandoning treatment once they achieve a 100 percent disability rating.[101] Other veterans wait to apply for disability once they reach retirement age.[102] The problem for the public official or the historian is differentiating between real need and outright manipulation of the system.

This is not to say that the community of sufferers is a passive group. The current nonprofit landscape contains hundreds, if not thousands, of 501(c)(3) organizations reaching into virtually every feature of a veteran's existence. Many are small-scale ventures. Iron Warriors helps with "debilitating injuries" caused by mental and physical trauma, specifically connecting veterans with service dogs. Soldier Sanctuary, an organization "BY combat vets FOR combat vets," operates in eastern Pennsylvania and follows a simple mission: it provides opportunities, as often stated by Soldier Sanctuary founder Tom Bucci, to "GTFO" (Get the Fuck Out) and sponsors a variety of activities—kayaking, hiking, tours of historical sites—all with the general purpose of adding something new and purposeful to a veteran's daily routine.[103]

On the opposite end of the spectrum is the Wounded Warrior Project. Founded in 2003, it is a well-funded national organization that serves as an umbrella for many types of assistance to veterans. The Wounded Warrior Project supports veterans' mental health, career counseling, attaining VA benefits, and emergency financial assistance, among many other programs.[104] Unfortunately, like other national charities, it has not been immune to controversy or scandal. In 2015, the Wounded Warrior Project took in $372 million in donations and spent almost 40 percent of this amount on salaries and overhead, including junkets for its executive staff.[105] Although these revelations prompted a shake-up of upper management, the organization has yet to completely recover its public standing.

CONCLUSIONS

Combat medicine rarely keeps pace with the evolving lethality of modern weapons. Yet, modern lifesaving methods have reached a point where the vast majority of war wounded make it home today. Men and women who would have died from massive concussions or multiple amputations in past wars now survive mental and physical trauma at unprecedented rates. Doing so begins a long process of lifetime recovery with many obstacles and few guarantees of success.

Despite bouts of budgetary belt-tightening, generational conflict over VA resources, and periodic scandals resulting from corruption and inefficiency, health care remains a deeply embedded expectation among veterans. For all their struggle with the older products of World War II, Korea, and Vietnam, contemporary veterans live in the accumulated wake of their predecessors. Treatment for service-related injuries and the costs of old age are a routine part of the VA medical portfolio. The entitlements won and expanded over the course of decades are the norm and will likely remain that way as more contemporary veterans join the system.

Contemporary veterans are also leaving their own mark on the health care system. By virtue of the complex dynamic of modern wounds and treatment, they present significant challenges to surgeons, clinical psychologists, and physical therapists who must contend with the interrelated problems of body and mind. These challenges are particularly relevant to the rapidly growing numbers of women who have been subject to enemy fire and systemic abuse within the military. Given the sheer number of disabled veterans produced by military operations since 2001, it is likely that the VA medical institution will spend additional decades and tens of billions of dollars to heal itself in its attempts to heal them.

CHAPTER SIX

The Economics of the Veteran

> Employers tell me it's not their problem that my military service cut me out of the job market. They say I've got no work experience. It's the old tired circle of no experience, no job, no experience. People don't care. They just don't care.
> —*Vietnam veteran Richard Dix, 1970*

> Starting a business by veterans, for veterans, is probably the closest I will ever come to re-creating the emotions I felt and the bonds I enjoyed during my time with the Army.
> —*Iraq and Afghanistan veteran Mat Best, 2019*

INTRODUCTION

One of the most important ways for a veteran to come home is to work. In this one simple action is the opportunity for individuals to make their own way, to pay bills or invest time and effort in a new profession or the possibilities of entrepreneurship and the American Dream. Work is also an opportunity to meet family obligations as soldiers mature into new responsibilities. Work is a means toward a new mission defined by spouses, mortgages, school tuition, and children.

Before even arriving at these basic tasks is an additional layer of questions. How does the military prepare a veteran for a civilian career? On the surface, a twenty-year-old draftee former infantryman had significantly different civilian employment prospects in 1973 than does a National Guard military police officer returning from his fourth Iraq deployment in 2012. How did military skills translate in an ever-changing job market?

The latter point is important. Unlike the immediate post-1945 transition, the subsequent Cold War and the period after Soviet collapse in 1991 lacked a clear economic delineation between war and peacetime. A civilian economy took firm hold after 1945. Although the "military-industrial complex" bequeathed to Americans after World War II continuously evolved over the succeeding decades, promoting the postwar boom and periodically shielding parts of the country from reverses of economic fortune, veterans after Vietnam entered a job market that was far more fluid and vicarious than it had been for their fathers and grandfathers.

One final point deserves some attention. In the transition from military to civilian life, we cannot assume that the veteran was a passive entrant into the U.S. marketplace. Many of the men and women departing the service saw their new status as veterans as something intrinsically valuable, not only for the more obvious organizational skills and self-discipline that employers sought but also as an *identity* that they could leverage in niche markets that would substantively recognize their service. Veterans have always taken this path. A quick look at C. Wright Mills *The Power Elite* (1956) reveals a host of former generals on corporate boards.[1] However, in the recent past, a whole new array of veterans have jumped onto this bandwagon and turned it into something of an entrepreneurial art form.

THE EVOLUTION OF "POSTWAR" ECONOMIES

The boom that dominated almost thirty years of the post–World War II era set the standard for three generations of veterans' expectations. Even counting the transition problems that plagued the U.S. economy immediately after 1945 or periodic recessions (1953–54, 1957–58, 1960–61, 1969–70), the country grew at a remarkable rate.[2] The gross national product increased from $206 billion in 1949 to over $500 billion by 1960. Ten years later, it would exceed $1 trillion.[3]

In stark contrast stood the economy of the seventies, a decade bracketed by the abandonment of the gold standard (1971) and two oil crises in 1973–74 and 1979. Multiplying these woes was a decline in American global trade, increasingly challenged by resurrected postwar European economies, particularly West Germany. In Asia, Japan led a regional economic resurgence and was joined by a number of lesser-developed nations.[4] As early as 1971, the United States had an unfavorable balance of trade, its first since 1893.[5] For the average American, or veterans being mustered out after Vietnam, terms like "recession" and "stagflation" translated into what seemed to be the permanent end of generational job security.

The Reagan era witnessed an economic dichotomy of boom and bust. It started in a deep decline, complete with high unemployment (10.8%) and an astronomically high prime interest rate (21.5%) in 1982.[6] The so-called Rust Belt, already suffering from the reverses of the previous decade, continued its slide. Referring to the auto, steel, lumber, and construction industries, a contemporary *New York Times* article noted that the "prospects there are grim and financial and psychological stress is intense."[7]

Progress in the Sun Belt states stood in sharp contrast to the old economic sectors. Texas, California, Arizona, and other states saw rapid expansion of the service sector, particularly in high-tech industries. Bill Gates and Steve Jobs became the exemplars of the new economy and the dawning information age. By 1980, Apple Computer was valued at $1.8 billion, which placed it ahead of Ford and the Chase Manhattan Bank.[8]

The economy eventually recovered and surged forward by the time Reagan achieved his decisive victory against Walter Mondale in 1984. When he left office, Reagan claimed that his administration was responsible for creating more than sixteen million new jobs, an impressive number offset by an average hourly wage, after inflation, that barely moved above its 1970 level.[9] More to the point, Reagan departed the political scene with a federal deficit that had tripled to almost $3 trillion during his eight years in office and a weakened regulatory structure that showed ominous signs of vulnerability, specifically during the savings and loan crisis on "Black Monday," October 19, 1987. The market dropped 508 points, 22.61 percent of its value, the largest one-day loss in U.S. history at that time.[10]

The nineties witnessed an extension of this bifurcated economy: a period characterized by massive macroeconomic prosperity accompanied by severe structural problems that became increasingly obvious as the country neared the new millennium. Pundits described it as a "postindustrial" or "information economy," one relying on data rather than finished goods. It was a time where Disney surpassed U.S. Steel in stock value and never looked back.[11] The nineties were a period of tremendous overall growth. The Dow Jones industrial average more than quadrupled (from 2,588 in 1991 to 11,722 in 2000), and by 2001, 51 percent of American families held some stock investments.[12]

At the same time, both white- and blue-collar employment became increasingly tenuous. An old standby like General Motors announced layoffs for 70,000 workers and 21 plant closures in December 1991.[13] Newer industries were also unsafe. Between the mideighties and the midnineties, AT&T reduced its workforce by 100,000 people and welcomed the New Year in 1996 with 40,000 additional firings, the largest in the telephone industry at that moment.[14]

Nineties economics represented a balancing act, being a time when investors and lawmakers celebrated a federal budget surplus.[15] However, these same people shared space with a growing underclass of unemployed and underemployed workers struggling for traction in a global economy. They were exemplified by Michael Moore's 1989 film *Roger and Me*, which depicted the rise and fall of Flint, Michigan, the automaking city intimately tied to General Motors. What Moore depicted, according to *Film Comment*, was "a portrait of America without the tools to fix what's gone wrong."[16]

Americans started the new millennium with economic hopes that proved to be very short lived. The internet-driven tech bubble, fueled by investor speculation on the newfound possibilities of online commerce, burst in 2001. Before the year was over, the country recoiled from coordinated terrorist attacks on September 11. Airline traffic briefly halted, and markets closed for a short time as Americans struggled for balance. As the incipient Global War on Terrorism (GWOT) began with the invasion of Afghanistan, most of the country hesitantly heeded George W. Bush's advice to return to a modicum of normalcy and not be afraid to go shopping again.[17]

More profound systemic changes to U.S. economic fortunes were around the corner. Bush kept his campaign promise to cut taxes, a pledge that resulted in an estimated additional $1.5 trillion added to the federal deficit, according to a 2012 Congressional Budget Office report.[18] Alongside this decision, in a move reminiscent of Lyndon Johnson's pursuit of domestic policy alongside the escalating Vietnam War, the Bush administration poured additional billions into the Global War on Terrorism. According to a 2019 report by Brown University, the total cost of overseas military contingency operations between 2001 and 2020 amounted to $6.4 trillion.[19]

Then came the Great Recession of 2007–9. As the new century began, the progressive and deliberate efforts to deregulate federal oversight of banking and the financial sector as a whole came to a terrible fruition. In the short space of a only a few years, stock market losses wiped out a staggering $7 trillion in value.[20] Millions were impacted by the loss of jobs, homes, savings, and personal investments. In 2008 alone, 43,500 businesses filed for bankruptcy, more than double the number two years earlier.[21] The country reeled. In 2013, journalist Matt Taibbi reflected on the enormity of the problems as he waited at a pretrial bank fraud hearing of Abacus, a community bank located in New York's Chinatown: "So who's the defendant? Is it Citigroup? Goldman Sachs? Wells Fargo? JPMorgan Chase? Bank of America? After all, these companies had been involved in countless scandals since the financial crisis of '08, a disaster caused by an epidemic of criminal fraud that wiped out 40 percent of the world's wealth in less than a year, affecting nearly everyone in the industrialized world."[22] A 2009 *Chicago Tribune* story touched the heart of the individual crisis for millions of Americans. "What does it feel like to lose your middle-class life?" author Barbara Brotman asked. "Like the solid ground beneath you turned to water. Like you woke up in a world you find unrecognizable. Like you are sick."[23]

To counteract the massive impact of the financial disaster, the federal government embarked on an equally massive multibillion-dollar bailout of the financial industry, automakers, and distressed mortgage holders under the Troubled Assets Relief Plan (2008–10).[24] As it became known, TARP was followed by the American Recovery and Reinvestment Act of 2009, a more massive, $800 billion stimulus package promoted by the incoming administration of Barack Obama. Federal money went to a tax cut as well as unemployment benefits, infrastructure projects, and support for state Medicaid funding.[25]

Much of the country recovered from the Great Recession. Prior to the COVID-19 pandemic, unemployment stood at historic lows in much the same way that the Dow Jones average reached unprecedented peaks at the end of February 2020. However, recovery has been uneven, and in some categories, ongoing economic hardships continued long after economists and policymakers declared victory. As late as 2017, key areas of the old industrial Rust Belt and the South had not recovered and were experiencing continuing economic decline. Certain portions of the former workforce, specifically those analysts described as holding "middle skill" jobs—requiring more than a high school diploma but less than a college degree, everything from manufacturing to telemarketing—were not seeing these positions come back.[26]

A SHORT HISTORY OF VETERANS IN ECONOMIC TRANSITION

As the section above indicates, recent veterans have had to navigate a far rockier economic path than did previous generations. The prospect of consistent growth, periodically interrupted by market fluctuations, clearly has not been part of the modern landscape. Yet, successive cohorts of veterans, produced by Vietnam, the latter days of the Cold War, and current ongoing overseas contingency operations, did and continue to traverse the new economy despite its many pitfalls. Just how they managed this is an interesting study in individual initiative and adaptive federal programs.

Veterans of the Vietnam War suffered from a combination of poor economic circumstances worsened by poorly crafted and executed federal policy. Generally better educated but younger than the generation that served in World War II and Korea, Vietnam-era veterans found a systemically weaker economy that was not prepared for them and, in some cases, treated military service as a liability for employment.

National economic policy often compounded these difficulties. As the Vietnam War wound down, federal officials did little to coordinate the rapidly increasing number of discharges—from 496,000 in 1965 to over 1 million by 1970—with private sector demand.[27] Moreover, as the draft gradually ended, inducting 152,000 men in 1972 and only 25,000 a year later, Nixon and his primary advisers framed the change in political terms, linking the measure to his 1972 reelection prospects, rather than considering the economic impact on veterans as a group.[28]

Vietnam-era military policies also complicated veterans' employment prospects. First among these was the Pentagon's response to the concurrent challenges of declining discipline and a significant uptick in military drug use. Military sanctions produced a noticeable increase in administrative discharges. Between June 1970 and June 1971, for example, almost one in five sailors left the Navy under terms that were "general," "undesirable," "bad conduct," or "dishonorable"[29] These types of discharges followed veterans immediately into civilian life. A dishonorable discharge automatically forfeited readjustment benefits under the Cold War GI Bill. Veterans discharged for drug use could also lose medical benefits at the discretion of the Veterans Administration.[30] Other sanctions, for drug use or bad conduct persisted on a veteran's record and tainted his job prospects.

A number of new federal programs did attempt to help recently discharged veterans. To facilitate job placement, the Pentagon sponsored direct connections with businesses that were defense contractors, such as IBM, to employ discharged veterans. In June 1971, the Nixon administration took this idea a step further by encouraging the National Alliance of Businessmen, which represented almost thirty thousand companies, to provide one hundred thousand jobs for Vietnam veterans.[31]

Both the Veterans Administration (VA) and the Defense Department cooperated with numerous Great Society projects intended to ease veterans' transition from the military to civilian life. Programs for employment placement in police and fire departments, Volunteers in Service to America, and Job Corps were all folded into "veterans in public service careers" (VIPS) initiatives. During the Nixon years, the Defense Department funneled veterans into Department of Labor vocational training as well as the U.S. Office of Education's Career Opportunities Program.[32] The VA encouraged veterans to serve as teachers in the "deprived areas" of rural America as well as the inner cities.[33] Project Remed and Operation MEDIHC (Medical Experience Directed into Health Careers) attempted to recruit military medical specialists in the civilian medical professions.[34]

By all official accounts, the overlapping layers of federal programs touched millions of Vietnam-era veterans, although the results appear to be mixed at best. For all its grand claims, Nixon's effort with the National Alliance of Businessmen was purely voluntary and netted only twenty thousand new jobs for veterans in 1971. The Nader Report found veterans' programs under Nixon to be poorly funded, sometimes with money taken from other job programs.[35] Government-sponsored job fairs commonly attracted far more applicants than available positions. In May 1972, frustrated veterans destroyed kiosks in what one witness described simply as a "riot."[36] Word of mouth, family, friends, and personal initiative accounted for the vast majority of employment, according to one Harris poll.[37]

Veterans' unemployment emerged as a major issue at the end of the Vietnam War. Although it stood at only 4 percent in late 1969, two years later, with the national economy in the teeth of another recession, the rate for younger veterans aged twenty to twenty-four was 12.4 percent. For all veterans, it was more than double the national figure.[38] Joblessness was far greater for minority veterans. Ironically, the vocations that offered higher rates of promotion in the military—the combat arms—translated as "low skill occupational specialties" in the civilian sector. This, combined with higher rates of less-than-honorable discharges among African American veterans, made employment far more difficult.[39] According to testimony by the National Urban League before the Senate Committee on Veterans Affairs, Black veterans' unemployment was 22.4 percent in the first quarter of 1972.[40]

Employers, buffeted by encroaching hard times and dubious about the prospects for the newest crop of returning soldiers, proved reluctant to assist veterans. When the 1970 "Jobs for Veterans" initiative sent out a mass mailing appeal to nine hundred thousand businesses to encourage hiring, it received a 2 percent response rate. Undersecretary of Commerce Rocco Siciliano put the matter bluntly in June 1970, noting: "It is hard to imbue businessmen with a social conscience when business is bad."[41] Unions proved equally reluctant to allow returning rank-and-file members with little seniority to jump the line ahead of hundreds of employees who had already been laid off.[42]

Despite these obstacles, Vietnam veterans endured and, in many cases, defied the odds. Existing data indicates a mixed record with respect to their postwar economic fortunes. One 1981 study recorded Vietnam veterans' unemployment rate in 1977 at 8 percent, more than Vietnam-era veterans (5%) but almost equal to surveyed nonveterans (9%). Race continued to be an important determinant of employment. Joblessness for African American veterans of Vietnam was more than five times that of whites.[43] Underemployment also remained a chronic problem unseen in the statistics. Combat veterans were already well versed with the problem of translating military skills to civilian work after discharge, but this dilemma also affected individuals with technical skills, particularly women. Although trained in literally hundreds of military occupations, female veterans of World War II discovered their most likely employment reduced to "clerical and kindred work."[44] Twenty years later, military nurses who rejoined hospital staffs after returning from Vietnam found the transition from valued colleague to "handmaiden" a difficult process, as one historian has observed.[45]

Studies of Vietnam veterans' earning power illustrate some departures and dispel a few myths. Obstacles specific to Vietnam-era veterans, from parsimonious readjustment benefits to the troublesome core of poorly educated men within the most advanced military in the world, created significant economic difficulties. In some respects, veterans experienced the same problems as their boomer generation: their incomes suffered from a glut of young applicants entering a soft economy in the seventies.[46] Unlike the much stronger periods of growth following World War II and Korea, it took time for them to build their own individual economic prosperity. Yet, through a combination of improving economic times and individual initiative, they did regain lost ground. One comparison of Korea and Vietnam veterans indicates that while the former group earned slightly more than comparable civilians, Vietnam veterans had not fallen behind their nonveteran peers at the end of the seventies.[47] One more recent (2003) evaluation of approximately thirty thousand veterans noted distinctions between Vietnam-era draftees and volunteers according to their race. Overall, men in the sample saw a 1.5 percent reduction in wages compared with to their civilian peers. White draftees suffered the largest losses (-5.0%), whereas African American draftees (+3.0%) and volunteers (+7.5%) recorded the largest increases over comparable nonveterans.[48]

*

In the eighties, the most noticeable feature for veterans leaving the service for civilian careers was a lack of official urgency regarding their transition. Once the country cleared the hardships that dominated the first year of the Reagan administration and growth returned, the assumption followed that returning good times would absorb the slow but steady number of people leaving the military.

As noted in Chapter Two, the early life of the Montgomery GI Bill reflected this trend, but compared with its Vietnam, Korea, and World War II predecessors, it paled in comparison. To qualify, service members had to contribute a $100 payroll deduction each month for their first year of service. With that accomplished, they would qualify for $9,000 in benefits after two years in uniform and $10,800 after completing a three-year enlistment.[49] Payouts were available on a monthly basis that covered up to four years of full-time college enrollment. Unlike the 1944 Serviceman's Readjustment Act, which offered both tuition and a stipend that opened both public and private colleges to veterans, the Montgomery GI Bill was inadequate to pay for just resident tuition and housing at most state colleges in 1986.[50]

Job training programs for veterans were similarly limited in the eighties. In 1983, Congress approved the Veterans Job Training Program, which was actually created for Korea- and Vietnam-era service members but revised to apply to all veterans. The program reimbursed employers for up to 50 percent of the training costs necessary for work. The vast majority (80%) of these workers were Vietnam-era veterans. Most trainees who finished the program eventually entered the machine trades, construction, and managerial occupations at a higher salary than did nonparticipants. However, almost two-thirds of the veterans who entered the program did not complete it. The highest dropout rates occurred among African Americans, veterans with disabilities, and women.[51]

*

The end of the Cold War with the Soviet Union introduced some new and important dynamics impacting veterans. For one, mass demobilization followed the end of the conflict. According to Peter Singer, approximately seven million individuals left or were forced out of all militaries around the world in the ten years following the fall of the Berlin Wall.[52] As the world celebrated, U.S. active duty forces faced the prospect of the incipient "peace dividend" and its consequences. A new term, "RIF'd" (reduction in force), entered the military lexicon, affecting hundreds of thousands in every service branch. Long-serving professionals were offered one-time cash payments as a demobilization incentive. As one official managing the program put it, "The drawdown isn't about quality, it's about quantity."[53] Between 1987 and 2000, the Pentagon cut the military from 2.17 million to 1.37 million, a reduction of 37 percent.[54]

For career soldiers, it was a profound moment. Colonel Alfred M. Baker, a Vietnam veteran who was tasked with closing down the Berlin Brigade in 1994, commented: "In some ways, this has been the toughest assignment I've ever had. It's saying goodbye to a city and a mission that has played such a role in history. It feels like amputating your own leg."

In personal terms, leaving the military was at best bittersweet. After being chosen for involuntary separation, one officer reflected: "I never thought it would come to this. But the best way to serve my country is by leaving the Army. Whether I want to or not."⁵⁵

Proposals varied as to what to do with the surge of veterans. There seemed to be a natural transition from military service to the public sector. One *New York Times* editorial suggested that individuals with military medical training could augment personnel in city hospitals. In the same vein, the author also saw a role for veterans in police departments to battle violent crime or as a means for teaching staffs to regain control of classrooms.⁵⁶

Like their Vietnam-era predecessors, a number of companies started veterans hiring programs. Employers as diverse as General Electric; Schneider National Carriers, an interstate trucking firm; and Kentucky Fried Chicken actively recruited former military personnel. Firms were attracted to the high percentage of veterans with high school diplomas (98% of the Army in 1991), current security clearances, and leadership skills among officers and noncommissioned officers. Recent history had also added an important cachet to military service. As Secretary of Defense Dick Cheney noted in October 1991: "Remember, these are the same people who dazzled and impressed the world during Desert Storm."⁵⁷

President Bill Clinton, like Nixon before him, also dedicated millions of federal dollars to facilitate veterans' economic transition. Clinton's administration continued the 1990 Troops to Teachers program that paid up to five thousand dollars for veterans to obtain their teaching certificates and move into K-12 classrooms.⁵⁸ The Department of the Army contracted fifty-five job assistance centers to provide counseling and training to build job-hunting and interview skills.⁵⁹ In 1995, the Defense Department announced the "Troops to Cops" conversion plan, which provided $15 million for individual training in the Community Oriented Policing Services Program.⁶⁰ Former soldiers seemed to be a natural fit for law enforcement. H. R. Barrera, who managed recruitment for the Harris County Sheriff's Department in Houston, Texas, noted: "Military people are drug-free, disciplined and used to abiding by rules and regulations."⁶¹ The measure also seemed a perfect means for the Clinton administration to meet its promise of placing one hundred thousand new police on the streets to fight crime.

Although these initiatives gained a great deal of public attention, they represented a relatively small number of veterans in the nineties. A close examination of Veterans Administration data indicates a few distinct characteristics of the veterans who left the military between

Vietnam and the Global War on Terrorism. With the exception of those briefly deployed for Operations Desert Shield and Desert Storm, the VA classified the individuals of this era as "peacetime veterans." This cohort was different from the Vietnam generation with respect to its career paths. Peacetime veterans participated in general labor, manufacturing, the trades, and services at higher rates than Vietnam veterans. For their own part, Vietnam veterans had an edge in managerial and professional specialties as well as technical fields.[62]

Given the limitations built into the Montgomery GI Bill, this divergence makes sense. Veterans who followed the Vietnam generation had less access to education, particularly at the college and university level. Instead, they pursued vocational training and degree programs attainable with the reduced benefits available after 1982. Demographics also obviously played a part. The "peacetime" veteran was younger, much less vested in career work, and typically unable to enjoy the benefits of seniority. Overall, post-Vietnam veterans' economic prospects were a good illustration of diminishing returns, in much the same way that programs and opportunities for Vietnam-era veterans were a step down from those who served in World War II and Korea.

*

The September 11 terrorist attacks altered the basic course of American national security interests, civil liberties, and politics. Veterans affairs were no exception. The most important change in service and veterans' status was the massive use of U.S. reserves and the National Guard in numbers unprecedented since the Korea War. Between 2001 and 2014, the Pentagon and state governments called up 815,000 of these personnel.[63] However, what distinguished this service from its 1950–53 counterpart was its duration and the multiple deployments of part-time soldiers. A few reserve and National Guard units moved to active duty status for only weeks or months following the September 11 attacks. Many more citizen soldiers—especially those in the military police, intelligence, civil affairs, transportation, and aviation—experienced frequent and lengthy overseas tours of duty.[64]

This new category of service placed distinct economic burdens on reservist veterans. Some specific sectors were affected more than others. A 2014 study, for example, noted that male reservists were overrepresented among first responders, specifically police, fire, and emergency medical services. During the GWOT, hundreds of police and fire departments across the country were saddled with extra workloads that could only be partially covered with overtime and temporary hires. Consequently, mobilization affected both the reservists, who lost valuable training, experience, and seniority, as well as their local communities, which had to adapt to lengthening emergency response times.[65]

Many businesses faced with these disruptions simply cut their losses. Companies blanched at the prospect of absorbing increased costs for overtime, temporary replacements, and ongoing pension benefits in some cases. Many firms took the deliberate step of preempting potential expenses by either firing reservists before they deployed or immediately after they returned home. In the first two years of the Global War on Terrorism, 5,690 veterans lost their jobs this way.[66] As late as 2011, the National Guard Bureau estimated that 20 percent of returning reservists were unemployed, twice the rate for all veterans after 2001.[67]

Federal law was supposed to protect these veterans, but implementation was often problematic. The Uniformed Services Employment and Reemployment Rights Act (USERRA) of 1994 was a modern update of the original GI Bill and predated the surge in overseas contingency operations.[68] In principle, its basic provisions seemed relatively straightforward. Deploying service members could expect to have their original jobs back once they returned home. Being able to count on civilian careers left behind was an obvious boon to part-time soldiers and reinforced the basic contract between the government and military volunteers.

In practice, the USERRA often produced incomplete or inadequate solutions. It did not apply indefinitely to reservists called away from their civilian jobs. Passed in an era before the September 11 attacks, the law protected employment for reservists recalled for up to five years. Lawmakers never anticipated multiple or multiyear deployments that went beyond this limit. Other provisions of the USERRA simply shifted costs from businesses to the reservist. For example, although the law mandated that deployed individuals could keep their employer health insurance and pension plans, it made service members responsible for payments, a difficult prospect for reservists on a military pay scale.[69]

Most returning reservists did not contest the loss of jobs or increased personal expenses. According to one estimate, as many as two-thirds of veterans did not bother to follow official channels for redress.[70] However, thousands did file complaints with the Department of Labor: in 2004, approximately fifteen hundred did so. Seven years later, the number of filings was almost identical.[71] Individuals could file complaints with the Veterans' Employment and Training Service in the Department of Labor. Federal employees serving in the reserves could use the same process or represent themselves before the Merits System Protection

Board, which handled appeals from federal civil servants.[72] To circumvent federal intervention, many businesses simply required new hires to sign preemployment agreements to take any disputes to binding arbitration, a tactic that has withstood subsequent challenges in federal courts.[73]

Active duty veterans of the Global War on Terrorism assumed their own distinct characteristics as the conflict dragged on. As a group, it seemed that veterans were shielded to a degree from the economic fluctuations of the early twenty-first century. According to the Bureau of Labor Statistics, former service seemed to be an insulator from unemployment. In 2018, the average unemployment rate for veterans was 3.5 percent as compared with 3.8 percent for civilians.[74]

However, the devil, as they say, is in the details. Veterans as a group included all ages, from Greatest Generation retirees to Vietnam veterans enjoying well-established careers and seniority to more contemporary veterans of the GWOT. Women, who were a growing part of the veteran demographic, experienced greater difficulty finding work. In 2007, female veterans were unemployed at more than twice the rate (9.6%) of civilian women (4.5%). This gap closed slightly only after the Great Recession began at the end of the year.[75] Younger veterans (18–24) also consistently experienced substantially higher rates of unemployment than their nonveteran counterparts. During the worst days of the economic downturn, civilian unemployment peaked at 10 percent in October 2009.[76] Among veterans aged eighteen to twenty-four, it was almost triple this figure at 29 percent in 2011.[77] Similar joblessness existed for African American veterans. In 2011, it ranged from 17.4 percent to as high as 21.3 percent.[78]

A 2014 RAND study commissioned by the Defense Department explained the reasons for the difference in unemployment between veterans and civilians. Some answers were simple. When a young veteran left military service, he or she technically became unemployed until moving into an alternative: work, college, or vocational training. In the first month out of uniform, it was not uncommon for veterans to experience a 25 percent unemployment rate.[79] Another important obstacle was health. The RAND study found that veterans in the age cohorts of eighteen to twenty-four and twenty-five to thirty reported significantly higher rates of mental and physical disabilities than did civilians in the same age groups.[80] As Sebastian Junger has observed, in the wake of contingency operations in Iraq and Afghanistan, the U.S. military has had the highest recorded rates of post-traumatic stress disorder in its history. Contemporary U.S. soldiers suffer from mental trauma at twice the rate of British forces, although only a small fraction of Americans actually participate in combat. According to a 2018 report by *Monthly*

Labor Review, 41 percent of more recent veterans claimed a disability, compared with one-quarter of all veterans. To put the issue in perspective, a 1990 study of Vietnam-era veterans recorded a 17 percent disability rate for those who served in-country. For veterans who served after Vietnam, 7.7 percent claimed some type of disability.[81]

A blizzard of federal programs appeared in the wake of this troubling data. Some were resurrected versions of old policy. In 2018, the Defense Department returned to the Troops to Teachers Program, which offered counseling and referral services, funding for certification, and grants to states that recruited veterans into K-12 schools.[82] The Transition Assistance Program was another retread from the nineties. The new version provided an additional year of Montgomery GI Bill benefits and an extension of vocational rehabilitation and employment benefits for disabled veterans.[83] After fielding numerous complaints about vocational rehabilitation training from Congress, the Government Accountability Office, and veterans, the Veterans Administration administered 110 recommendations that would "focus on employment and place more emphasis on its clients' skills rather than their disabilities."[84]

One piece of new legislation was the VOW (Veterans Opportunity to Work) to Hire Heroes Act of 2011. The law mandated job, health, and financial counseling as part of out-processing from the military.[85] It also provided businesses with a $5,600 tax credit if they hired a veteran who had been unemployed for six months or more.[86] These solutions resembled the cooperative approach taken immediately after World War II, when the VA assembled private entrepreneurs—from Ford and Westinghouse to International Harvester—and offered veterans, particularly combat wounded who were disabled, an opportunity at rehabilitation through new vocations.[87] Contemporary companies that invested additional effort to implement the VOW to Hire Heroes Act were more in tune with the modern service industry and included Disney, Penske, and Shell.

State and local governments also offered more than twenty-five hundred American Job Centers by 2018. These offices provided "skills translators" and "occupational crosswalks," which translated into guidance on funding for training and school as well as specific employment recommendations.[88] Veterans could search the My Next Move: For Veterans website, sponsored by the Department of Labor, for careers. The site offered a simple tool that could translate a former military occupational specialty code into a range of civilian equivalents.[89]

These efforts were successful for the most part. Veterans' unemployment steadily declined from 2010 to 2019. By February 2018, post-9/11 veterans had reached parity with civilian unemployment, whereas veterans from other periods actually enjoyed better status.[90] As late as March 2021, these figures had changed. All veterans over the age of eighteen experienced a 5.0 percent unemployment rate, although more recent "Gulf War II" veterans, a label created by the Labor Department, witnessed an uptick to 6.1 percent. One explanation for the trend was the increasing number of discharges produced by the most recent round of military downsizing.[91]

Some recent successes varied according to race in interesting ways. One author identified the trend according to the "bridging hypothesis," which primarily applied to the economic advancement of African American and Hispanic veterans from disadvantaged backgrounds.[92] Prompted by recruiting standards mandating a high school diploma, military discipline that carried over into civilian work, and education benefits, minority veterans tend to have historically higher employment rates, hourly wages, and annual income than their civilian peers.[93] According to a 2011 Department of Veterans Affairs report, minority veterans had a higher annual personal household income at every age group from seventeen to eighty-four.[94]

COYOTE BROWN

There are points in time when a work of fiction can capture an important facet of history. Such a moment came from William Gibson's observation in *Zero History* (2010) about the hybrid relationship between the military and the private sector. In this case, it was the symbiosis between military utility and fashion sense, something that a character in the novel described as "the new Walter Mitty demographic." Gibson continues: "It's an obsession with the idea not just of the right stuff, but of the special stuff. Equipment fetishism. The costume and the semiotics of achingly elite police and military units. Intense desire to possess same, of course, and in turn be associated with that world. With its competence, its cocksure exclusivity."[95]

Ten years after *Zero History*, Gibson's fictional point is now illustrated in seemingly endless lines of clothing and merchandise actively trading on the military image. It is exemplified in the color coyote brown, a particular tone for boots, shirts, pants, and hats that mimics military camouflage and regularly appears in outlets as particular as US Patriot Tactical or as mundane as WalMart, where active duty troops also shop for gear before deployment. A 2019 *Washington Post* story commented on the seemingly endless appeal of "Tacticool" marketing to a new generation of consumers: "To an extent, there seems to be value in putting the word "Tactical" in front of your company's name. On a dummy Instagram feed

I created—all tactical, all the time—I have encountered these products and services: Tactical Keychains, Tactical Pterodactyl Knives, Tactical Photographer, Tactical Distributors, Tactical Tailor, Tactical Outfitters, Tactical Walls."[96]

This crossover effect is as old as the combination of advertising and military recruitment. The French marshal Maurice de Saxe quipped in 1757: "Troops are raised by enlistment with a fixed term, by compulsion sometimes, and most frequently by tricky devices."[97] Today, de Saxe's "tricky devices" are still present, only much more sophisticated for modern recruiting.

When the draft ended in 1973, the need for military advertising took on a particularly important meaning. As Beth Bailey notes in her study of marketing for the all-volunteer force, the Pentagon had to confront the fact that its "product" was incredibly unpopular to the point of open public hostility. In response, the Defense Department essentially attempted to demilitarize the public face of military service. Recruitment advertising enticed potential recruits with such tangible benefits as job training, travel, and funding for college education. One 1971 print ad touted military service as an entry into sightseeing and romance. "Take the Army's 16-month tour of Europe," it read, accompanied by the image of a young man and woman sitting together at a café.[98]

Military recruiting succeeded after Vietnam when it could separate service from the institution and place it closer to the individual. The slogan "Be All That You Can Be," married with increased benefits under the Montgomery GI Bill, proved to be highly successful in drawing better-caliber recruits. As was the case during the Vietnam era, military service was a highly attractive alternative for minorities, who saw fewer opportunities for salaries, benefits, and advancement in the civilian economy after 1973. By 1991, although African Americans were 12 percent of the U.S. populace, they comprised 23 percent of active duty forces.[99]

Corporate military affiliation was another means to commodify service that benefited both companies and the military establishment. During World War II, if a company could find a way to position itself as an asset to the war effort, a veritable cornucopia of federal dollars awaited them. Philip K. Wrigley talked the War Department into the proposition that a stick of gum in every K ration would increase dental hygiene, alleviate "false thirst," and reduce "nervous tension."[100] When the war ended, entrepreneurs also understood how this affiliation could help them with a new peacetime marketplace composed of millions of veterans. In a 1945 tract, Shell Oil cultivated solidarity with the public by claiming that it "merely acted in the line of duty in doing better than its best to speed the war's end."[101] By appealing to a sense of mutual wartime service, companies like Shell very carefully positioned themselves in a post-1945 boom dominated by millions of veterans.

A more modern, updated version of this approach involved the National Football League in the sixties. To challenge baseball as "America's pastime," the National Football League (NFL) commissioner Pete Rozelle capitalized on the infant league's close affiliation with the U.S. military. Players in the NFL began accompanying United Service Organizations (USO) tours overseas as early as 1965. In 1968, Buffalo Bills quarterback Jack Kemp led a group of football luminaries, including Bobby Bell, Lance Alworth, and Super Bowl I and II most valuable player Bart Starr, on visits to military bases in Vietnam. Los Angeles Ram defense tackle Rosie Greer would later join Bob Hope on tour in Vietnam that same year.[102] The Defense Department promptly returned these attentions. As early as 1968, the U.S. Air Force undertook flyovers of professional football games.[103] Since that point, military color guards became another fixture of the pregame ritual. During Super Bowl XIX (1985), in addition to these now-standard military trappings, the halftime show included the Tops in Blue, a five-hundred-member Air Force singing group, and President Ronald Reagan, who conducted the opening coin toss from the Map Room of the White House.[104]

This practice increased exponentially after the September 11 attacks as officials pursued public demonstrations of normalcy with increasingly overt displays of patriotism. Game standards now included a massive American flag brought out by first responders and veterans. The sledgehammer-like approach to nationalism inevitably invited parody, something accomplished very well in Ben Fountain's 2012 *Billy Lynn's Long Halftime Walk*.[105]

As the war continued, the NFL's partnership with the military was more deeply embedded than most people realized at the time. A 2015 investigation by Senators John McCain and Jeff Flake revealed that the National Guard and the Department of Defense were channeling millions of dollars into the league for recruitment. The Atlanta Falcons ($1 million) and Green Bay Packers ($400,000) were the largest recipients of military funding, what the *Washington Post* described as "paid patriotism."[106]

The relationship between the military and corporate America is more complex when it directly involves veterans. Many firms market themselves as employers for former service members. In part, this is simple, good public relations. The "veteran friendly" label is a deliberate move to enhance a corporate image in the marketplace. In another sense, employing veterans is also a very practical move for members of the "military-industrial complex" in America. Veterans have an abundance of technical skills prized by companies, an attraction embedded in aerospace engineering, software development, nuclear power, and many other industries around the country. The relationship is very often incestuous. During World War II, the Grumman Aircraft Engineering Corporation built fighters for the U.S. Navy and employed hundreds of former sailors, a very common practice at the time.[107] Presently, the military-corporate revolving door exists on a scale that is an order of magnitude greater than World War II. Stephen H. Walker, who served as director of the Defense Advanced Research Projects Agency is now vice president and chief technology officer for Lockheed Martin. Thomas Donnelly, former chief financial officer for the Defense Intelligence Agency, currently serves as a senior executive for SOS International, a company that provides intelligence analysis, logistics, and training support.[108]

Another facet of the military-corporate relationship involves new start-up companies owned by veterans that offer practical products and leverage their unique cultural standing. *Forbes* magazine somewhat glibly described the trend as "vetrepreneurship" in 2016.[109] An excellent example is Sandboxx, a company founded by retired Marine Corps veterans Sam Meek and Ray Smith. Sandboxx markets itself to a very specific slice of the public: its main service is expediting the delivery of regular letters to recruits in training and units deployed overseas. According to a 2018 press release: "Recruits perform at higher levels in boot camp when they receive encouraging letters and photos from loved ones at home. With Sandboxx web and mobile applications, users can type a message from their phone, add a photo and hit send. Sandboxx will securely print the message and deliver it to the recruit or Marine, usually on the next business day."[110] It was a shrewd business model, one clearly cognizant of the separation anxiety common in new military families. For a fee, Sandboxx offered peace of mind for spouses, partners, and anyone interested in maintaining reliable communication with loved ones in uniform or, according to its website, "connecting you to what matters most." Other services followed the same theme. Sandboxx is now also a travel agent for military families, facilitating lodging, flights, and car rental to both military bases and tourist attractions.[111]

A variation on the territory explored by Sandboxx comes in the form of veterans who lean very hard into their personal identity to carve out a market niche. This story is not exactly new. In *Flags of Our Fathers*, James Bradley recounted a story his father told him about the expectation among some of the Iwo Jima flag-raising survivors that they could cash in on their hero status. This was particularly true of Rene Gagnon: "'All the bigwigs on the tour would slap us on the back and promise us a job if we ever needed one,' he told me once. 'I didn't think much of it, but Rene's eyes lit up. He thought he had it made.'"[112]

Mat Best is a perfect example of contemporary "vetrepreneurs." Best is a former Army Ranger who deployed on multiple tours to Iraq and Afghanistan. After leaving active duty, he became extremely adept at developing a public persona through YouTube and social media. His song parodies "How to Be an Operator" (2013) and "How to Be a Crossfitter" (2015) attracted millions of hits online.[113] Best created Article 15 Clothing and cofounded Black Rifle Coffee Company with Special Forces veteran Evan Hafer. His 2019 autobiography, *Thank You for My Service*, rose to number one on the best-seller lists of both *Publishers Weekly* and the *Wall Street Journal*.[114]

Best and Hafer have a number of tools at their disposal to advance their business interests. One of them is humor that is crude and absolutely unapologetic about its choice of topics. Some are relatively innocuous, like the Black Rifle Coffee series on YouTube where veterans react to a variety of movie genres (e.g., war, horror). But Best also portrays himself as an antidote to the #MeToo culture and its attack on "toxic masculinity" by embracing what is, in effect, its polar opposite. He offers a scathing critique of the "pathetic chorus of first-world whining."[115]

Best often portrays such sentiments as satire, but there is an edge to them, one that resonates with his audience. What is striking about the approach is how he and Hafer have used their status as veterans to deflect what might otherwise be disastrous, self-inflicted wounds to their public personas and business fortunes. They do it by shielding such controversial sentiments within the cocoon of veteran's status. Best does this very deliberately in *Thank You for My Service*: "I wanted the world to know that veterans like me, who loved man shit like beards and whiskey and guns and hot chicks in American flag bikinis, weren't ticking time bombs waiting to explode. We were normal people who just so happened to have gone through some extraordinary experiences and come out the other side proud of our accomplishments, grateful for our brothers and sisters, and ready to apply all that experience to the next chapter of our lives in the civilian world . . . *and thrive*."[116]

The same conflation of product and veterans status applies to the positioning of the Black Rifle Coffee brand. In a 2018 CBS interview, Hafer went out of his way to explain that his company was the furthest thing from another boutique coffee maker. "Name me another CEO that's carried a SAW [Squad Automatic Weapon] through an alley at three o'clock in the morning in Baghdad, Iraq."[117] Company slogans on its website and product packaging are constant drumbeats of "fresh roasted freedom" and "coffee or die." In an interview with *Forbes*, Hafer simply described what he was doing as "selling freedom, one cup at a time."[118]

These methods have made Black Rifle Coffee an incredibly successful business. In 2018, the company grossed over $30 million. Just one year later, it was projecting $80 million in revenue.[119] Other aspiring entrepreneurs have taken note. Presently, the market is blanketed by new entries, veteran-owned and not, selling everything from workout gear with concealed carry pockets (Alexo Athletica) to a company called Tactical Baby Gear.[120]

*

Unfortunately, this type of marketing may be both lucrative and ripe for abuse. The problem is timeless. There has and always will be a seamy underside to war and relations between civilians and soldiers. "Allotment Annie," a woman who simultaneously married multiple GIs heading overseas to collect their paychecks, was something of an urban legend bound up in fact during World War II. Vivian Eggers, a Kentucky woman married to seven servicemen, became a national sensation when she was discovered and promptly arrested in 1943.[121] Today, any visitor to a major U.S. military base will find pawnshops, check-cashing businesses, and used car dealerships that surround the installation, each intent on separating a soldier from his or her money.

Scams like these have been given a modern upgrade in the twenty-first century. One example is the University of Phoenix, which aggressively marketed itself as an ideal solution for veterans interested in obtaining college degrees. As one spokesperson for the University of Phoenix put it: "Veterans continue to come to our schools because they can get an accelerated, focused, academic program that moves them quickly from the battlefield into the workplace in a career of their choosing."[122] Recruiters emphasized the school's online programs, which offered flexibility and, according to University of Phoenix advertisements, direct access to major corporations who helped develop curriculum. They promised easy transfer of military training to academic transcripts.

The University of Phoenix aggressively pursued GI Bill benefits by directly paying the Pentagon for access to active duty service members on dozens of military facilities. Recruiters gained access to the Army's Family and Morale, Welfare, and Recreation Programs, where the University of Phoenix sponsored pop music acts and laptop computer giveaways. It also paid to be present at job fairs held at reserve, national guard, and active duty bases and used the opportunity to market its online programs to service members about to leave the military.[123]

The enterprise was hugely profitable. The University of Phoenix joined other for-profit schools such as DeVry University and ITT Technical Institute in a bonanza of federal educational funding. Between 2009 and 2015, the University of Phoenix alone earned $1.2 billion from GI Bill benefits.[124]

Yet problems began to emerge regarding the quality and cost of veterans' education. A Senate investigation in 2014 found that two-thirds of the students attending for-profit colleges never received a degree.[125] However, at the University of Phoenix, the percentage of matriculating students was significantly lower. Its online campus, where most veterans took their programs, had just a 7.3 percent graduation rate in 2015.[126]

Sanctions and investigations followed quickly on the heels of these revelations. The Defense Department officially suspended University of Phoenix recruiting on military bases in 2015. In 2017, the Federal Trade Commission began an investigation of University of Phoenix business practices. Over the next two years, the VA fielded nearly six hundred complaints against the school.[127]

At the end of 2019, the Federal Trade Commission (FTC) found that the University of Phoenix had made false claims that it worked with companies like AT&T and the American Red Cross to develop courses and deceived veterans about how much GI Bill benefits would cover tuition. In his official statement, Rohit Chopra, FTC commissioner, took the school to task, saying it "scammed its students by luring them in with false job placement promises." The government ultimately fined the University of Phoenix and its parent company, the Apollo Education Group, $50 million and determined that it would void $141 million in student debt.[128] In March 2020, the Department of Veterans Affairs officially announced that it was suspending new enrollment in the University of Phoenix owing to practices that were "erroneous, deceptive or misleading either by actual statement, omission, or intimation against G.I. Bill beneficiaries."[129]

The marketing of "military friendly" credentials is another example of high-tech fraud applied to both business and higher learning. The term Military Friendly® is owned by a Pennsylvania advertising company called Viqtory Media (formerly Victory Media) which maintains publications like *G.I. Jobs*, *Military Spouse*, and *STEM Jobs*. According to the company website: "Military Friendly® is the standard that measures an organization's commitment, effort and success in creating sustainable and meaningful opportunity for the military community."[130]

Viqtory Media awards the Military Friendly label to organizations after they fill out a proprietary survey that tests just how well they treat customers with military backgrounds. Some of the companies awarded this status include AT&T, Comcast, and Boeing, among many others.[131] Colleges and universities also seek out the status as a marketing tool for veterans who are prospective applicants. According to Viqtory Media, "The Military Friendly® Schools survey is the longest-running most comprehensive review of college and university investments in serving military and veteran students. Our 2019–2020 Military Friendly® Schools list is more exclusive than ever, and covers institutions offering certificate programs to doctoral degrees."[132]

However, serious problems emerged when the nonprofit group Veterans Education Success (VES) filed a complaint with the Federal Trade Commission regarding some of Viqtory Media's practices. In 2015, VES noted that more than 257 schools awarded Military Friendly status were not approved by the Department of Defense for tuition assistance or voluntary military education programs. Moreover, despite Viqtory Media's claims, there is no outside assessment of the Military Friendly survey. Ernst & Young auditors, the firm contracted by the company for this purpose, clarified in a public statement that its only function was to ensure Viqtory Media follows its own methodology. Perhaps the most damning evidence uncovered by VES was Viqtory Media's practice of selling "lead generators," that is, veterans' personal information, to colleges for recruiting purposes without veterans' knowledge or consent.[133]

The FTC investigation resulted in a settlement with Viqtory Media. In his *Inside Higher Ed* article in 2017, Andrew Kreighbaum noted that "under the terms of the settlement, Victory is required to prominently disclose to readers that its rankings are paid endorsements. No financial penalty was included in the order, but each violation could result in a fine of up to $40,654." Despite the relatively mild penalty, federal officials offered a pointed rebuke of Viqtory Media practices: "Service members and their families put themselves on the line every day to protect our nation," the acting FTC chairwoman, Maureen K. Ohlhausen, said in a statement. "We owe it to them to make sure that when they look to further their education, they get straight talk instead of advertising in disguise."[134]

CONCLUSIONS

Taking the long view of U.S. economic history, it is clear that serious fluctuations followed the extended post-1945 boom period, making the path for veterans and citizens in general increasingly difficult. Lifetime employment security in manufacturing and industry had already begun to erode by the time the Vietnam War ended in 1973, and the process would only escalate by the end of the decade. Wages for most people stagnated despite remarkable increases in productivity. By the end of the twentieth century, a new premium on education and technical training defined success or failure in the postindustrial information economy.[135]

The impact of these changing economic conditions on veterans has varied over time. As a group, veterans outperformed civilians throughout much of the post–Vietnam era. However, much of this advantage was bolstered by the maturing career tracks of World War II and Vietnam veterans. A more careful examination of the individual data reveals important weaknesses within specific veterans' constituencies. One of key determinants is youth. The economic hardships of today's young veterans—eighteen to twenty-four years old—are reminiscent of Vietnam, when benefits and job opportunities paled in comparison with those of World War II veterans. Other factors involve race as well as gender. Both women and minority veterans often register lower employment rates than do their white male peers.[136]

Programmatic responses to address these difficulties are notable for their breadth and lack of depth. The federal government has renewed the GI Bill periodically since the eighties and constructed a potpourri of training and education programs to address the transition into the civilian economy. In the case of the former, GI Bill benefits have not kept adequate pace with rapidly increasing college costs. "Transition assistance," which covers a range of activity from out-processing counseling to tax incentives and direct grant aid for businesses and public entities hiring people leaving the military, has produced mixed results, particularly for the newest crop of Gulf War II veterans.

Self-help has emerged as one simple solution, particularly for the newest generation of young veterans. Yet although the private sector has the potential for remarkable success, risks are ever present and profound. A cleverly positioned market strategy is no guarantee of profitability in an increasingly crowded landscape of veteran-owned companies. Moreover, tens of thousands of veterans trusted Department of Defense–affiliated education programs only to find themselves with student debt far above the national average.

CHAPTER SEVEN

Lost on Campus: Veterans and a College Education

> Soldiers typically are not a shy bunch and may seem aggressive when addressing an issue or disagreeing with a particular point. This presentation style is not meant to be unprofessional but rather is considered professional in that it demonstrates confidence and conviction.
> —*An educator, quoted in 2016*

INTRODUCTION

Americans have a long and interesting historical relationship with education. We appreciate its purpose and utility yet suspect elites who possess special knowledge and the status that knowledge confers. As Alexis de Tocqueville observed of foreign visitors to the country: "If he only singles out the learned, he will be astonished to find how rare they are; but if he counts the ignorant, the American people will appear to be the most enlightened community in the world."[1] Americans have treated learning as a multipurpose tool: It can break the grip of intermediaries on knowledge and empower, lending credence to the concept and the reality of the autonomous, self-made man (or woman). Education is also a means toward an end, a device able to transform basic ability into upward socioeconomic mobility.[2]

Federal policy applied many of these basic principles to veterans at the end of World War II. Education benefits embedded in the original 1944 Servicemen's Readjustment Act served multiple purposes. In the short term, placing veterans in school allowed the country to buy time as it transitioned from wartime production to a civilian economy, avoiding a flooded job market and another economic depression. For individuals, school at any level allowed for the pursuit of self-interest, upward mobility, and a better way to meet growing postwar family responsibilities. For the country as a whole, a better educated constituency such as the 16 million men and women who exited the war offered the prospect of a deep reservoir of talent ready for the public and private sectors. Few at the time predicted how important GI Bill education benefits would be for the country. However, we know today that a large part of the post-1945 U.S. economic boom came from the minds of veterans taught and trained through this one federal program.

Multiple generations of veterans have discovered since World War II that gaining access to college was only a first step in a very long and difficult process. Successive versions of GI Bill drew back from the generous benefits prevalent throughout the original. Consequently, finding a way to pay for escalating tuition costs along with housing, books, and other fees proved to be a challenge for many veterans. Navigating campus culture was another challenge. Where veterans were a fascinating novelty in the forties, they found the next generation of students, faculty, and administrators far less welcoming during and after the Vietnam War. Even when schools dedicated themselves to welcoming veterans to their campuses and rectifying past mistakes, the academic landscape remained littered with obstacles, some more apparent than others.

A FOOT IN THE DOOR

Prior to World War II, college was a sanctuary for American elites. With rare exceptions, the ivory tower was an abstraction for most. As late as 1945, only four in ten Americans graduated high school. Of these, 16 percent went to college.[3] That exclusivity was already changing during the war, whereupon math and science were as instrumental to modern warfare as a fighting spirit. The Army Specialized Training Program, the Navy's V-12 Program, and the Army Air Corps College Training Program sent hundreds of thousands of officers and enlisted to school. By 1943, 21 percent of them were women.[4]

Wartime training programs sponsored by the War Department presaged the flood of veterans who would enter postsecondary education after 1945. During the forties, most veterans used their benefits for vocational training in skilled trades, a spectrum that introduced tens of thousands to work in construction, manufacturing, and industry.[5] This talent proved instrumental to the growth of labor unions and more generally in meeting pent-up demand for housing, consumer goods, cars, and a host of products. To keep pace with the booming postwar airline industry, for example, the total number of aircraft mechanics almost tripled from 28,000 to 75,000 in 1950.[6]

The U.S. college population experienced a similar boom. In 1947, 1.1 million veterans enrolled in colleges and universities, 49 percent of all students.[7] Three years later, that number increased to 2.5 million. Tuition payments available through the GI Bill opened virtually any private or public university to veterans.[8]

Universities quickly adapted to the influx of students. Campuses at private and public colleges experienced a building boom as construction struggled to keep pace with the demand for new dormitories, dining halls, and classrooms. Faculty hiring entered into what could best be described as a golden age, where it was not uncommon for graduate students to receive job offers and complete their terminal degrees while on the tenure track. By 1970, there were 7.9 million students enrolled in American colleges and universities. Of these, approximately 700,000 were veterans.[9]

The irony of this story is that as college became more available for Americans, particularly the baby boomers who entered schools en masse after World War II, it became progressively less so for veterans of that generation. The primary problem was federal funding, which leveled off during the Korean War and basically stagnated for the next twenty years. Even after Congress increased benefits for tuition and living expenses in 1974, they were still grossly inadequate for most universities. That year, a single veteran received $1,980 for all college expenses even though tuition alone cost between $890 for state college and as high as $5,000 for private universities.[10] Only a few months into his term, Gerald Ford vetoed a new GI Bill that attempted to close the benefits gap. Although massive majorities in the House and Senate overrode Ford, he successfully obstructed additional spending increases for the remainder of his time in office.[11]

These decisions had a profound effect on veterans returning from Vietnam. Individuals who could bridge the federal funding gap did so through their own savings, student loans, and full or part-time jobs. Veterans who could not fell through the cracks. This outcome was most notable among African American veterans, particularly those who came from the working-class poor. After he came home from Vietnam, U. N. Railey noted that "it's really a problem.... All the food expenditures, gas and so forth are going up. On [the GI Bill benefits] you can't make it."[12] In 1973, 25 percent of Black veterans used their GI Bill education benefits compared with 46 percent of whites. By 1980, the percentage improved somewhat to 36.4 percent versus 60.2 percent of whites.[13] However, it was clear that African Americans, who comprised an increasing percentage of the U.S. military after the Vietnam War, were not enjoying one benefit of that service.[14]

Limits to educational programs also dictated where veterans might go to college. Unlike the 1944 GI Bill, which allowed them to enroll in virtually any institute of higher education in the country, the versions that followed after 1973 were much more restrictive and did not keep pace with rising costs, particularly at private universities. Consequently, veterans became fixtures at public four-year institutions and community colleges, as their overall participation began to precipitously decline in higher education. In 1976, almost two million attended college, but by 1985 that number had declined to approximately three hundred thousand.[15] In the meantime, veterans' representation in the Ivy League diminished to the point where it became extremely rare. A 2016 survey of fall semester undergraduates found eleven veterans at Yale, three at Harvard, and just one at Princeton.[16]

Veterans experienced a brief lapse in education benefits when the Vietnam-era GI Bill expired in 1977.[17] It was not permanent. After some initial resistance from the White House and the Defense Department, Congress passed the Montgomery GI Bill in 1984, which provided a monthly education allowance for veterans who entered active duty after June 30, 1985. Actual benefits could be as high as $10,800, an amount that included monthly payments for tuition, housing, books, and fees for up to 36 months of instruction.[18] The new policy was highly popular among new recruits, although it proved inadequate to pay for resident tuition and housing at most state colleges at the time.[19] Regardless, the connection between higher education and the United States military continued unabated through the eighties and nineties, bolstered by Reserve Officers' Training Corps (ROTC) and active duty military personnel enrolled in academic degree programs for professional development (see table 3).

TABLE 3. VETERANS' EDUCATIONAL PROGRAMS, 1974-2011

1974	Veterans and Dependents Education Loan Program
1976	VEAP (Post-Vietnam Era Veterans Educational Assistance)
1981	Educational Assistance Test Program
1981	Educational Assistance Pilot Program
1983	Veterans' Job Training Act
1985	MGIB-AD (Montgomery GI Bill-Active Duty)
1985	MGIB-SR (Montgomery GI Bill-Selected Reserve)
1990	Refunds for Certain Service Academy Graduates
1992	Service Members Occupational Conversion and Training Act of 1992 (SMOCTA)
2005	REAP (Reserves Educational Assistance Program)
2008	Post-9/11 GI Bill
2011	Veterans Retraining Assistance Program (VRAP)

Source: Cassandria Dortch, *GI Bills Enacted Prior to 2008 and Related Veterans' Educational Assistance Programs: A Primer*, R42785 (Washington, DC: Congressional Research Service, October 6, 2017), 4.

The period after September 11 was a clear tipping point for veterans, higher education, and federal policy. For one, there were simply more people entering the Department of Veterans Affairs (VA) system than at any time since Korea. By 2012, approximately two million men and women qualified for federal educational benefits under the new Post-9/11 GI Bill. They were joined for the first time by their children and spouses, to whom they could delegate benefits.[20]

The Post-9/11 GI Bill was also far more generous than were past programs. In 2019, it paid for full tuition and fees at a public college or up to $24,477 a year at a private institution. Support additionally included $1,000 a year for books as well as a housing allowance.[21] Not surprisingly, the new GI Bill proved to be hugely popular. In fiscal year 2018 alone, 800,000 received education benefits at a cost of $12 billion to the federal government.[22]

In many cases, the Post-9/11 GI Bill's very popularity proved to be a problem. The Department of Veterans Affairs could not keep pace with college enrollment and benefits applications to the point where more than half of the 167,000 veterans who used their education benefits for the Fall 2009 semester experienced delays.[23] Although officials promised the addition of more staff to keep pace, processing continued to lag behind demand. As late as October 2018, the official VA backlog was 120,000 unfilled applications, and some veterans had to wait up to sixty days to receive finished paperwork.[24]

Not all obstacles originated with the VA, and student veterans suffered, nonetheless. Many college registrar's offices struggled with translating military training into academic credit. Upon departing the service, veterans could obtain a Joint Services Transcript, which listed all the military schools, occupational specialty experience, and college-level test scores accumulated while on active duty. To a civilian layperson, basic training in any branch was a logical transfer as a physical education credit. However, the more arcane (to civilian eyes) training, such as Advanced EMS Operations or Emergency Preparedness, was harder to shift onto an academic transcript.[25]

Repeated deployments posed problems for student veterans when they interrupted study and triggered loan repayments. As previously discussed, it was not uncommon for the National Guard or reserves to mobilize repeatedly for duty in Iraq, Afghanistan, or both during the long course of the Global War on Terrorism. In some cases, student veterans received ample notice to pass along to their faculty and administrators. In others, they had a few weeks to make arrangements. Unit activation might fall in between semesters, although the military rarely included that contingency in planning. Military deployments also triggered the student loan repayment process. Unbeknownst to many veterans, loan companies deferred payment only under the condition that they maintained full-time college enrollment. There was often no contingency for absences caused by mobilization. When Todd Bowers was recalled to active duty by the Marine Corps in 2004, he left school behind and did not return home until after being wounded by a sniper near Falluja later that year. Part of his homecoming was a letter informing him that his student loans had been referred to a collection agency.[26] Bowers's experience was not uncommon among student veterans.

The for-profit educational industry treats veterans' benefits as a gigantic cash cow, a major problem for these students. According to a 2019 Congressional Budget Office report, the Post-9/11 GI Bill cost $65 billion between its creation and 2016.[27] Clearly, there was an enormous amount of money to be made in the student veteran market (see table 4).

TABLE 4. TOP TEN RECIPIENTS OF POST-9/11 GI BILL BENEFITS, 2010–2011

Apollo Education Group	$133 million
Education Management Corporation	$113 million
ITT	$99 million
DeVry University	$96 million
Career Education Corporation	$71 million
Strayer University	$49 million
Corinthian Colleges	$39 million
University of Maryland System	$31 million
Kaplan	$27 million
University of Texas System	$25 million

Source: Hanover Research, *Veterans Marketing Research* (Arlington, VA: Hanover Research, 2012), 20. Courtesy of Hanover Research.

For-profit colleges soon dominated the veterans' educational landscape. They offered flexible online programs and aggressively marketed their programs on military bases with the direct cooperation of the Defense Department. The University of Phoenix employed six hundred veterans as part of its "military division" for direct outreach. By 2012, eight of the top ten institutions receiving Post-9/11 GI Bill funding were for-profit colleges or universities.[28]

Veterans offered a number of advantages for businesses like DeVry, ITT Tech, Capella, and the University of Phoenix. One was a loophole in federal policy known as the 90/10 rule, which capped the amount of money a school could receive from federal financial aid sources at 90 percent of its total revenue. Through a quirk in federal law, GI Bill funding did not count toward that percentage.[29] For-profit schools like the University of Phoenix also shrewdly hired large contingents of veterans not only to build a rapport with potential customers but also for the knowledge of the labyrinthine military bureaucracy, which enabled them to process credit transfers and general paperwork more easily than could other colleges. Taken as a whole, predatory institutions treated veterans like "cash piñatas," as one University of Phoenix alum put it, but were able to increase their share of federal veterans educational benefits by 600 percent to near parity with public colleges and universities.[30]

For veterans, time spent in for-profit colleges proved to be extremely problematic. Contrary to what recruiters often promised, many programs were not accredited by state or national authorities. Veterans who graduated found out that their degrees were essentially worthless. In most cases, graduation was rare. A 2018 congressional report found that only 30 percent of Kaplan students enrolled in two-year programs completed them. A third finished four-year degrees.[31] These numbers were impressive when compared with the University of Phoenix, owned by the Apollo Group. In 2008, it graduated only 6 percent of its students.[32]

TEACHING THE VETERAN

When higher education contemplated the prospect of introducing massive numbers of veterans into college classrooms after World War II, some of the most respected voices in academe were not optimistic. At the University of Chicago, Robert M. Hutchins famously claimed that "colleges and universities will find themselves converted into intellectual hobo jungles. And veterans unable to get work and equally unable to resist putting pressures on colleges and universities will find themselves educational hoboes." James Conant, the president of Harvard University, questioned the impact of the numbers themselves, arguing that veterans would introduce mediocrity to U.S. universities because the GI Bill did not "distinguish between those who can profit most by advanced education and those who cannot."[33]

Returning GIs proved Hutchins and Conant wrong. As students, they impressed faculty. Veterans turned out to be disciplined, diligent new entries who challenged fellow students and instructors. One professor at the University of Illinois complimented "the dynamic working standards and the mental vigor which they bring to campus." Lacking the time or interest to indulge in fraternity life or freshman hazing, veterans challenged faculty to abandon outdated pedagogy and introduce courses that addressed foreign policy, current events, and contemporary politics. A new generation of doctoral students trained through the GI Bill carried these changes forward for decades to come.[34]

Between the Korean War and the end of selective service, military service was less a point of comparison than a clear point of departure in colleges and universities. In an effort to preserve intellectual currency during the height of the Cold War, policymakers made the deliberate decision to expand educational deferments to college-bound young men. Millions of baby boomers took the Selective Service College Qualification Test to be reclassified 2-S (deferred for college). In 1955, three hundred thousand students were deferred to finish their studies.[35] In 1970 alone, selective service deferred 2.3 million men to pursue school, a number close to the total number of Americans who served in South Vietnam during the entire war.[36]

Robert Timberg's elegantly constructed *The Nightingale's Song* (1995) captured a cultural point that both defined and divided baby boomers on and off campus. Regarding Reagan's characterization of Vietnam as a "noble cause," he wrote: "I was thus surprised to find myself seeing red when Reagan's remark met with ridicule, not just by Carter aides in Austin but by press colleagues who dismissed it with superior grins and smug put-downs, the newsroom equivalent of boos and hisses."[37] Timberg was not a neophyte or an ideologue. As he notes in *The Nightingale's Song*, he shared the same background with Oliver North and James Webb: the Naval Academy, the Marine Corps, and South Vietnam. When he witnessed the Iran-Contra scandal, Timberg noted: "I picked up a familiar and troubling aroma. Others saw greed, naked ambition, abuse of authority, a breathtaking disdain for Congress and the federal bureaucracy. I saw those things, too, but what I smelled was cordite, burning shitters, the disinfectant odor of hospitals."[38] The cleavage that Timberg identified was not a matter of "have" or "have not" but "served" or "did not serve." He was articulating the bright lines separating a veteran's constituency not just from the rest of the country but also, more important, from the elite products of American colleges and universities.

After Vietnam, as student veterans became a shrinking minority on most public and private universities, these bright dividing lines faded somewhat. By 1997, slightly more than four hundred thousand attended college out of a total of more than 14 million nationwide.[39] Campus culture in the eighties and nineties treated most student veterans as a small, largely benign campus constituency. The remnants of Vietnam persisted and periodically flared, but not at the same sharp level of past friction.

That qualified anonymity changed with the new century. The surge of student veterans produced by the Global War on Terrorism and subsequent Post-9/11 GI Bill introduced them back onto campuses in numbers not seen since the late seventies.[40] However, these particular individuals differed from past arrivals. About 60 percent had some combat experience, a rate almost twice as high as groups with earlier service.[41] They were more likely to be first-generation college students than their civilian peers. They also tended to be much older than traditional undergraduates, even more so than the veterans who went to college after World War II. In 2012, the average age of veterans enrolled in four-year colleges was thirty-three.[42]

When they entered classrooms, veterans tended to use their military experience as the first yardstick available to measure college. Contemporary literature on student veterans prominently features constant comparisons between campus life and military life. Many found the former lacking in quality. Veterans commonly mentioned their appreciation of military routine, clarity of purpose, and overall predictability—things college life lacked in many cases.[43] Veterans also repeatedly returned to problems experienced with their fellow students, from the general absence of self-discipline and selfishness to their obsession with trivial celebrity culture.[44] Fairly or not, when matters turned to the military and America's ongoing wars, veterans found other students disconnected and insincere. One veteran cited in a 2012 article was openly disdainful: "Some guy in my class came up to me and told me he really supports the troops and thank you for your service. I was just back and I was in one of those moods. So, I said, oh yeah, so what do you do to support the troops? He kind of looked at me . . . that attitude . . . they are kind of stumped and stare at you. Do you buy a bumper sticker? Do you join a Facebook group? I was upset with the whole thing."[45] Veterans who transitioned into K-12 student teaching and education careers spoke of similar experiences. They were surprised when exposed to the new culture in schools: "Former service members can be bewildered by teachers who are not willing to share successful lesson plans or instructional materials and by the cliquishness and rivalry among faculty subgroups sometimes present in schools."[46]

Early large-scale surveys of student veterans receiving Post-9/11 GI Bill benefits pointed to a variety of problems they were experiencing on campuses. A 2010 RAND study found, for example, that public college performed the worst with respect to accepting military credits.[47] In class, only about a third of veterans in both public and private universities believed that they were able to meet faculty academic expectations, although significant majorities considered their faculty as a source of support.[48]

Race also played an important part in veterans' educational decision-making success. One 2015 study found that the military served as a critical "bridging environment" for better educational outcomes. Armed with improved benefits, post-9/11 Black veterans (53.6%) use education benefits at a higher rate than did earlier cohorts (41.3%) and attended college at a higher rate than Black nonveterans.[49] The combination of military discipline and higher entry-level educational standards for recruits also translated into a higher probability of graduation for Hispanic veterans.[50]

Like Vietnam-era veterans, minorities had a higher likelihood of going to community college. As was the case during that time, the decision was prompted by both rapidly escalating costs and problems unique to this group. Hispanic veterans tend to have some of the lowest pre-enlistment academic scores and, as a result, tend to gravitate to the combat arms in the Marine Corps and Army, where they consequently suffer from disproportionate rates of physical wounds and post-traumatic stress disorder (PTSD).[51] However, many choose two-year institutions because they best suit these veterans' circumstances and goals. Community colleges offer a better selection of technical training and have more extensive night programs than traditional universities. This is important to Hispanic veterans who are more often married with children than are average postsecondary undergraduates.[52]

For the most part, colleges and universities around the country devoted significant time and energy to address these shortcomings. Accommodation policies, already well advanced through the Americans with Disabilities Act, were applied to the veterans' campus population. The physical needs of veterans with physical disabilities generally came under the rubric of building access and modifications to basic facilities. Mental trauma was a different story. College health centers that commonly dealt with psychological counseling for an eighteen- to twenty-five-year-old clientele generally lacked the expertise for PTSD, military sexual trauma, and the problems associate with traumatic brain injury. Veterans with transportation and regular access to regional VA centers received better care than those who did not.

Adapting classroom pedagogy to student veterans presented a different challenge. Faculty took to the idea with a variety of overlapping, self-supporting goals in mind. Beyond the obvious need to teach discipline-related skills, they also attempted to address "transitional needs," as one publication put it, by incorporating a sensitive approach to veterans' culture.[53] To accomplish this task, they analyzed what academics considered to be veterans' strengths and weaknesses, some of which recalled similar discussions following World War II. Veterans were more diligent students than were nonveterans. They spent more time preparing for classes and were more likely to engage faculty in class and during office hours. Most studies noted that they were less interested in socializing at college functions or off campus.[54] Student veterans also tended to function better in group settings, although this work included some important caveats. They generally did less well among civilians or, interestingly, with veterans from other service branches, where traditional rivalries persisted. The same divisions also appeared when former active duty veterans mixed with members of the National Guard and reserves.[55]

One common solution was academic segregation. Many colleges created veterans-only classes and "learning communities" to facilitate academic progress. One pilot composition course designed specifically for veterans described itself as "a space where if you want to write about service, it is a safe space."[56] Stripped of its contemporary jargon, the concept is relatively straightforward. Given the room to work without distraction, a cohort of students sharing the same basic characteristics could then focus on academics. In the best cases, shared culture augments academic progress. The principle is common in education in a variety of contexts, particularly with respect to gender.[57]

Perhaps one of the most successful examples of this approach is the Veterans Writing Project.[58] Founded by Army veteran Ron Capps in 2012, the nonprofit is dedicated to promoting writing skills among veterans while using them to improve veterans' lives. In seminars around the country, Capps and a cohort of instructors offer small seminars that delve into all facets of writing, grammar, setting, and narrative structure. To connect with veterans, the program utilizes the fiction and nonfiction of veterans from Siegfried Sassoon to Philip Caputo and James Webb.[59]

But there is more to the Veterans Writing Project than literature. Scattered throughout its handbook, *Writing War: A Guide to Telling Your Own Story*, are self-referential nods to the need for truth and the difficulties in reconciling art with "our deadliest creations." Capps intends his program to be therapeutic. The Veterans Writing Project is designed to provide agency to a shrinking contingent of Americans with a shared experience. More than that, the project offers a chance at a legacy. As noted in the introduction to *Writing War*: "We write to make our voices eternal, to give a sense of permanence to our ideas."[60]

Two qualities make the Veterans Writing Project effective. First is the emphasis on high academic standards. Ron Capps and his fellow writing faculty begin with the premise that quality is important and will not be subverted by the special needs of his audience. Essentially, the Veterans Writing Project overtly observes the basic principle that it will not discriminate against veterans, but equally so, it will not discriminate *for* them either. The second quality that Capps's program successfully constructs and maintains is its authenticity. The shared experience—between teacher and student—of being veterans establishes a rapport that is organic rather than forced or artificial. This bona fide nature, a difficult prospect in normal circumstances, establishes a starting point for instruction, constructive criticism, and progress.

Changes to curriculum accompanied efforts at better institutional attention to veterans' needs. A 2012 survey of 690 colleges found that almost two-thirds had programs purposefully built for veterans. The number with a dedicated veterans' service office increased from 26 percent in 2009 to 56 percent in 2012.[61] Many of these addressed the "transitional needs" of veterans, which included dedicated orientation sessions for incoming students, financial advising, academic counseling, and sensitivity training for faculty and staff. The University of Wisconsin, Madison, veterans service office, for example, held forty-one such summer orientation sessions so that staff could meet incoming student veterans.[62]

Many schools conducted "Green Zone Training" as part of their veterans' outreach efforts. Although the programs varied from college to college, they pursued consistent goals. The University of Oklahoma Veteran Support Alliance held seminars so that faculty and staff could "realize veterans are nontraditional students, a special population of financially independent adults often juggling family, work, and studies." The Purdue University Veterans Success Center offered a "VA Campus Toolkit," which provided links to federal resources for veterans.[63] A number of schools also partnered with nonprofits to augment their veterans' programs. The entire University of North Carolina system contracted the San Diego–based company PsychArmor for training modules as well as the development of best practices for campus policies.[64]

A literal cottage industry sprang up around evaluating the quality of veterans' programs in higher education. Schools began to compete for national ranking, a process that served both prospective student veterans as well as the parent school's marketability. One of the most prestigious awards is the "Best for Vets" designation by *Military Times*, a highly respected publication founded in 1940.[65] Every year, *Military Times* issues a comprehensive survey to participating colleges. It asks for information on accreditation, eligibility for Department of Defense tuition assistance, retention rates, and school assistance to cover gaps in GI Bill aid, among many other important factors.[66] Schools that earn a high ranking actively advertise their "Best for Vets" designation on their home websites.[67]

While *Military Times* is an excellent example of a legitimate process, nonprofit partnerships with universities have a decidedly mixed record. Some, for example, PsychArmor, are too new for full evaluation of their business practices, although they appear to offer a high degree of transparency.[68] Still other companies, such as Viqtory Media, covered in Chapter Six, have been found to be manipulating veterans for their own profit. The watchdog group Veterans Education Success (VES) investigated Viqtory Media and found its rating systems flawed, its assessment practices questionable at best, and an ongoing practice of selling veterans' personal information as "lead generators" for schools without consent to be unethical if not borderline illegal.[69]

Despite problems like these, university support for student veterans did improve. When the American Council on Education published a 2013 report on veterans, it noted progress in an array of areas. The number of schools with dedicated veterans' centers almost tripled between 2009 and 2012. A significant majority (71%) incorporated veterans' programs into their strategic planning. Most had increased staffing for veterans and a majority conducted training for veterans' counseling.[70] A separate 2012 American Council on Education study indicated that a significant majority (72%) of veterans thought they were receiving appropriate institutional academic support, a percentage almost equal to that for nonveterans. Schools received lower grades in some aspects of student life. Slightly more than one in four student veterans agreed that their colleges helped them with nonacademic responsibilities. Two-thirds did not believe their schools provided support to help them "thrive socially."[71]

Data on one key metric remained opaque in the early stages of the Post-9/11 GI Bill. Between 2009 and 2015, the Department of Veterans Affairs lacked complete data on graduation rates.[72] This gap prompted a national organization, the Student Veterans of America, to conduct a comprehensive survey to unearth more accurate details. Published in 2017, the resulting study found a six-year graduation rate of 53.6 percent for veterans who used Post-9/11 GI Bill benefits, slightly higher than contemporary nonveterans (52.9%). This rate was lower than for veterans who went to college under the Montgomery GI Bill (57.8%) and substantially lower than all veterans who attended college between the Korean War and September 11 (66%–68%).[73]

CAMPUS ACTIVISM AND VETERANS

History demonstrates that veterans are rarely a passive presence on college campuses. Despite the responsibilities of family and academics, they traditionally have been joiners and leaders, breathing new life into existing organizations and striking out on their own with new enterprises. At some universities, veterans' clubs left dormant since the post–Vietnam era gained a new lease on life after September 11.

The evolution of individual organizations varied, although some consistent details are apparent. Many existed simply as a way to fill gaps left open by university administrations. Veterans organized to compare experiences and discuss the best ways to navigate college bureaucracy or seek out supportive faculty. Others simply wanted a cushion as they reacquainted themselves with civilian life. It was not uncommon for campus veterans' groups to enjoy the sponsorship of older veterans' organizations. In 2011, for example, a group of young Iraq and Afghanistan service members created the University of Kansas Collegiate Veterans with the assistance of the local Veterans of Foreign Wars Post 852.[74]

Over time, national organizations emerged and appeared in colleges and universities. One of the largest, the Student Veterans of America (SVA), was incorporated in 2008 and is committed to "empowering veterans" and "providing an educational experience that goes beyond the classroom."[75] By 2019, the SVA claimed 1,583 chapters and advocacy for 700,000 "military affiliated students" in all fifty states and four countries.[76] Much like the Service Women's Action Network, covered in Chapter Nine, the Student Veterans of America sponsored scholarships, hosted mentorship programs with the private sector, offered leadership training, and conducted annual conferences for its campus affiliates. Other nonprofits, such as the National Association for Black Veterans, provide guidance for educational certificate programs and military transfer credits to a more specific body of undergraduates.[77]

Other veterans' groups were notable for being critics of the wars in Iraq and Afghanistan and U.S. policy in general. Operation Truth was organized in August 2004 and provided a platform for veterans to express their discontent regarding the lack of adequate body armor, the military's stop-loss program that extended service terms beyond their contracted deadlines, and the lack of overall coherence to counterinsurgency efforts in occupied countries. The Iraq Veterans Against the War (IVAW) borrowed a page from the past, sponsoring Winter Soldier: Iraq and Afghanistan in March 2008. The event brought together two hundred active duty military and veterans to talk about their wartime experiences.[78] Founded in 2004, IVAW was a regular fixture in antiwar protests and gatherings around the country during the early stages of overseas military operations. As U.S. troop withdrawals commenced under the Obama administration, the IVAW shifted to issues prevalent among veterans: suicide prevention, PTSD, and other health care issues.[79]

For the most part, however, most of the energy that came out of contemporary veterans' organizations resembled that which followed World War II. Aside from being advocates for themselves, contemporary veterans embraced altruism for deployed troops and their local communities. Collection drives for active duty military personnel—foot powder, baby wipes, and snacks able to withstand heat were particularly popular—developed into annual campus campaigns. Student veterans also cosponsored charity events with other nonprofits such as the Wounded Warrior Project and its various offshoots. One of the most popular was the 5K run/walk, which allowed younger veterans to compete with one another and older veterans with "more mileage" a chance to show support.[80] Essentially, campus veterans' groups pursued "activism as grounded in the ideals that motivated them to become soldiers in the first place," as one author put it more recently.[81]

CONCLUSIONS

The original Servicemen's Readjustment Act set a precedent that subsequent educational aid programs for veterans did not match. Although the original 1944 law threw open the doors to virtually any college in the country, that window of opportunity began to close as lawmakers pulled back on funding the escalating costs of higher learning. By the time Vietnam veterans began entering campuses, most could afford only community colleges and public four-year institutions. The 1984 Montgomery GI Bill and the Post-9/11 GI Bill were certainly more generous but never successfully closed a monetary gap that was decades in the making.

Military operations after September 11 focused a great deal of scrutiny not just on federal funding for college but also on the overall local level of support veterans might expect once they arrived on campus. Initial indicators were not promising. However, between 2009 and 2015, hundreds of colleges and university made a concerted effort to ease veterans' transition by offering clear pathways for academic counseling, financial assistance, and mental health support.

The end results were mixed. A 2014–15 poll conducted by Gallup and Purdue University found that 55 percent of post-9/11 veterans strongly agreed when asked if they were satisfied with their federal benefits, compared with only 28 percent of veterans overall. Veterans were much less sanguine about campus life, however. Only 25 percent strongly agreed that their universities "understood their unique needs."[82] Public colleges, which post-9/11 veterans attended at a higher rate because of costs, performed worse than did private for-profit and nonprofit institutions.[83]

The polling data points to the fact that constructing a cultural balance for veterans on campus was far more difficult than addressing such tangible needs as financial aid or academic tutoring. Faculty and staff may have been well-intentioned in their pursuit of tolerance, sensitivity, and safe spaces for Iraq and Afghanistan veterans, but treating military service as a borderline disability alienated many of the people they intended to help. Ron Capps's Veterans Writing Project was a rare example of a best practice that is effective. His pedagogy is able to connect with his target audience by virtue of a shared experience before moving on to the mechanics of literature. One of the strengths of Capps's approach is that he does not dwell on the liabilities of military service but rather treats the totality of the veterans' experiences as a resource for reflection and expression. It can be first step toward learning or healing. Or both.

Finally, where student veterans found gaps in the campus experience, they filled them with their own organizing skills. Like their predecessors in the American Veterans Committee and the Vietnam Veterans Against the War, principle informed practice. Some worked to improve life for their brothers and sisters in uniform and build tangible links between them and the civilian community. Others focused more broadly on the betterment of their campuses and the people who lived in and around them. Throughout, student veterans sought a means to find their way in the new terrain of higher education, while they continued their mission of providing service for the greater good.

CHAPTER EIGHT

The Veteran in Politics

> "Sir, you should run for Congress someday.
> So this shit doesn't happen again."
> —*A Marine in Rep. Seth Moulton's (D-MA) platoon, Iraq, 2004*

INTRODUCTION

In many respects, veteran's status is a gold standard in American politics. For a country rooted in conflict, be it on the early frontier or prosecuting counterterrorism operations, military prowess is a way to stand out among peers in a potent demonstration of individual bravery for the purpose of collective survival. Even the more mundane types of military service carry with them the superlatives associated with patriotism, leadership, and sacrifice for the greater good. Accepting even the prospect of risking everything illustrates a form of heroism that places the veteran on a theoretically higher plane than most citizens back home. This is why political leaders have lost few opportunities to tell their constituents, "I served."

Consequently, military service and politics are inextricably linked and have been for the country's entire history. There are legitimate war heroes who continued their careers into the political ranks: George Washington, William Henry Harrison, Andrew Jackson, Zachary Taylor, Ulysses S. Grant, Theodore Roosevelt, Dwight Eisenhower, John F. Kennedy, and George H. W. Bush among them. A number of presidents, Harry Truman, Richard Nixon, Jimmy Carter, Gerald Ford, and George W. Bush had military careers that could perhaps best be described as relatively nondescript. Some, such as William McKinley's service in the Civil War, have simply been overlooked. Other military records, like Lyndon Johnson's, are the product of pure fabrication.

Regardless, military records matter, especially to voters with the same shared experience. It is political currency. Good Union men endorsed by veterans organized around the Grand Army of the Republic prospered in late nineteenth-century America. For politicians like Teddy Roosevelt who were too young to have served in the Civil War, new conflicts had to suffice. Upon returning from Cuba, the young colonel authorized not one but two secret campaigns for his nomination as Republican candidate for governor, all the while telling the press he was an officer first and "I feel that my place is with the boys."[1] When he finally mustered out of the Army in September 1898 and embarked on the campaign in earnest, Roosevelt took a cohort of Rough Riders on the stump, all in full uniform. His former bugler, Emil Cassi, would announce Colonel Roosevelt's arrival at whistle-stops, and his former comrades, including Color Sergeant Albert Wright, bracketed the candidate as he spoke about the glory of San Juan Hill.[2]

Although it is hard to debate that military service and veteran's status has value in modern U.S. politics, the idea does beg a few questions worth investigating. Veterans clearly represented a distinct twentieth-century voting bloc. A quick count of veterans of the two world wars and Korea reveals at least 24 million political constituents with military experience. The larger question is, How uniform was this constituency? Did military experience trump the other facets of a voter's political identity? The same questions equally apply to lawmakers. Did their veteran's status transcend politics? To what extent did it protect them? The onset of war in 2001 offers an opportunity to revisit these issues to determine if it marked notable departures or political consistency.

BUCKING THE SYSTEM

As is the case with most parts of modern veterans' narratives, World War II is a good starting point. In political terms, the war had an impact similar to that which followed the Civil War, producing a generation of leaders who remained in various political offices for the next half century. The 80th Congress (1947–49) serves as a useful baseline and illustrates the broad variety of military service within U.S. politics. In 1947, the majority of those in Congress had spent some time in uniform, presenting something of a living military history lesson. Joseph J. Mansfield, a Texas Democrat, raised two companies of National Guard troops in 1886, the year Geronimo surrendered. Republican Edward V. Robinson of Wyoming served with the British against the Boers from 1899 to 1902. A large contingent, 164 in all, including the entire Iowa delegation, had Great War service. Ninety fought or served in World War II, some with distinction (John F. Kennedy), others (Joseph P. McCarthy) much less so. More than a few were legitimate war heroes, albeit lesser known to history. Texas Democrat Olin Earl Teague joined the Army and became part of the 79th Infantry Division, earning in the process three Silver Stars, the Bronze Star, and three Purple Hearts.[3]

Military service was the social and political norm and increasingly remained so in the years following World War II. Between the war and the extension of selective service into peacetime, it permeated most corners of American society and politics after 1945, so much so that by 1967, 75 percent of House of Representatives members were veterans. The Senate peaked in 1975, with 81 percent of its membership having served in the military.[4] Veteran's status was a simple way to establish a rapport between a prospective candidate or sitting lawmaker and a large portion of the electorate who shared a common experience. Perhaps the best example is Dwight D. Eisenhower, who had no political record whatsoever in 1952 but was immediately recognizable and, more important, credible to the millions with whom he served in the European Theater of Operations.

While they may have held federal office in large numbers, veterans' experiences did not guarantee support for policy or shield the government from corruption during the Cold War. Although the need for military readiness was obvious after 1945 given the severe challenges affecting the early war effort, Congress rejected the idea of universal military training. Instead, it instituted an increasingly flawed peacetime selective service program that continued for almost thirty years. Nor did the high proportion of veterans in Congress protect the Defense Department from budget cuts in the 1950s, particularly its ground forces.[5] The sizable number of veterans in office did not produce a critical mass of support to mobilize the National Guard and reserves for Vietnam; most politicians chose to protect their local constituencies at the expense of draftees who could not vote.

As the Cold War moved forward into the fifties, veterans in Congress populated the so-called iron triangles—public officials, defense contractors, and the military establishment—that emerged from the nascent modern military-industrial complex, in many instances cementing these incestuous relationships with both their political and military status.[6] New York's Third Congressional District was home to the Grumman Aircraft Engineering Corporation, which made its name producing such fighter aircraft as the F4F Wildcat during World War II. Its successor corporations continue to produce planes for the Navy. During and after World War II, Grumman heavily recruited veterans from the Navy for both their expertise and good public relations. These employees settled throughout Long Island and made up a good portion of the Third District's constituency. Not surprisingly, the district was represented by Henry J. Latham, a Navy pilot who served in the Pacific during World War II and was elected to seven consecutive terms from 1945 to 1958.[7]

The large number of veterans in Congress did not prevent cuts to the Veterans Administration immediately after World War II or in the years to come. When Omar Bradley departed the Veterans Administration

(VA) to become chairman of the Joint Chiefs of Staff in 1948, Congress pounced on the agency. Between 1947 and 1948, lawmakers cut the VA budget from $38.9 billion to $32.9 billion, or 15.4 percent. In the year before Communist forces crossed the 38th parallel to invade South Korea, further reductions prompted the VA to terminate seven thousand employees and shutter thirteen branch offices.[8]

The conclusion of the Korean War did not stop ongoing debates about how best to recognize veterans through public policy. In practical terms, the Veterans' Readjustment Assistance Act of 1952 (otherwise known as the "Korean GI Bill") was a step down from the original GI Bill. It provided a lump sum for college assistance: $110 a month for individuals, $155 for veterans with one dependent, $160 a month for veterans with two or more dependents. None of these provisions kept pace with actual college costs or accounted for inflation in the years following World War II. William P. Tolley, the chancellor of Syracuse University, described the Korean War GI Bill as a "shabby deal."[9]

The Eisenhower administration contemplated further cuts to veterans' benefits. In 1955, the president created the Bradley Commission with the express purpose of curbing the costs of health care and pensions associated with the burgeoning numbers of veterans.[10] Although the White House was unable to halt the growth of the Veterans Administration budget, it successfully introduced means testing for veterans' pensions in 1959.[11]

Costs were not the only concern to lawmakers, and the subsequent debate revealed interesting divisions within Congress. Of particular interest was the nature of Cold War military service and how veterans' programs should recognize it, if at all. Many politicians, like Olin Teague, who chaired the House Committee on Veterans' Affairs, were stanch opponents of parity. Teague argued that veterans who served after Korea and did not assume the same risks as individuals with wartime service did not deserve the same benefits. He conveniently ignored the millions of World War II veterans from his generation who performed logistical tasks and never saw a moment of combat. Regardless, Teague was joined by budget hawks in both parties as well as the American Legion, which maintained the official position that Cold War service was relatively less disruptive to military personnel.[12]

The main proponent of the new, post-Korea GI Bill was another World War II veteran, Senator Ralph W. Yarborough of Texas. He was joined by compatriots in Congress such as Senators George McGovern (D-SD), Daniel Inouye (D-HI), and Representatives Frank Horton (R-NY) and Phillip Burton (D-CA). Yarborough's argument for a new benefits plan was straightforward: He believed that military service merited official recognition and benefits regardless of its nature or risk. He pointed out that amendments to the Korean War–era Veterans' Readjustment Assistance Act extended the window for eligibility to 1955, two years beyond actual wartime service. Moreover, in testimony before Teague's committee, Yarborough offered details, by military branch, of World War II veterans who qualified for the original GI Bill but never saw combat.[13]

The escalating war in Vietnam took away the issue of combatants' status, and the overall expansion of federal programs under Lyndon Johnson's Great Society added impetus to passage of a new veterans' benefits program. The result was the Veterans' Readjustment Benefits Act of 1966, otherwise known as the "Cold War GI Bill." The new law was the product of a series of compromises, which its substance reflected. Education benefits were meager compared with even Korean War–era payments. A single veteran received a monthly allowance of $100 for tuition, fees and "subsistence" for up to thirty-six months. Veterans with two or more dependents received $150 a month. In either case, the total dollar amounts indicated even further ground lost to inflation and regular college tuition increases.[14]

As the sixties drew to a close, veterans programs stagnated at the federal level, a trajectory that lawmakers were reluctant to challenge. When the Vietnam War and the Great Society were in their early stages, they contributed momentum to the logic of recognizing service through public policy. The wars against communism and poverty started with a sense of what was possible in an era of trust in effective government. Only a few short years later, this optimism had faded and was replaced with the harsh logic of fiscal retrenchment. It was this new article of faith that led the former Navy commander Richard M. Nixon to encourage veterans to be "champions of responsible government."[15]

Into this era of diminishing expectations Vietnam veterans began entering politics. They did not appear in large numbers, nowhere near that of the World War II generation. One of the first was John P. Murtha of Pennsylvania. Murtha joined the Marines in 1952 and completed his three-year obligation before moving to the reserves. He was still in that component when Vietnam began to escalate. Murtha took the rare step of volunteering for active duty and deployed to South Vietnam in 1966, where he worked as an intelligence officer.[16] In the process, he was wounded twice and was awarded a Bronze Star for valor. Shortly after coming home, Murtha entered state politics and served as Pennsylvania state representative from 1969 to 1974. Murtha won a seat in the House of Representatives by just over 220 votes in a 1974 special election. His victory allowed Democrats to occupy a position held by the Republican Party for 24 years.[17]

Murtha's story was an exception to the rule at the time. He was the first Vietnam combat veteran to serve in Congress.[18] His path to service was very much unlike the generation of World War II veterans who had preceded him. Murtha was a rare reservist during Vietnam who decided to give up a comfortable life as a local businessman to deploy to an active war zone. He was a "retread" like his Korean War peers but as a matter of choice. What likely gave his 1974 campaign traction was his veteran's status, particularly in his largely rural Pennsylvania district, but it also reflected the national revulsion surrounding the Watergate scandal, Richard Nixon, and the Republican Party in general.

John Kerry, a decorated Navy veteran who served in Vietnam between 1968 and 1969, took a somewhat different tack. After his discharge in 1970, Kerry joined Vietnam Veterans Against the War (VVAW) and quickly became its public face. In addition to participating in VVAW events such as Operation RAW (Rapid American Withdrawal) at Valley Forge, Pennsylvania, he appeared on popular programs such as the *Dick Cavett Show* to promote his antiwar views.[19]

Kerry's testimony before the Senate Foreign Relations Committee on April 22, 1971, as the VVAW protest Operation Dewey Canyon III raged outside, was one of the highlights of his early political career. In direct contrast to other VVAW members who made angry speeches and hurled their medals over hastily erected barricades at the foot of the U.S. Capitol, Kerry was a case study in passionate calm and respect. He spoke of the anger and frustration of his generation of veterans born out of the hypocrisy of needlessly sacrificing American lives in Vietnam for the "mystical war against communism."[20] Although Kerry was clearly willing to observe the protocols of authority rather than alienate sympathetic political leaders like J. William Fulbright, his moderation cost him support with the VVAW. Many members resented his sudden media fame and suspected that Kerry had political ambitions beyond the antiwar movement. He left the organization at the end of 1971.[21]

As it turned out, the veterans' activists who believed Kerry was on his way into politics were correct, although his path was anything but easy. He first ran for Congress in 1972 at the head of a well-funded and managed campaign for the Massachusetts Fifth District. However, Kerry never overcame the accusation that he was a carpetbagger, or "blow-in," as locals called it. Kerry embraced his outsider status, campaigning under the slogan: "He's not a politician. He listens."[22] Interestingly, Kerry's status as a veteran hurt him in the race, specifically because he had applied it as a way to lend gravity to his antiwar activity. Local conservative newspapers in his district had a field day with his antiwar record, particularly after an earlier *New York Times* story by Neil Sheehan found many of the references to atrocities highlighted in his Senate speech to be false.[23] Kerry tallied only 44.7 percent of the vote against his Republican opponent, Paul W. Cronin, who received 53.4 percent of ballots that November.[24]

When he ran for the Senate in 1984, Massachusetts Democrats did not endorse Kerry's candidacy. The national party leadership was equally dubious. The U.S. Speaker of House and scion of Massachusetts politics, Thomas "Tip" O'Neill, put his weight behind Kerry's opponent, James M. Shannon.[25] Despite his party's resistance, Kerry prevailed in the Democratic primary and the general election that fall. In office, Kerry was a proponent of a nuclear arms freeze during the Reagan years and opposed Republican increases in defense spending. In 1991, he voted against authorizing use of military force for the Gulf War and proposed steep cuts in the military budget after the fall of the Soviet Union.[26] Although Kerry did devote time to domestic issues such as child abuse prevention and Medicare reform, most of his legislative portfolio focused on foreign affairs and international trade.[27]

John McCain reentered American life after more than five years as a prisoner of war in North Vietnam. When he officially retired from the Navy in 1981, McCain settled on politics as his new vocation. Like Kerry, he decided to run as a new arrival to his post-military state of residency, in this case Arizona. McCain conducted what seemed to be a throwback campaign. His staff estimated that he knocked on twenty thousand doors in total during the 1982 congressional contest. McCain paralleled Kerry in that he was also well funded and enjoyed the service of a high-end consulting firm that produced slick TV ads for his run.[28]

McCain also defused the allegation that he was a carpetbagger in a manner much different from Kerry. Referring to his Vietnam experience at a candidates' forum, McCain noted: "We in the military service tend to move a lot. We have to live in all parts of the country, all parts of the world. I wish I could have had the luxury, like you, of growing up and living and spending my entire life in a nice place like the First District of Arizona, but I was doing other things. As a matter of fact, when I think about it now, the place I lived longest in my life was Hanoi."[29] What McCain found was a veterans' status that transcended even normal combat experience and gave him traction regardless of his participation in a divisive and unpopular conflict. As a prisoner of war, McCain garnered sympathy for the severe injuries he suffered at the hands of the North Vietnamese. In a broader sense, the national mood was far different in 1982: Americans were seeking ways to commemorate Vietnam War service and make amends for the past.[30] Commenting on the public mood in 1985, pollster Daniel Yankelovich, remarked: "Those who didn't serve have a bad conscience. Those who did and those who supported the war and then changed their minds have a bad conscience. And the way we treated the soldiers who served there gives us all a bad conscience."[31]

Vietnam veterans began to run for office in increasing numbers. Larry Pressler, a Republican from South Dakota, became the first to join the Senate in 1978. He was followed soon after by Al Gore, who won as a Democrat from Tennessee in 1984. In the 1980s, such combat veterans as Tom Ridge (R-PA) and Duncan Hunter (R-CA) joined lawmakers who had also served in Vietnam like Martin Lancaster (D-NC) and David Skaggs (D-CO) in the House of Representatives. In all, fifteen Vietnam veterans served in Congress by 1987.[32]

When he embarked on his campaign for the U.S. Senate in 1986 to fill the seat opened by Barry Goldwater's retirement, John McCain returned to his Vietnam roots. He described surviving the war as a "second chance," which McCain dovetailed into a chance "to give something back to this nation which has given so much to me and to all of us. With your help I can be of even greater service to Arizona and America in the U.S. Senate." McCain won his race by twenty points, trouncing Democrat Richard Kimball.[33] He was joined in the Senate by fellow Vietnam veterans Bob Kerrey of Nebraska in 1989, Chuck Robb in 1989, and Max Cleland in 1997. In fits and starts, the Vietnam generation reintroduced itself to politics, much like it did to the rest of the United States.

ESTABLISHMENT MEN

As they entered the political discourse, it became clear that veterans' status was not proof against political partisanship any more than it had been in the past. During the Reagan years, ongoing debates about foreign policy, particularly the issue of American intervention in Nicaragua, drew constant comparisons to Vietnam. Some veterans of the conflict, like Al Gore, saw it as a cautionary tale, making the point that Vietnam "creates a strong determination to pick conflicts carefully and not get into a situation that is a no-win proposition."[34] Republicans resurrected the Cold War concept of falling dominoes and warned of a new Soviet beachhead on America's doorstep. John McCain took a careful approach to the issue. He was a consistent supporter of aid to the Nicaraguan Contras who were attempting to overthrow the Sandinista government and warned against congressional "micromanaging" in 1985, but he would not abandon the idea of legislative oversight from the Republican Party.[35] In the ensuing Iran-Contra hearings, arguments broke along familiar party lines.

Foreign policy bombshells aside, at almost the same time, McCain and other lawmakers discovered that their veteran's status was not a protective shield against allegations of personal corruption. One of the most infamous scandals of the eighties involved the relationship between financier Charles Keating and a group of five senators who interceded on his behalf when federal regulators were investigating the corrupt business practices of Lincoln Savings and Loan Association.[36] The so-called Keating Five, as they came to be known, included Alan Cranston (D-CA), Dennis DeConcini (D-AZ), Donald Riegle (D-MI), John Glenn (D-OH), and John McCain. The *Arizona Republic* would reveal that Keating and his associates donated $112,000 to McCain's House and Senate campaigns. The *Phoenix New Times* accused McCain of making a Faustian bargain with Keating, trading campaign donations and deals that benefited his wife and father-in-law for political access.[37]

At the time, the Keating Five were linked not only to a corrupt bargain between a handful of senators and their wealthy benefactor but also to the collapse of the savings and loan industry, which ruined thousands of lives and cost the country hundreds of billions of dollars.[38] An academic journal article published in 2005 characterized Keating's criminal scheme as "the tactically brilliant but strategically disastrous step of deliberately targeting nonwealthy widows to scam using *un*insured junk bonds."[39] The human face of the scandal appeared in the form of Shirley Lampel, a widow ruined by Lincoln Savings and Loan, who joined a long line of retirees appearing before Congress in November 1989. In measured but pointed tones she reduced the complexities of corruption and the financial regulatory system to a simple conclusion: "The henhouse door was open and the fox got in."[40]

McCain weathered the political storm caused by the Keating scandal, but it haunted him for the rest of his political career, returning during his 2000 and 2008 campaigns for the White House. One columnist wrote during his second run: "McCain, long a maverick and the infallible, unassailable, war hero engineer of the 'Straight Talk Express,' is now just another Republican—an obstacle to the Democratic Party to be denigrated, besmirched, harassed, undermined, gossiped about and ultimately destroyed. Welcome home, John."[41]

Oliver North also found that scandal could eventually rub away the veneer of a Vietnam War hero. And he was that: a Naval Academy graduate and combat Marine who led a rifle platoon much as had James Webb. As an ambitious member of the National Security Council (NSC) staff under Robert "Bud" McFarlane, North inserted himself into a variety of secret projects, including the Reagan administration's extralegal efforts to support the Nicaraguan Contras. For many Americans, North became the public face of the Iran-Contra investigation, particularly when he appeared in full uniform to testify before Congress in July 1987. North was defiantly honest during his appearance and admitted his role in the scandal, arguing that his efforts and those of like-minded NSC staffers and cabinet officials were necessary to defend U.S. interests against international communism.[42] Early in his testimony, he invoked Vietnam and the honor explicit in military service. While North's actions appalled many, contemporary polling was split. A *New York Times*/CBS survey found that 62 percent considered him a "true patriot," but most (by a five-to-three margin) believed he "had gone too far in his actions." He was indicted on fourteen felony counts in March 1988.[43]

A judge dismissed all charges against North in 1991 on a series of technicalities. One of his first subsequent actions was an entry into politics. In 1994, North decided to run for an open Virginia senate seat with tepid support from the Republican Party but millions in mail-in donations for the campaign. Once he plunged back into the public sphere, the relatively fresh Iran-Contra scandal returned with him.

North's treatment of his opponent, fellow Marine and Vietnam veteran Chuck Robb, introduced an interesting, focused sort of partisanship into the contest. In stump speeches, North often referred to Robb as an "Eighth and I Marine," implying that he enjoyed a safe, meaningless support position during the war. In fact, nothing was further from the truth. Robb, like North, was a combat veteran, and the accusation rankled some of his better-known peers. Consequently, on October 7, 1994, James Webb, Bob Kerrey, and four other Vietnam veterans publicly endorsed Robb in a press conference held in front of the Iwo Jima memorial.[44] They took the opportunity not to attack North's military record but the man himself. Former Navy SEAL and Medal of Honor winner Bob Kerrey stated: "This isn't about who is the better officer. This is about who lied and who told the truth." For his own part, James Webb said: "Over the years, many people who have known Oliver North well have marveled at the distortions and exaggerations he has brought to the public arena."[45] It was a devastating public indictment, one that challenged the bedrock of North's claim to the integrity of service for the greater good. However, despite this last-minute challenge, the final election was close, with Robb defeating North by only three points, 46 percent to 43 percent.

One of the most important recent examples of how veterans and politics commingled was the 2004 "swift boating" of John Kerry. Although the Vietnam War resurfaced during Bill Clinton's 1992 run, the issue emerged with a vengeance when Kerry challenged incumbent George W. Bush.

Kerry wielded his Vietnam War service to both embellish his credentials and criticize Bush's handling of ongoing, unpopular wars in Iraq and Afghanistan.[46] The constant refrain was also a way to question the value of Bush's service as a Texas Air National Guard pilot who never deployed to Vietnam.

The response to this particular tack came from an interesting direction: a nonprofit group comprising men who had served with Kerry that identified itself the "Swift Veterans" (later the Swift Boat Veterans for Truth, or SBVT). Its introductory letter, published in May 2004, offered what amounted to its mission statement: "It is our collective judgment that, upon your return from Vietnam, you grossly and knowingly distorted the conduct of American soldiers, marines, sailors and airmen of that war (including a betrayal of many of us, without regard for the dangers your actions caused us). Further, we believe that you have withheld and/or distorted material facts as to your own conduct in this war."[47] The group essentially made two claims. The first was that Kerry had misled the country in his 1971 Senate testimony during Dewey Canyon III, repeating unverified and false stories about U.S. war atrocities. Second, these veterans believed that Kerry had also embellished his own war record for personal and political gain.

Kerry himself admitted that his 1971 Senate statement was "a little bit excessive" in an April 2004 interview with Tim Russert.[48] His awards for wounds received in combat and recognition for heroism were another matter. During the war, Kerry received the Silver Star, the Bronze Star, and three Purple Hearts. Although there was no question that the military awards system was inflated during Vietnam, it was difficult to prove that this context applied specifically to Kerry.[49] In fact, Kerry's commanding officer, George Elliott, who endorsed Kerry's Bronze Star, was also a member of SBVT.

In the ensuing public scrum between Swift Boat Veterans for Truth (and their supporters) and the Kerry campaign (and its supporters), accusations about political bad faith arced back and forth between the two camps. Pundits traced SBVT financial support back to Bush allies. Commentators noted that many elements of the traditional political smear were at work. Cable news tended to focus on accusations and responses rather than the root source of the alleged scandal.[50]

Veterans on both sides of the story collectively formed a media blind spot in 2004. Although some publications such as the *Washington Post* and the *Boston Globe* invested the time and effort to obtain affidavits and track down specific portions of the Swift Boat story, too many news outlets simply granted the respective groups of contending veterans credibility without context or proper fact-checking.[51] This process damaged not only Kerry but also George W. Bush after a story emerged about favoritism during his National Guard service. Dan Rather suffered from his own self-inflicted scandal when CBS News failed to verify the authenticity of documents pertaining to the incumbent president's service. Capping the episode was the bizarre *New York Times* headline: "Memos on Bush Are Fake but Accurate, Typist Says."[52]

Although Vietnam veterans trickled back into politics after 1973, the war provided, at best, limited protection from partisanship and retained many of its own sharp edges. For John Murtha, service was a means to establish a rapport with part of the country that regularly sent its sons to Southeast Asia. For an aspiring politician like John McCain, the war engendered sympathy at a time when the country was interested in making amends for the past. Service had its limits, however. Status was not proof against scandal, as McCain and North discovered for very different reasons. Perhaps more important, status as a veteran was not only an imperfect shield against scandal but also a sword to lend political attacks credibility. This trend is not new. However, it is currently augmented by cable news and the internet, which are more prone to granting a superficial form of agency to veterans with too little concern for the consequences.

THE NEXT WAVE

The events of September 11 touched many parts of American life, and politics was not an exception. Two wars refocused national attention on issues such as military affairs, terrorism, and national security. Veterans' status seemed to be an essential credential necessary to gain traction in a new and dangerous twenty-first-century world.

This was particularly true for the Democratic Party. In the years after World War II, it was common to depict Democrats as warmongers, who aggressively led the country into conflicts like Korea and Vietnam. However, in the years following Vietnam, a distinct shift took place. During the period that encompassed the 1973 War Powers Act and constant debates about the use of U.S. military forces abroad, the Democratic Party shed its aggressive legacy, but also its credibility with respect to national security issues. A 2002 Gallup poll recorded a massive GOP advantage over Democrats—50 percent to 31 percent—on the question of which party would do a better job of protecting the country from international terrorism and military threats.[53]

Promoting veterans as candidates in the political environment of the new Global War on Terrorism seemed to be an ideal solution, particularly with respect to recent returnees from U.S. conflicts. These young men and women had experienced the consequences of U.S. foreign policy, a quality that gave them the gravity to critique it. Further, by restoring its direct links with the military through these veterans, the Democratic Party could also potentially increase its relevance in congressional districts lost to Republicans for decades in states like Pennsylvania, Texas, Ohio, North Carolina, and Virginia.[54]

By 2006, as public opinion began to move against the war, the Democratic Party introduced the country to its slate of veteran candidates.[55] House minority leader Nancy Pelosi referred to them as the "Fighting Dems" that October. She went on to say: "The military credential is important in that it gives them standing on national security, but they are also battle-tested. They're ready for these campaigns. They share a determination to make our country strong—not only militarily but also in the health and education of our people. It inspires all of us in the larger fight."[56]

In total, Democrats ran more than fifty veterans in 2006 congressional contests, including nine Iraq veterans. As a group, they created a human link to the party's critique of Republican military policies. Individually, they were a departure from the polished norm, possessing a "raw authenticity," as a writer for the *Atlantic Monthly* described it, that appealed to a public tired of party mudslinging.[57] Some, like John Kerry before them, were outspoken critics of the U.S. military operations. Patrick Murphy, an Iraq veteran who won a narrow victory in his eastern Pennsylvania district, called for an end to the war itself.[58]

Tammy Duckworth entered her race for a seat in the Illinois Democrat delegation voicing similar sentiments. Duckworth was a rare candidate at the time, a wounded female combat veteran of Iraq who had lost both legs as a result of enemy fire. Like John McCain, she used her unique status to flay political opponents for their conduct of the war. Duckworth gained the endorsement of the progressive Iraq and Afghanistan Veterans of America Political Action Committee as well as the Democrat establishment.[59] Party leaders like Bill Clinton, Barack Obama, and John Kerry spoke on her behalf and raised money from the faithful.[60]

The end results of the "Fighting Dems" strategy were disappointing. Duckworth did not prevail in her bid for office. Only five Democratic candidates won seats: Murphy in Pennsylvania, who was joined Joe Sestak and Chris Carney in the state's delegation, as well as Tim Walz of Minnesota. James Webb, the former Marine infantry platoon leader who won a Navy Cross in Vietnam, won a Senate seat in Virginia.

Despite these early races being dominated by Democratic candidates, Republicans soon recovered and launched their own slate of veteran hopefuls. In 2010, Mark Kirk, a Navy reservist, won the Illinois seat formerly held by Barack Obama in Illinois.[61] In Ohio that year, Republican Steve Stivers, a National Guardsman who had deployed to both Iraq and Afghanistan, defeated Mary Jo Kilroy in the Fifteenth District. The party also included Vietnam veterans in its cohort of candidates. Paul Cook, a Marine infantry officer wounded twice in Vietnam spent time in the California Assembly and local government before running for Congress in 2012. That year, backed by local media, veterans groups, and state and national party officials, Cook easily carried California's Eighth Congressional District by sixteen points.[62] The retired Marine Corps lieutenant general and pilot Jack Bergman followed by capturing the Michigan's First District in 2016.

By 2020, post-9/11 veterans were an increasingly visible element in national politics.[63] Candidates set a tone that would have been familiar to an observer of politics during the heyday of the Kennedys. David Halberstam beautifully captured the moment then and now: "The new men were tough—'hard-nosed realists' was a phrase often used to define them, a description they themselves had selected. They had good war records; they were fond of pointing out that they were the generation which had fought the war, that they had been the company commanders, had borne the brunt of the war and lost their comrades. This gave them special preparation for the job ahead, it was the company commanders replacing the generals, and even here was seen virtue."[64] The new breed of veterans were pragmatists, tempered by war and ready to bridge political gaps for the betterment of the country. This theme appears often during and after elections. When asked by an interviewer about his goals if elected, Jack Bergman replied simply to "get Congress working together." It was a desire echoed by candidates and the public alike.[65]

One lawmaker who embodied this approach at the outset of his political career is Republican Dan Crenshaw. A decorated Navy SEAL with multiple deployments to Iraq and Afghanistan, he was an accomplished veteran of America's current wars. Crenshaw shrewdly wove his military achievements into his political persona. His campaign slogan, "Choose to Do Hard Things," was accompanied by a biography which featured rigorous special forces training, dangerous special operations missions, and the loss of an eye on his third tour of duty to an improvised explosive device.[66] To generate publicity and demonstrate his literal fitness for office, Crenshaw conducted a five-day one-hundred-mile run through his Texas district in 2018.[67]

After briefly engaging in a public spat with *Saturday Night Live* comedian Pete Davidson about his eye wound, Crenshaw gained public sympathy not only for being the victim of a joke in poor taste but also for his handling of it.[68] He used the moment as an opportunity to emphasize tolerance and commonality in a November 2018 *Washington Post* editorial: "There are many ideas that we will never agree on. The left and the right have different ways of approaching governance, based on contrasting philosophies. But many of the ultimate goals—economic prosperity, better health care and education, etc.—are the same."[69] At the outset of his first term in Congress, Crenshaw appeared ready to follow through on his rhetoric. Soon after his victory in Texas, he signed a pledge with New Jersey Democrat Mikie Sherrill, a Naval Academy graduate and helicopter pilot, to cosponsor legislation and serve with civility.[70]

That is not to say veterans have escaped recent politics unscathed. During the 2016 presidential campaign, among many of the generally held norms that fell by the wayside was the one that protected veterans from criticism. Contrary to conventional wisdom, advice from his staff, the Republican Party, and a wide spectrum of commentators, candidate Donald Trump attacked both John McCain and the family of Humayun Khan, a U.S. Army captain killed in action in 2004 by an Iraqi suicide bomber.[71] Once it came to office, the Trump administration would reverse and obstruct long-standing policies that expedited the citizenship process for immigrants in uniform. Officials terminated the Basic Training Naturalization Initiative, which allowed noncitizens to be naturalized as soon as they completed entry training.[72] U.S. Citizenship and Immigration Services reduced the number of overseas locations for naturalization of service member from twenty-three to four. In just the first year of the Trump administration, the number of military members attaining citizenship dropped from eight thousand a year to four thousand.[73]

CONCLUSIONS

The number of veterans elected at the national level today may never reach the numbers of preceding generations. When the 116th Congress started business in 2019, there were ninety-six veterans, slightly down from the previous term. Two-thirds were Republican. However, the new generation of post-9/11 veterans was a predominant part of this group. More than half of the men and women in the Congressional Veterans Caucus served after 2000.[74]

What they can and will accomplish remains to be seen. However, it is clear that former members of the military contribute to the often contrary nature of American politics. Republicans found that veterans were just as useful as critics of Barack Obama's national security policies as they had been for Democrats who spoke against the Bush administration. When

Iraqi authority collapsed under the ISIS onslaught and Syria devolved into a brutal civil war, these Republican veterans argued for a stronger stand against long-term threats to American interests. As the country continues to wrestle with the "forever war," voices like Dan Crenshaw's and those like him are amplified by his status and remain at the center of policy debates.[75]

As was the case with past collections of veterans, their service made them relatable but not immune to political wounds. Patrick Murphy lost his seat in 2010 largely because of broad dissatisfaction following the Great Recession, something that made his wartime service irrelevant. Similarly, though Tammy Duckworth's sacrifices in uniform were unique and irreproachable, her moderate positions on immigration and the military's "don't ask, don't tell" policy drew criticism from activists.[76] When Duckworth started her campaign for the Senate in 2016, the *Chicago Tribune* ran an exposé on her modest policy achievements and relationship with corrupt Illinois governor Rod Blagojevich. In the recent past, Duckworth became, like John McCain before her, the target of conservative media attacks on her patriotism.[77]

Lastly, it is clear that civility and cooperation among post-9/11 veterans was an early casualty of contemporary U.S. political partisanship. The 2019 impeachment proceedings took away the possibility of moderation when lawmakers, with the exception of Tulsi Gabbard, were compelled to take a stand on the issue. Mikie Sherrill found out just how much in a New Jersey town meeting where, as one reporter recounted: "The space rippled with a mixture of boos, cheers, and angst." She was not helped by her compatriot Dan Crenshaw, who denounced impeachment in a press release before a formal inquiry began: "The Democrats' true intentions have always been impeaching the President. It's been a core piece of their agenda since 2016 and today they were finally honest about it. Opening an impeachment inquiry without having all the information is irresponsible. It's the result of a political party blinded by their dream of taking down the President."[78]

CHAPTER NINE

The Women Praetorians

"We should be proud to shoot like girls, fight like girls, train like girls, and win battles like girls."
—*Lieutenant Colonel Kate Germano*, Fight Like a Girl, *2018*

INTRODUCTION

Women have always been intrinsic to U.S. wars. As colonists and citizens of the Republic, they directly participated in every facet of the national defense. When war became industrialized, women produced the vast amount of material consumed by modern militaries. As the Industrial Revolution magnified casualties on an unprecedented scale, women devised ways to mitigate suffering through organizations like the America Red Cross and United States Sanitary Commission. When William Tecumseh Sherman spoke of Mary Ann Bickerdyke, who was instrumental in organizing medical treatment and sanitary conditions throughout the Civil War, he famously said: "She ranks me."[1]

For most of modern American history, the number of women in uniform has been comparatively small. Of the sixteen million citizens mustered to fight in World War II, women comprised 400,000. Although there were periodic discussions of extending the draft to women during the course of the war, the United States never took that step.[2] Still, despite their numbers, the quality of women's service was broad and diverse. During World War II, the number of military occupational specialties open to women grew from 4 to 239.[3]

World War II set an important policy precedent that would affect generations of women in uniform in ways not anticipated or understood at the time. In keeping with their wartime representation, the Women's Armed Services Integration Act of 1948 officially capped female enlisted strength in the U.S. military at 2 percent of the total force. When the Korean War began, women constituted only twenty-two thousand of active duty personnel, approximately a third of whom were in medical services.[4] The women who subsequently served in Korea, Vietnam, and Cold War posts throughout the world would be a well-educated, self-selected group of specialists, particularly in administration and military medicine. They served with distinction but were a rarity by virtue of federal law, institutional practice, and, importantly, military culture.

The 1948 law, which finally lapsed in 1968, created a vast undertow throughout the military establishment.[5] It was, by its own terms, a male institution, one that treated female members as an afterthought. At best, women were considered capable participants, but it was rare to see them considered integral to the military's mission. This foundation affected changes that began to appear within the military immediately after Vietnam, specifically recruitment, training, promotion, and retention. A generation of practices influenced one of the most strident debates within the military—assigning women to combat units—that continues to this day. The depth of this one debate is reflected in a 2015 Marine Corps gender integration study that bluntly stated: "Risking the lives of a military unit in combat to provide career opportunities or accommodate the personal desires or interests of an individual, or group of individuals, is more than bad military judgment. It is morally wrong."[6]

Consequently, women praetorians are a more rarified group among an already shrinking contingent of American veterans in general. Some of their experiences parallel those of the larger body of male veterans. They joined the military for reasons familiar to any enlistee: patriotism, tradition, boredom, a search for new skills and challenges. However, from the point that women actually entered the military and, later, after joining the ranks of veterans, their narrative significantly diverges from that of men.

WOMEN JOIN THE RANKS

The type of woman who joined the military remained remarkably consistent between World War II and Vietnam. As a group, they tended to be better educated than men. In one surveyed group of World War II servicewomen, 54 percent had some college training. The study recorded similarly high college attendance for women during the Korean War (44%) and the Vietnam era (53%).[7] Educational proficiency translated into higher mental classification than men. According to standardized mental aptitude testing, in 1972, there were more than twice as many women in the highest classification, Categories I and II, than male recruits.[8]

Prior to 1973, most women in the military were white and the products of middle-class families. In terms of age, female volunteers tended to parallel men. During World War II, a third were twenty-five or older when they entered the armed forces. During the Vietnam era, only 8 percent fit that category. However, in some occupations, the age gap between men and women actually widened. A surveyed group of Army nurses stationed in Vietnam had an average age of 23.6. Air Force and Navy nurses averaged 28.2 years old.[9]

Spoken, but mostly not in the public domain, was a clear social stigma attached to women's military service. When she asked her parents to sign for her enlistment in 1969, Ann Powlas met with resistance: "In my mom and dad's day, during World War II, women in the service were considered to be bad people. They just knew I was going to come out a whore."[10] Homosexuality was a constant source of concern. By 1971, military recruiters seeking out female enlistees were well versed with the issue. Marine Captain Maureen Fullerton assured parents that if their daughters "might encounter Lesbianism," the perpetrators would be immediately discharged from the military.[11]

The end of Selective Service altered many of the opportunities available for women, if not the lingering stigma. Anticipating a significant shortage of men willing to accept voluntary enlistments, military officials were prompted by the Gates Commission to examine entry testing standards, training, and military occupations open to women.[12] One particular concern was the low retention rate for female recruits. Between 1966 and 1971, the Navy had the highest retention rate (46.2%) for women with thirty months of service, whereas the Marine Corps had the lowest at only 27.6 percent.[13]

By 1977, concerns about women staying in the military had eased. The military retained women at about the same rate as men and at a higher rate in the medical, administrative, intelligence, and communications specialties.[14] As mentioned above, higher test scores accounted for part of this improvement. A Defense Department manpower study also pointed to the fact that women were applying to recruiters at a much higher rate than men and the process had become increasingly more selective.

What characterized women in the new all-volunteer military was a mixture of old and new traits. Many joined out of a sense of tradition. Recounting her reasons for entering the Marine Corps, Lieutenant Colonel Kate Germano noted her father's prior service as an Army officer. However, her real inspiration came from watching a graduation ceremony of Naval Academy midshipmen.[15] Georgia Jane Ford cited the same sense of family history when she joined the Air Force in 1951 after her father expressed concern that Korea would be the first war since the American Revolution in which a Ford had not fought.[16] After her friends enlisted, Constance Anderson, who served as an Army nurse during the Korean War, was "determined to catch up with them and find them." She recalled that service offered exciting possibilities: "I was always looking over the hill for a greener pasture.... I felt maybe there was something out there that I haven't seen or needed to see."[17]

Economic motives were also clearly at work. Military pay and benefits were one way for women to overcome the long-standing civilian wage gap with men. In 1970, total compensation for a private (E-1), the entry-level rank in the military, was $5,419 a year. This compared very favorably with professional ($5,099), clerical, ($4,451), mechanical or maintenance crafts ($4,557), and semiskilled "operatives" ($4,309) positions available at the time for women between the ages of 18 and 24.[18] The same advantage held in 1999. According to a Department of Labor study, entry-level positions for women in retail, food service, and education paid approximately the same median wage, between $15,000 and $16,000. Military pay for a private (E-1) with four months' service, in comparison, was significantly lower at $11,513 a year.[19] However, taking into account a housing allowance, pension contributions, GI Bill benefits, and, most important, health care, it is clear that the lowest military rank was competitive, if not superior, to entry-level civilian jobs for women.[20]

For these and other reasons, increasing numbers of women joined the ranks. By 1976, their numbers had doubled to 5.3 percent of active duty enlisted personnel. By 1990, the proportion of enlisted women in all branches of the service doubled again to 11 percent. In 2018, the figure was 16.5 percent. The largest representation is in the Air Force (24.9%), with declining percentages in the Navy (24.7%), Army (16.8%), and Marine Corps (9.5%). Female representation in the officer corps has lagged behind these numbers. In 2017, women comprised just 18 percent of officers of all ranks.[21] Again, the totals varied according to the branch. In *Fight Like a Girl*, Kate Germano commented, "Seeing a female general in the Marine Corps is akin to seeing Bigfoot riding a unicorn."[22]

Most military occupational specialties in combat support and combat service support were available to women. These included communications, medical fields, administration, electronics, food service, transport, civil affairs, and military police among hundreds of others.[23] Many of these would be critical to overseas contingency operations after 2001. In 2013, on the unanimous recommendation of the Joint Chiefs of Staff, the Pentagon ended the exclusion of women from the combat arms. Implementation proceeded apace in subsequent years. By August 1, 2019, all infantry, field artillery, and armor battalions within Army brigade combat teams included female soldiers.[24]

The racial composition of female veterans changed dramatically in the decades following the end of the draft. Where service had once been the domain of college-educated white women, it increasingly reflected a much larger minority representation. By 2011, 31 percent of military women were African American, 13 percent were Hispanic, and 4 percent were Asian.[25]

As women joined the Global War on Terrorism in increasing numbers, they also suffered the effects of military service to a great degree, which official statistics failed to reveal for a number of years. In terms of combat with the Taliban, al-Qaeda, and ISIS, women in the military seemed far less likely to be wounded or killed in action. According to a Congressional Research Service study, women constituted only 2 percent of combat wounded in Iraq and Afghanistan between 2001 and 2017. Similarly, women suffered slightly more than 2 percent of combat deaths during the same time period.[26]

The figures underplay the overall exposure to risk endured by military women. Regardless of their occupational specialty, they were constantly in danger. Military police and civil affairs units consistently left the relative safety of forward bases to commingle with the local population. Logistics work required frequent travel on hotly contested supply routes. As Matt Friedman, the executive director of the National Center for PTSD, put it: "Frankly one of the most dangerous things you can do in Iraq is drive a truck, and that's considered a combat support role."[27] Moreover, what was true for medical personnel in Vietnam was equally so in Iraq or Afghanistan. Writing about first responders in Vietnam, Shelley Saywell could have been speaking for her peers fifty years later: "What nurses saw in those operating rooms was an unrelenting procession of the bits and pieces of people arriving from the battlefields. What they felt, working twelve-hour shifts in a kind of 'twilight zone' removed from the war yet dealing with its effects, was a sense of unreality, of helplessness, of anger."[28]

Exposure to this "unrelenting procession" of trauma, compounded by isolation and recurrent sexual harassment, produced its own consequences for military women, although they were poorly understood at the time by veterans' institutions and the general public. Postwar examinations of Army nurses in Vietnam saw a high incidence of post-traumatic stress disorder (PTSD): one 1988 study indicated a rate as high as 20 percent among nurses exposed to "high war zone stress, e.g., exposure to enemy fire, death and dying, and environmental hazards."[29] For women who served in the 1990–91 Gulf War, the PTSD rate was 16 percent, double that for men.[30] For women who served after September 11, the official incidence of PTSD was even higher, at least 20 percent, which placed it on the high end of the spectrum for all veterans of these wars. Private studies noted an even higher occurrence of PTSD, between 21 percent to 27 percent, among female veterans in the first six years of the war.[31]

More ominous were ongoing revelations from women veterans regarding military sexual trauma (MST). Its sources varied from person to person. In 2007, 3 percent of women indicated that they were sexually assaulted, with more reporting sexual coercion (8%) and unwanted sexual attention (27%).[32] In a relatively short space of time, military sexual trauma evolved as a separate form of post-traumatic stress that appeared to be rampant in the armed forces. According to official Veterans Affairs (VA) statistics, 22 percent of women reported MST, as did 1 percent of men. However, dozens of studies published between 2001 and 2009 found that these official rates were almost certainly too low. Clinical research of MST found that between 20 percent and 43 percent of female veterans suffered from such trauma. Veterans affected by MST demonstrated higher rates of substance abuse, anxiety, and depression; physical problems associated with MST included fatigue, gastrointestinal distress, and pelvic pain.[33]

On one level, the tragedy of MST is the fact that the largest source of injury to military women is the U.S. military itself. The facts speak for themselves. Between 2001 and 2017, slightly more than one thousand women were wounded in Iraq and Afghanistan.[34] In comparison, between 2016 and 2018 alone, the VA processed thirty-six thousand claims of PTSD related to military sexual trauma.[35]

In another sense, military sexual trauma reflects a fundamental breach of trust within the military institution. One group of researchers likened MST to family violence in that many of its perpetrators were known to their victims, in positions of authority, and supposed to be governed by accepted norms of behavior. In the case of the last point, expectations were rightly higher given established codes of military conduct and years of public policy reforms dedicated to the treatment of women in uniform.[36]

The demonstrable gap between reasonable expectation and military reality made military sexual trauma that much worse for its victims. Women bought into the premise that military culture, defined by the core concept of unit cohesion, would apply to them as equals. Military sexual trauma ruined that expectation when it occurred and again when both active duty women and veterans reported the crime. Veterans Affairs policy avoided collecting specific evidence of MST claims for years, a practice that impeded provision of proper disability benefits.[37] In too many cases, military units also tended to close ranks after women leveled accusations of MST, treating their desire for justice and medical help as a betrayal. In either instance, as one writer observed, "Camaraderie becomes cruel captivity."[38]

WOMEN VETERANS AND THE DILEMMA OF INSTITUTIONAL LIMITS

The most important factor limiting the proper care and treatment of women veterans was their numbers. As a result of World War II mobilization and twenty years of subsequent federal policy, women were a tiny part of the overall population of U.S. veterans. According to the Veterans Administration, in 1972 women comprised only 1.9 percent of all living veterans.[39] While that number has increased significantly, as of 2020 the figure stands at 10 percent.[40]

These numbers tell a story. They dictated priority, budgets, and the allocation of resources. Placed in this context, the tiny contingent of women veterans was largely lost among the tens of millions of their male peers. These tendencies became embedded parts of the Veterans Administration and, later, the Department of Veterans Affairs. The axiom that bureaucratic inertia is one of the hardest forces to fight in a modern nation proved abundantly true time and again for military women.

Evidence of this inertia is scattered throughout the historical time line. In 1946, Omar Bradley quashed a pamphlet that addressed specific medical care for female veterans, arguing that the existing VA system was already adequate to their needs.[41] The system, built for a male-dominated military, persisted into the Vietnam era. Clinicians regularly misdiagnosed PTSD symptoms in women. Administrative protocols proved confusing for female veterans who actively sought help. As late as 1982, a General Accounting Office (GAO) report indicated that VA hospitals failed to provide women with complete physical exams, domiciliary care, or psychiatric services.[42] Lacking both adequate institutional support and the peer groups available to men in need of assistance, women became a different form of "invisible veteran" after Vietnam.[43]

One of the most important areas impacted by this trend was VA health care. A 1998 study found that female veterans tended to use VA health services less than men, in part because women enjoyed better private insurance and did not need to rely on the government.[44] However, and more important, private health care was far better able to address specific women's needs than was the VA. Gender-related blind spots permeated the government system. Hospitals and medical centers in the VA system lacked segregated female wards, for example. Women admitted for inpatient care had to share bed space in open areas with men. Well into the early nineties, most VA facilities lacked basic amenities like bathrooms and showers for women.[45] The absence of facilities was not only inconvenient but actively hampered the proper treatment of service-related disabilities, particularly psychiatric ones.[46]

Psychological care, particularly for sexual assault, proved inadequate for years and only slowly began to catch up after repeated scandals. Gaining recognition of the problem was difficult. A 1988 Defense Department report indicated that at least 5 percent of military women were raped while in uniform. This conclusion was challenged just two years later by a study finding that at least a third of women experienced some type of sexual harassment or assault while in uniform, a conclusion driven home by Senate hearings on the problem of sexual abuse following the Gulf War and the 1991 Tailhook scandal.[47] Repeating a sentiment echoed by many women at the time, Barbara Franco, an Army veteran raped by three soldiers in 1975, testified that "most women veterans do not go to the V.A. because it is the same male-dominated, abusive system and environment which hurt us before."[48]

As a result of repeated public exposure, in 1998 the Department of Veterans Affairs budgeted $67 million to improve facilities for women and address privacy concerns. The department also created a Women Veteran Coordinator in each VA medical center to act as an advocate for female veterans.[49] Officials redoubled outreach to include seminars and town meetings held in VA facilities as well as the annual conventions of the American Legion, the Women's Army Corps, Women Marines, and Disabled American Veterans following the theme "Women Are Veterans, Too."[50]

In relatively short order, it seemed as if these efforts had generated positive progress. A January 1999 GAO report noted that the "VA has made considerable progress in removing barriers that prevent women veterans from receiving care." It recognized increased outreach to women mentored by women veterans' coordinators and a "significant increase" in available facilities and their use.[51] It also seemed that the military might have turned the corner on treatment for sexual assault. The number of women receiving counseling for MST increased significantly from 2,350 in 1993 to almost 9,000 in 1997. Officials saw this as an encouraging sign that more women were seeking help.[52] A 2003 VA study reached a similarly optimistic conclusion that the data showed *"unprofessional, gender-related behaviors declined significantly between 1995 and 2002.*[53]

Research sponsored by the Department of Defense challenged this optimism. A 2003 article published in the *American Journal of Industrial Medicine* completely contradicted the VA's findings, noting that 37 percent of surveyed female veterans acknowledged that they had been raped at least twice during their military service. An additional 14 percent reported that they had been gang-raped while in uniform. Perpetrators were usually noncommissioned officers or peers of similar rank. Three-quarters of victims did not report their rapes to their commanding officer.[54] The claims were disturbingly reminiscent of the 1992 Senate hearings following the Gulf War.

These revelations and a growing body of scholarship initiated yet another round of institutional reforms. The Department of Veterans Affairs began specifically screening veterans for military sexual trauma as early as 2002.[55] Lawmakers, equally mindful of the seriousness of the problem and its impact on ever growing numbers of women being deployed to Iraq and Afghanistan, passed Public Law 108–422 in 2004, which provided disability benefits for MST.[56]

While these were important and necessary steps, problems have since plagued the system. When the VA Office of Inspector General sampled a set of 2017 MST claims, it found the almost half were improperly processed by administrators.[57] A Yale Law School study looked at an earlier period, 2008 to 2012, and determined that military sexual trauma claims were much less likely to be approved than other types of PTSD.[58] Similarly, a number of investigations by the Government Accountability Office demonstrate an ongoing absence of specialized programs for women as well as persistent noncompliance with privacy standards that the VA had identified more than thirty years earlier.[59] Although the Department of Veterans Affairs as an institution recognizes the need for additional treatment resources, the evidence suggests a troubling lack of consistent progress.

SELF-ADVOCACY AND REFORM

Since the Civil War, it has become a common practice for veterans to organize to gain public recognition and agency in domestic policymaking. Postwar eras witnessed the creation of the Grand Army of the Republic (1866), the Veterans of Foreign Wars (VFW, 1899), and the American Legion (1919) for the purpose of veterans' advocacy. These organizations became instrumental actors in U.S. politics and effectively lobbied for both public commemoration and new federal law.[60]

As established groups like the American Legion and VFW settled into positions of power, they were challenged by new arrivals. The American Veterans Committee (AVC) and the Vietnam Veterans Against the War (VVAW) typified the generational friction that periodically emerges within the veterans' community. The tension reflects the impatience over the pace and direction of advocacy as much as the internal organizational culture. Members of the AVC wanted a stronger voice in the emerging civil rights movement of the 1940s and 1950s and actively resisted McCarthyism.[61] The VVAW fought against both U.S. foreign policy in

Southeast Asia and the reflexive nationalism of the American Legion and VFW.

Cleavages rooted in representation and advocacy continued throughout the post-1945 period, in many instances based on gender. A brief examination of traditional and nontraditional veterans' organizations reveals that they rarely granted women veterans the attention they routinely demanded from the public and the government. The American Legion approved a temporary charter to its first all-female post in 1945. The Four Branches Post 303 in Minneapolis initially included sixteen women.[62] Others followed in Chicago and Philadelphia, but overall women remained a tiny minority within the largest veterans' organizations. When June A. Willenz became the executive director of the American Veterans Committee in 1965, she was a rare pioneer at the national level. The American Legion did not elect a female national commander until 2017, when Denise H. Rohan earned the position.[63]

Women veterans did not wait for permission to organize as their own advocates. Many of the earliest groups came from their professional affiliation with the military. The first chapter of the Women's Army Corps Veterans' Association was chartered as a nonprofit corporation in 1946.[64] The Retired Army Nurse Corps Association was founded in 1977 to facilitate social contact between veterans and "establish a means of communication by, for, and about Army nurses."[65] Other groups are built around a specific branch of the service. The Women Marines Association (founded in 1960) pursues the same standards as other established veterans' groups, with a focus on tradition, camaraderie, and community service; it also embraces the same exclusivity as its parent military organization. As one online publication put it, "Women Marines Association: Representing the Fewer and Prouder ... Generations of Service."[66] These groups, like the American Legion and the VFW, emphasized the historical preservation of their service, community outreach, the promotion of female service in the military, and the professional development of its members.[67]

A major turning point came with the formation of the Vietnam Veterans of America (VVA) in 1979. When the VVA was formed, organizers included Lynda Van Devanter, an Army nurse who served in South Vietnam between 1969 and 1970, as part of the leadership. Van Devanter initiated the VVA Women's Project in 1979 with the dual objectives of generating greater recognition for female veterans by projecting women into the public discourse, like many traditional male veterans' groups, and promoting badly needed reforms within the VA and the military. Van Devanter was an early advocate for improved health care for women.

She focused on access to routine gynecological care and breast cancer screening. Under her leadership, the VVA lobbied for official acknowledgment and care for women suffering from PTSD.[68]

Health care concerns proved to be a consistent rallying point for women veterans. The increasing proportion of female service members deployed for Operations Desert Storm and Desert Shield (6.8%) resulted in a surge in physical problems associated with Gulf War syndrome after 1991.[69] As noted earlier, almost one-third of veterans of this war suffered some type of sickness as a result of their service. Birth defects experienced by women who had served in Saudi Arabia and Kuwait created a sad solidarity with the female spouses of other veterans. Women veterans subsequently joined more than fifty separate groups that spent years pressuring Congress for disability assistance.[70]

What they wanted was not just help for themselves but for their children as well. One woman who served in the Gulf War put it this way: "I don't care if they [the U.S. government] say they did it or not. I don't care if they admit that it is real or not. I don't want any money from them. I want to make sure that my daughter is covered, health insurance wise, for the rest of her life."[71] In a very real and important sense, the women affected by Gulf War syndrome were motivated to reinvent veterans organizing for new and unprecedented reasons. In the past, men affected by severe physical wounds, post-traumatic stress, or both sometimes presented dangers to their families. These could be resolved with treatment or institutional intervention. In the case of Gulf War syndrome, women were transmitting the consequences of military service at an inescapable, genetic level to the most innocent victims imaginable. What "justice" or a "social safety net" meant in this context transcended virtually anything experienced by veterans to that point in history.

Women veterans became a dynamic force in the veterans' community. They adopted, like many private advocacy groups, the early internet as an organizing tool. The World Wide Web allowed veterans to share their experiences and struggles in a manner that created valuable community support. Online communications also allowed for geographically disparate groups to share information, develop methodologies for action, and pursue these in a unified manner. Women who served in the military also applied training and organizational skills derived from their service in highly effective and precise ways. One veteran who served as a nurse compiled a list of Gulf War syndrome symptoms and matched these to VA medical codes, so that claimants could receive appropriate compensation. This list was periodically updated and shared through newsletters and groups linked via the internet.[72]

The escalating numbers of women in uniform and the increasing incidence of their involvement in combat after September 11 has run concurrent with activism. Today, the older organizations mentioned above have been augmented by successive waves of veterans' nonprofits. They tend to be holistic in their approach to female service, starting with military policy affecting women and moving through the assimilation process that women follow after being discharged. The Service Women's Action Network (SWAN), founded in 2007, sued the Defense Department in 2012 to allow women into the combat arms and renewed litigation five years later when the Trump administration appeared ready to reverse existing policy.[73] The SWAN mission statement—contained in the terms "Support, Connect, Advocate"—addresses a long list of services that range from health care and housing to financial advice, employment counseling, and legal services.[74]

These modern veterans' nongovernmental organizations seek out and maintain corporate ties, which is beneficial to both parties. As part of its support for women veterans' employment transition, Women Veterans Interactive (founded 2009) maintains a relationship with large corporations like Amazon as well as somewhat smaller companies with existing links to the government and the military such as USAA Insurance and Northwest Federal Credit Union.[75] It is a highly attractive arrangement: USAA, which already has a long-standing relationship with veterans as clients, can burnish its public image through its own community outreach. For others, such as the private military contractor Booz Allen Hamilton, adopting a progressive client like SWAN is a useful means to recover a public image damaged by recent federal price gouging investigations.[76]

Nongovernmental organizations for female veterans are far more sophisticated regarding the internet than were organizations established after the Persian Gulf War. They maintain daily and, in some cases, real-time communications through a variety of platforms. They can access older veterans through Facebook or broadcast messaging to younger women through Twitter. The June 2020 SWAN Twitter feed covered an array of issues as diverse as military access to birth control, body armor specifically for women's physiology, and LGBTQ rights.[77] Similarly, in the wake of the COVID-19 crisis, women veterans' organizations offered direct support for individuals affected by the disease. Both SWAN and Women Veterans Interactive created links to VA health resources, domestic abuse counseling, and ongoing fundraising for COVID relief.[78]

CONCLUSIONS

Women have been and are a distinct subgroup within the larger body of military veterans. Though they have consistently contributed to American wars, the military and its adjunct veterans' organizations have largely treated women as outliers. As is the case with minority veterans, there is a distinct difference between serving and full recognition of service.

The absence of institutional and cultural recognition has without question hurt women in uniform and afterward. It has slowed their access to military occupations and promotions and, until recently, has constructed a cultural blind spot with respect to how the larger body of society acknowledges their service.

Both veterans' institutions and women veterans have adapted to their increasing numbers, although the former has done so in ways best characterized as inconsistent. Controversy has prompted periodic reform, but progress within the Department of Veterans Affairs has been halting in a number of areas, in some cases regarding the most basic accommodations imaginable. Inertia, a foundational element present throughout the VA, continues to be an obstacle to reform.

Confronting these challenges, women veterans have taken charge of determining their own destiny with the VA and throughout society as a whole. Nonprofit organizations dedicated to women veterans have proliferated in the recent past, evolving from bodies linked to professional service to institutions built around the entire military experience. Demographics are in their favor. Even as the number of veterans in the United States continues to decline, the overall proportion of women with military service will grow. By 2040, women are projected to be approximately 16 percent of veterans overall.[79]

CHAPTER TEN

The Veteran in Popular Culture

> Lacking direct experience, many Americans have turned to film and television representations to try to understand these events as they continue to unfold, as new forms of warfare, including secret surveillance and drone assassinations, have increased under President Obama's tenure as commander in chief.
> —*Anna Froula, "What Keeps Me Up at Night," 2016*

INTRODUCTION

War is a prevalent theme in popular culture. Its attraction comes from the qualities of human drama, a broad range of emotions and behaviors, that war expresses and amplifies. In film, television, theater, literature, and a variety of popular culture media, war invites the audience into deeper insights about the personal stakes and suffering produced by conflict. In a short poem, Siegfried Sassoon captured the qualities of this struggle in life of a soldier:

> Shaken from sleep, and numbed and scarce awake,
> Out of the trench with three hours' watch to take,
> I blunder through the splashing murk; and then
> Hear the gruff muttering voices of the men
> Crouching in cabins candle-chinked with light.[1]

Sassoon wrote "Trench Duty" in 1918, but it could easily apply to a soldier on a night exercise at Camp Mackall, a few miles outside Fort Bragg, or on deployment in the Korengal Valley of Afghanistan.

The wartime experience offers the artist a broad opportunity. As one writer observed in 1991, Hollywood treats the experiences of soldiers as "its basic building blocks."[2] War, for example, offers the juxtaposition between cold, calculating strategic planning and its human consequences. Depicting this process can be an artistic version of a Rorschach test. For a prowar audience, battle is the fulfillment of a "just" war, a vindication of patriotism, or a demonstration of manhood. Placed before viewers more prone to antiwar sentiments, the same art is a tale of corruption and incompetence, where the soldier (and the enemy) are victims of the military institution.[3] This explains why Anthony Swofford and his fellow Marines saw *Apocalypse Now* in completely different terms from Francis Ford Coppola. Regardless, war is a staple in the entertainment industry because of its inherent ability to engage audiences at a very visceral level.

Contemporary media often follows a completely different approach, applying war as a cheap device to garner the audience's attention. Post-9/11 television, particularly "reality" programming, which primarily consists of conflict, liberally applies the term "war" to featured shows. In the past few years, audiences have been treated to *Parking Wars* (A&E, 2008–12), *Storage Wars* (A&E, 2010–19), and even *Cupcake Wars* (Food Network, 2009–). By conflating essentially meaningless conflict with the hard realities of actual bloodshed, reality television deadens and trivializes its actual meaning.

Popular culture generally treats veterans with more restraint. Thematically, this may be because the veteran, though subject to some of the same dramatic influences as the warrior, is a topic more about the consequences of war than its glory. What gives the veteran agency in popular culture are the causes of these consequences and the response to them. Bravery and perseverance are present in the story, albeit in a different form, one with potentially more muted and subtle undertones. In a more pragmatic sense, veteran-themed works are much less popular than art that addresses war, and box office receipts show it. *Stop-Loss* (2008), which dealt with the post-deployment struggles of a group of Army soldiers, earned only $11 million. In contrast, 2013's *Lone Survivor*, a film dramatizing the exploits of a special forces team in Afghanistan, brought in more than $154 million worldwide.[4]

However, as Anna Froula notes, art is an essential means to draw audiences closer to the topic of war and veterans. This is not unimportant in that most contemporary Americans lack personal experience in uniform and also obtain an increasing percentage of their information and perceptions from nontraditional sources. The Pew Research Center noted in 2016 that millennial and Generation Z individuals increasingly derive what they know from entertainment rather than mainstream news media, much more so than do their parents and grandparents.[5] John Oliver is today what Walter Cronkite meant to baby boomers. This is not to say that these generations of young people are unique. In their memoirs, Vietnam veterans like Ron Kovic and Philip Caputo recalled the impact of John Wayne on their perception of war and military service.[6] Wayne had a significant influence on millions of Americans during the course of the Cold War. Yet, the importance of information in postindustrial, post–Cold War America should not be understated either. Opinion shapers and "influencers" exert a tremendous impact on contemporary society, which is something that even the Pentagon recognized after 2001 as it pursued "information dominance" with respect to U.S. military conflicts.[7] This has resulted in partnerships with the gaming industry and, much like it was during World War II, Hollywood.[8]

Popular cultural depictions of veterans travel through a number of filters, some derived from thematic approaches to the topic, others the result of the chosen medium. The treatment of veterans in popular culture is a complicated process that invites detailed examination. Much of the discussion begins with artistic choice. Have the respective playwrights, directors, or actors chosen broad depictions of the veteran or more subtle ones? Other components relate to prevailing audience preferences in a particular historical context. Still others are dependent on the simple reality that popular culture can be a marketable commodity and the bottom line often determines the finished artistic product. This chapter will examine a few of the main thematic approaches to veterans in films, theater, poetry, and other genres since the Vietnam War. As we examine these works, it will be important to discern their distinct qualities, consistency over time, and departures from established norms. It will be equally important to see the degree to which the products of popular culture resonated with their audiences in the last half century since Vietnam.

THE VETERAN AS A CAUTIONARY TALE

In many respects, veterans are the human embodiment of the costs of war. From this perspective, a great deal of art approaches war as a transformative experience that damages its participants. The veteran consequently is a victim of not only violence but also a broad spectrum of negative attributes: corruption, incompetence, indifference, or open hostility. This victimization returns with the veteran from war to home, where the former combatant experiences the same negative qualities from both institutions—Veterans Affairs (VA) is a recurring culprit—and society as a whole.[9]

Various types of popular culture media often treat veterans as a motivating device. Films produced during the Vietnam War and immediately afterward used the veteran as a convenient way to illustrate a larger problem, be it crime, violence, or the decline of authority and social stability. In a callback to film noir in the forties, both low-budget sixties-era motorcycle movies or more mainstream crime dramas such as Clint

Eastwood's *The Enforcer* (1976) featured the veteran as an unstable part of America's criminal element who crossed the line into domestic terrorism.[10]

Other types of art move beyond tropes and focus more specifically on the very personal damage that war inflicts on an individual's psyche. Brian Turner's book *Here, Bullet* (2005) attempts to impart the intimate relationship that a veteran has with violence. Speaking to the bullet, Turner writes: "If a body is what you want, then here is bone and gristle and flesh." Speaking for its target, "Here is where I complete the word you bring hissing through the air."[11] Part of Turner's genius is his ability to convey the permanence of the relationship. The passage of the bullet through "bone and gristle and flesh" is only the beginning of a story that starts on a battlefield but carries on long after impact. The rest of the veteran's life is spent contemplating the moment when the war entered his or her body and remained permanently emplaced in their mind.

The extent to which this damage affects veterans' relationships with other people has been the subject of many artistic works. Steve Tesich's play *The Speed of Darkness* (1989) offered one of the most stark portrayals of the gulf created between the veteran and the rest of the world in a scene where the daughter's boyfriend, Eddie, asks her father, Joe, about Vietnam:

> EDDIE: The worst part, I hear, from the little I know, was not knowing who the enemy was.
>
> JOE: No. The worst part was finding out. See. For all you know, I'm the enemy.[12]

In this context, war creates an unbridgeable gap. Violence forms not only the boundaries delineating civilian from veteran but also presents a point of demarcation from which the veteran poses a direct threat to society. In *Taxi Driver* (1976), Travis Bickle is a deranged misfit who holds the outside world in contempt. His final redemption at the end of the movie comes from a badly mistaken interpretation of a killing spree. Missing is the understanding that violence was the only social currency the veteran Bickle ever possessed or was interested in using.[13]

Sexuality is another barrier formed between veterans and people outside their experience. In his classic work *The Warriors: Reflections on Men in Battle*, J. Glenn Gray observed that love, more specifically "preservative love," between men is a survival mechanism produced by an "atmosphere of violence." According to Gray, "This love is, in men, evidently pervasive and immanent rather than ecstatic. It does not seize us from without but arises out of our own nature. Hence it may be less periodic and more dependable than erotic love, though less able to dominate many men in moments of crisis." Veterans often find, as illustrated in *Stop-Loss* or *Coming Home* (1978), that this "preservative love" lasts far beyond military service. The shared experience of war draws veterans together into a closer bond than they have with their wives or girlfriends.[14] In other cases, the emasculating nature of war carries forward into the core of a veteran's postmilitary experience. Bruce Dern's character in *Coming Home*, Captain Bob Hyde, reunited with his wife only to discover that he was rendered impotent by the war and made a cuckhold by another veteran.

Not all damage was permanent in cautionary depictions of veterans. Many works constructed a redemption arc that followed in the wake of tragedy. *Heroes* (1977) took a simplified route, attempting to interject humor into a story of personal destruction. Henry Winkler's Vietnam veteran was damaged in a way that was not a direct threat to himself or the people around him. His erratic behavior was recast as a "madcap," as one commentator described the film's protagonist Jack Dunne. In an interview, Winkler characterized Dunne as "a guy back from Vietnam who's a little touched."[15] As the plot unfolds, *Heroes* transforms a story about a man suffering from post-traumatic stress into a more conventional romantic comedy. Winkler's Dunne meets Carol Bell (Sally Field), adventures ensue, and love conquers all.[16]

The prospect of healing offered by women is a long-standing component of films devoted to veterans. Perhaps the best known and earliest rendition of this theme appears in *The Best Years of Our Lives* (1946). The three returning veterans, Homer (Harold Russell), Fred (Dana Andrews), and Al (Fredric March), find their female counterparts and eventual redemption in Wilma, Peggy, and Milly, respectively. Like *Heroes*, the story is simple. The love of a good woman is the key to normalcy and happiness. Normalcy had rules specific to the period, however. Long-term stability comes with marriage, as *The Best Years of Our Lives* highlights in its climax. Reassimilation and healing is the end result of heterosexual monogamy. Just how much of the veteran's latent military experience might remain is a mystery, although it seemingly would be delegated to the past.

Veterans films that adopted the theme of healing through relationships with women altered course after the Vietnam War. By the seventies, neither war nor gender relations conformed with the rules of the earlier generation. The cumulative effect of Vietnam and the women's liberation movement was to challenge the accepted norms of the Greatest Generation. Consequently, in *Coming Home*, Jane Fonda's Sally Hyde is a much different woman from her predecessors in *The*

Best Years of Our Lives. Her marriage is a sham. She loves both her husband and the wounded veteran Luke played by Jon Voight. In the end, she refuses to choose either man. Unlike *The Best Years of Our Lives*, healing came with the love of a good woman, but without conventional certainty of monogamy.[17]

Regardless of its incorporation of the complexities of contemporary gender relations, critics took *Coming Home* to task for the same reasons as *Heroes*. One complained it was a "trite love story with a now-possible happy ending rather than a significant portrayal of the destructiveness of the Vietnam War."[18] Reviews like this pointed to the problem of striking a balance between a conventional story involving a veteran and a story that gave the veteran special agency. Artistic works like *Coming Home* walked a fine line, almost a zero-sum cultural balance, between relatability to a larger audience and delving into a range of emotions and motivations difficult for a nonveteran viewer to comprehend.

The lesser-known film *Jacknife* (1989) returned to the theme of normalcy through a relationship but with some interesting additions. A statement by Vietnam veteran David (Ed Harris), speaking about his buddy who died in the war, goes to the heart of *Jacknife*: "Bobby said we'd all find girls. And then things would make sense."[19] But any real relationship is severely limited by the barriers built by David and Megs (Robert De Niro), who served with Bobby. Much as she wants to build a relationship with Megs or her brother David, Martha (Kathy Baker) is completely shut out of the discourse. "She don't know. She wasn't there," Megs tells David at one point in the film. Martha's choice is to accept Megs and heal him while being excluded, like all the rest of the civilian world, from the root source of his pain. Martha understands this distance in much the same way as Wilma, Peggy, and Milly did in *The Best Years of Our Lives*, but without the certainty of his commitment. The audience never finds out if the relationship between Megs and Martha is sanctioned by marriage.

Not all healing came from personal nurturing. In *Born on the Fourth of July* (1989), Tom Cruise's Ron Kovic finds his family sympathetic but unable to comprehend the impact of the wounds that made him a paraplegic. In his one interaction with a fellow Marine with World War II service, Kovic expects empathy but is rebuffed and criticized by a combat veteran who saw suffering on a scale that dwarfed his own. Oliver Stone used several such failed encounters to illustrate the gaps that prevailed throughout the United States during the Vietnam War and drove apart the country.[20]

Not surprisingly in a film directed by Oliver Stone, vindication comes in the form of politics. *Born on the Fourth of July* introduced overt political topics where most films about the veteran's experience avoided them. In this context, the source of Kovic's sense of loss and suffering is not the war but the establishment responsible for thrusting him into a pointless cause. Consequently, although most of Kovic's attempts at reconstructing his life through personal interactions fail, his ultimate vindication, and presumably his healing, begins when he is a featured speaker at the 1976 Democratic National Convention.[21]

Finally, there are representations of damaged veterans returning home without any resolution whatsoever. Prevalent in films depicting the experience of African American veterans after Vietnam is the theme of war as a continuation of the same struggles experienced at home. *Dead Presidents* (1995) features a seamless segue between battlefield survival in Vietnam and the poverty, violence, and racism of the Bronx in the early seventies.[22] Spike Lee revisited the same themes in the recent *Da 5 Bloods* (2020) and did an impressive job of marking the intricate linkages of U.S. history and war for African Americans.[23] Both films mark the profound difficulties of finding peace much less survival, whether at home or at war.

THE VETERAN AS A HERO

It is comparatively easy to portray the veteran as a hero, even in recent popular culture representations. Men and women who demonstrate valor in combat are rare and celebrated by the military institution and society alike. They carry that clearly delineated status with them into civilian life. After September 11, Americans extended the same treatment to first responders and, until recently, the police.

In popular culture, the war hero is a common device. Establishing a protagonist (or antagonist) as a veteran is a useful shorthand method of exposition to establish authority and relevance. *Lethal Weapon* (1987) followed this pattern for both in its depiction of Riggs (Mel Gibson) and his nemesis "Shadow Company," led by "the General" (Mitchell Ryan). *Lethal Weapon* also provides a good illustration of how superficial a device the veteran could be. The audience knows Riggs is disturbed because of his actions but never learns of the exact source of his problem. Shadow Company is composed of stock villains such as Mr. Joshua (Gary Busey); we never learn much about its motivations beyond simple greed.

This form of the veteran as war hero proliferated on television programming in the eighties with many of the same shortfalls magnified by the major networks.[24] One of the most popular was *Magnum P.I.* (1980–88). Thomas Magnum (Tom Selleck) was, in many respects, a throwback. He was a masculine archetype, a virtuous, relatable resolver of problems.²⁵ In fact, Magnum was one of three Vietnam veterans featured in the show. His friends T.C. (Roger E. Mosley) and Rick (Larry Manetti) were also experienced combat veterans but notable for how little it affected them afterward. The characters at their core are like Magnum: earnest, honest, and successful. In practice, *Magnum P.I.* used their gravitas as an interesting counterpoint to the exotic settings of Hawaii and the wealth constantly on display.²⁶

An even more popular contemporary of *Magnum P.I.* that simplified the veteran hero even further was the NBC series *The A-Team* (1983–87). Most people who consume media through a variety of platforms today do not recall just how popular it was at the time. Among the big three networks, *The A-Team* was a giant. During the 1983–84 season, it averaged 48 million viewers every week. An important part of the show's appeal was its simplicity. As one journal noted in 1987, "It presents a constant good vs. evil dialectic: the good people are proletarian, clean-living, often transient or newcomer workers subjugated by the villains, the latter usually corrupt capitalists, ugly red-necks often using the local government, status quo, or fear to justify their actions."²⁷

Like Magnum, *The A-Team* members apply their skills as former Vietnam special forces soldiers to resolve conflict affecting the disenfranchised, almost always with spectacular (and bloodless) violence. The four members of the team are a collection of stereotypes. "Hannibal" (George Peppard) as the leader is the white patriarch. "Face" (Dirk Benedict) is the con artist and ladies' man. B. A. Baracus (Mr. T) is the team's one minority member who serves as driver and muscle. "Howling Mad" Murdock (Dwight Schultz) is a helicopter pilot who literally had to be rescued from a mental institution to rejoin his comrades. Suffering from schizophrenia, paranoia, and manic depression, he is played for comic relief with barely a mention of post-traumatic stress disorder (PTSD).²⁸

The one noticeable departure present in *The A-Team* is the nature of the enemy. The main target of their elaborate, almost Rube Goldberg–type plans is invariably the establishment. This is consistent with the internal logic of the show. As viewers were reminded week after week, the A-Team comprises fugitives from military justice, "framed for a crime they didn't commit," according to the opening narration. It is a direct encapsulation of the Vietnam War as it transfers from military authority to different forms of civilian power. Interestingly, one of the most popular depictions of veterans during the peak of the Cold War in the 1980s is essentially a story about antiheroes.

Featuring the Vietnam veteran as an antihero was not uncommon after the war. Popular culture depictions of the veteran frequently portray them as a vessel for alienation.[29] Before *The A-Team*, *Billy Jack* (1971) and *Taxi Driver* (1976) illustrated the veteran in terms of how much he was disaffected by the war and injustice at home. The veterans' remedy, which was part of their appeal, was violence. De Niro's Travis Bickle wielded a variety of handguns. As Billy Jack, Tom Laughlin uses Hapkido as his remedy in the literal good fight, co-opting the growing popularity of contemporary martial arts movies.[30] He presents an interesting paradox, protecting women, Native Americans, environmentalists, and pacifists with his fists and feet.

The more recent *Stop-Loss* (2008) depicts the same alienation without the recourse to violence. The film features a soldier, played by Ryan Phillippe, who met his military obligations in good faith and finds himself betrayed by the government.[31] As noted in Chapter Two, *Stop-Loss* tapped into public dissent building around a well-known and controversial military policy of extending soldiers beyond their military service contracts. However, where it delved into subtleties of emotional responses to conflict, it never resorted to violence or dramatic action scenes as a means to resolve that conflict. Its avoidance of these popular culture tropes partly accounts for its lack of appeal at the box office. As one critic put it, "It's the film equivalent of a weary shrug—capturing the national mood at a moment when we'd all prefer some mood enhancers."[32]

One of the best-known veteran antiheroes in the post–Vietnam era is John Rambo. Rambo is both a victim and a hero. It is interesting to see that, at the outset, *Rambo: First Blood* (1982) establishes the protagonist with counterculture credentials. His long hair and fatigue jacket mark him as a hippie or a vagrant to Will Teasel, the town sheriff. When he sees the flag on Rambo's jacket, he warns: "Wearing that flag on that jacket, you're looking for trouble around here, friend."[33]

Once it becomes apparent that Rambo is a dangerous enemy, he is framed in new terms more applicable to his standing as a veteran. In the original book, Rambo's mentor, Colonel Trautman, acknowledges the profound separation, between a trained soldier who kills for his country and the civilian society that sends him to war: "You tolerate a system that lets others do it for you. And when they come back from war, you can't stand the smell of death on them. . . . He was a vagrant, you said. What the hell else could he have been? He gave up three years to enlist in a war that was supposed to help his country, and the only trade he came out with is how to kill. Where was he supposed to get a job that needed experience like that?"[34] The theme of work appears throughout *First Blood*. When Trautman first meets Teasel, he suggests police halt their pursuit of Rambo, so that they could arrest him at his next menial job. In his final speech, Rambo contrasts all the skills in the military that were worthless in the civilian world. This approach may have struck a chord, particularly among the millions of Americans affected by the deep recession in the country when *First Blood* appeared in theaters in 1982.

Rambo: First Blood Part II (1985) adds new levels to the betrayed veteran narrative. In this instance, it tapped into an issue that captured a great deal of attention in the eighties: prisoners of war left behind by a government more interested in avoiding culpability than protecting its military veterans.[35] The villain in *Rambo: First Blood Part II* is the CIA, a pop culture utility outfielder for this particular genre of movie. The agency, backed by hired mercenaries and the best possible technology, cannot hide the truth or prevail over Rambo in the end. Stallone, interviewed when the film was released, was clear about his intent to project Rambo beyond the veterans' community into the mainstream of a viewing public suspicious of authority: "I stand for ordinary Americans, losers a lot of them. They don't understand big, international politics. Their country tells them to fight in Vietnam? They go fight."[36] Again, Stallone's timing was impeccable. Revelations about the Iran-Contra affair became public a little more than a year after the movie premiered.

Rambo III (1988), the final sequel to the original trilogy, allowed the protagonist to evolve into what amounted to a cartoonish version of a hero able to literally take on whole armies of antagonists, in this case Soviet troops in Afghanistan. Overall, the original series was extremely successful, accumulating more than $600 million at the box office. Notable was the fact that *Rambo III* earned slightly more than half of its 1985 predecessor.[37] Although it is possible that the viewing public was becoming oversaturated with rescue movies in general (e.g., *Delta Force*, 1986) or with Sylvester Stallone in particular, it is still interesting to note that the further Rambo moved from a flawed, human hero of the original, the less popular his archetype appeared to be.[38]

FINDING A WAY HOME

A subgenre of films is specifically dedicated to the journey of a veteran returning home. They are distinct from works like *Coming Home*, which use the veteran as a motivating device for traditional drama or as a means to illustrate a broader conflict. *The Messenger* (2009) is a good example. It is one of the most literal representation of this genre, following two soldiers—Staff Sergeant Will Montgomery (Ben Foster) and Captain Tony Stone (Woody Harrelson)—who make up a military detail responsible for accompanying the bodies of fallen comrades to their families.[39] *The Messenger* speaks to the idea of separation, to boundaries that exist and are created between Montgomery and Stone and the constant stream of shocked and grieving family members they meet during their travels. The veteran in this instance is an object separate from the soldiers who bring him or her back, a distance Stone wants to maintain out of a sense of professionalism and, more honestly, for the sake of his own self-preservation. Montgomery cannot keep this distance, allowing himself to begin empathizing with the subjects of his mission. Having lost friends in the war, the space between Montgomery and the families is a bridgeable gap because he can understand what their grief means.

Other works of popular culture speak directly to the impact of the veteran coming home. The 1972 Tony Award–winning play *Sticks and Bones* depicts an Army sergeant who travels the country delivering blinded and maimed veterans to their families. David, the blind veteran protagonist, comes back embittered by his experience and unable to adapt to his disability. His parents, named Ozzie and Harriet by playwright David Rabe in a nod to the popular fifties' sitcom, are equally unable to cope with David's anger and his dependency. His need pierces their superficial happiness to have their son back. In the end, Ozzie and Harriet decide to talk him into dying by suicide in their own living room.[40]

Michael Cimino's better-known *The Deer Hunter* (1978) took on the same narrative of the passage between war and home. It portrays the main characters Michael (De Niro), Steven (John Savage), and Nick (Christopher Walken) as average Americans. The opening scene is an extended look into a wedding in a Pennsylvania steel town that forms the center of their work and life.[41] The Vietnam War permanently separates them from this home. For Nick, who never comes back, choosing to remain behind to compete in endless rounds of Russian roulette, the separation is literal. But the war does follow his two friends back to Pennsylvania. Steven is disabled by his wounds. Michael carries the war inside himself and struggles to contain it. He tries and fails to save Nick but refuses to invoke his rage against his friends back home, particularly the gun-waving Stan (John Cazale). De Niro's character is a significant departure from *Taxi Driver*'s Travis Bickle, who saw the world through one violent lens. The final scene where Michael, Steven, Linda (Meryl Streep), and their assembled friends sing "God Bless America" projects ambivalence and a sense of sadness, dignity, and hope for the future.[42] Cimino captured a moment in his work. *The Deer Hunter* won five Oscars, including best picture and best supporting actor for Walken.

Since September 11, documentaries have entered into the popular culture sphere and become important vehicles for representing the veteran's experience. As Anna Froula notes in the epigraph at the chapter's beginning, these works, alongside fictionalized accounts of conflict in Iraq and Afghanistan, are important as an inscrutable war intersects with a public increasingly dependent on media rather than traditional education.[43] There are dozens of films depicting the harsh realities of America's current wars, from *Soldiers Pay* (2004) to *Gunner Palace* (2005) to the better-known *Restrepo* (2010). Documentaries on veterans are more recent but follow standard themes of the disconnect between the military and a society that has no direct investment of time or pain. In an interesting echo of *Sticks and Bones*, these films often depict a public that is superficially supportive of former service members but ultimately indifferent in practice to the struggles of veterans.

One of the best is *Hell and Back Again* (2011). It chronicles Marines deployed to fight in Afghanistan and their transition on returning to Camp Lejeune, North Carolina. The documentary's main focus is Sergeant Nathan Harris, whose story starts out very simply. He enlisted because "I wanted to be a roughneck, to spit tobacco, and kill the enemy. I was a young cowboy."[44] On his third tour, Harris suffered a serious hip wound during a firefight in Afghanistan that ended his military career at the age of twenty-six.

Hell and Back Again offers an unfiltered account of the agony accompanying Harris's shattered hip. His lengthy and painful recovery highlights not just the physical suffering that accompanies a wound but also the profound loss of purpose. "Being a grunt is over, and that is all I ever wanted to be."[45] Harris is a man without a mission. He is without the reason for being he chose when he entered the Marine Corps, and he has the rest of his life to think about it. This loss and realization are the first part of a ripple effect that flows outward to touch his young wife, Ashley, his fellow Marines, and his family. It is driven home each time Harris repeatedly and openly contemplates suicide.[46]

Too few post-9/11 documentaries feature women veterans. As the number of women deployed to serve in Iraq and Afghanistan increased, popular culture struggled to keep up with this phenomenon. In the meantime, women remained in the same roles as they had during *The Best Years of Our Lives*: as spouses, girlfriends, and family members who anxiously orbit around their veterans.

Documentaries on women warriors offer one alternative to this artistic sequestration. They illustrate that women, whether fighting on active duty or coping with its aftermath as veterans, bear the burden of the responsibilities incurred by war, along with the costs, without the subsequent safety net awaiting men. The stated purpose of the documentary *Lioness* (2008) was "retrieving these women from the Pentagon memory hole."[47]

Codirected by Meg McLagan and Daria Sommers, the film follows five protagonists as it depicts the substantial pitfalls evident in a military culture that did not take women's contributions in combat seriously and the lack of recognition that shaped their homecomings. One of the five, Shannon Morgan, returns home to Arkansas reliant on her adoptive grandparents' and her own personal strength to work through PTSD caused by the war. She compliments the VA for its efforts, describing them as "phenomenal" in one interview, but noted the lack of female counselors: "I've had several encounters with male therapists where it just actually can't work."[48]

Lioness illustrates bridgeable and unbridgeable gaps faced by women veterans. Shannon Morgan finds solace in her family when coping with PTSD. Her uncle, a Vietnam veteran and inspiration for enlisting, became a particularly important source of advice and support. Yet, even including the VA, her circle of support is limited by institutional inertia and cultural disconnects—official and otherwise—regarding women in combat. Further, as Susan L. Carruthers commented in 2008, when women return to civilian life, the expectation follows that they will be nurturers and caregivers not to themselves but to their spouses, children, and families.[49] This is the case with Morgan, who is linked to her elderly grandparents by ties of love and reciprocity. In the final analysis, women veterans are separated from their peers in that they have greater responsibilities awaiting them without the concurrent institutional, social, or cultural resources. They are neither the women who would transform their men in *The Best Years of Our Lives* nor like men in almost any other popular culture representation of the veteran expecting help on their way home.

CONCLUSIONS

Vietnam is a constantly present touchstone in popular culture approaches to the veteran. Vietnam establishes a baseline for the whole spectrum of the veteran's experience, from the trials invoked by the horror of war to the qualities of individual perseverance that allow the veteran to build a life afterward. Vietnam is a yardstick for institutional failures to win the war or mediate the peace. This war provides context for the home front and the people who awaited the veteran when they came back.

In many respects, Vietnam serves as a mediator in the veteran's story, being a dynamic participant in popular culture representations of the topic. Colonel Trautman serves that purpose in *Rambo*. The same is true of Shannon Morgan's uncle in *Lioness*. A recent example of this narrative may be found in *Last Flag Flying* (2017), in which three Vietnam veterans reunite to bring the body of one of their sons, killed in Iraq, home.

Their journey is an opportunity to offer perspective on old and current conflicts. A common criticism of *Last Flag Flying* was its tendency to sidetrack this story with a more conventional fish-out-of-water trope regarding the cultural struggles of old men in the twenty-first century.[50]

Popular culture treatments of veterans are not immune to oversimplification. The figure of the veteran presents a tempting vehicle for epic revenge fantasy, overpowered superheroes (e.g., Chuck Norris), conventional romance, or screwball comedy. What reinforces this temptation is marketability. Franchises built around some of these characteristics have earned hundreds of millions of dollars and continue to do so.

However, directors like William Wyler, Michael Cimino, Clint Eastwood, and others have demonstrated that complexity is possible. They have reached into the depths of the veteran's experience to find unique elements of the veteran's pathos. There are some risks to this approach. The further artists pursue authenticity, the more they risk moving away from an audience less and less directly vested in the subject. When David Chase created the miniseries *Generation Kill* (2008) it was a rare point of pride that he valued an accurate depiction of military culture regardless of whether the characters were relatable.[51] That approach is hard to find in today's popular culture milieu.

The nature of contemporary veterans and their wars presents a number of challenges in the popular culture realm. *Lioness* demonstrates that the fundamental nature of combatants has moved far beyond existing convention and that art needs to catch up. Whether audiences are ready is a difficult question. In the wake of September 11, the public seemed more vested in fantasy—beginning with the *Lord of the Rings* trilogy and finishing with the Marvel Universe—than the hard realities associated with war. In contrast, very few recent movies about veterans did well at the box office. As Anna Froula points out, the lack of success does not diminish the importance of popular culture to future discourse about veterans.

CONCLUSIONS

> When the war is over, you pick up your gear, walk down the hill and back into the world, where people smile, congratulate you and secretly hope you won't be a burden on society now that you've done the dirty work they shun.
> —*Iraq veteran John Crawford*

INFLECTION POINTS

Throughout this book, I have addressed a series of inflection points between the military and civilian worlds and within the military itself. The former begins with the basic historical fact that military service has never been a holistic American experience. The motives for joining—in peace and in war—are as diverse as the reasons for not becoming part of the military. Patriotism balances against self-preservation. A family tradition of service moves against the hard logic of family obligations to spouses and children. A modern reality, particularly since World War II, is that most civilians never put on the uniform.

In American history, conscription has never resulted in universal service. The Civil War practice of paying bounties and hiring substitutes was replaced by an evolving post-1945 system of deferments. Men with critical skills, educational pursuits, conscientious objection, and host of other factors that encompassed millions of citizens were freed from the risks associated with military service. Interestingly, despite their universal integration into all facets of the military and growing numbers, women remain exempt from the draft today.[1]

The all-volunteer military deliberately reset the public discourse regarding participation in the military. After 1973, the government officially surrendered this particular authority over its citizens, who now set the parameters of individual selective service. The result was a force structure clearly more diverse in terms of race and gender but much more distant from mainstream society, which for years looked askance at anything associated with the Vietnam War. From that initial post-Vietnam separation, a new military subculture was born.

For those who did volunteer, their military experience was anything but monolithic, and each person had their own inflection points. Various factors shape veterans that begin with their first steps into the military:

their branch, unit, and occupational specialties, which lean heavily in the direction of logistics rather than combat. Each incarnation of the contemporary defense establishment adds more and more logistical layers to an increasingly complex military organism.

One more recent (2014) creation, the Army Cyber Branch, professes to be a hybrid of high-tech logistics and combat. Officially, it is "a maneuver branch with the mission to conduct defensive and offensive cyberspace operations (DCO and OCO). Cyber is the only branch designed to directly engage threats within the cyberspace domain."[2] Placed in contrast to recent bitter contests in places like Fallujah or the Korengal Valley, it is amazing how much the basic definition of combat has changed in such a short time.

Yet there is nothing new about these periodic military culture shocks. World War II veterans marveled at the new aspects of "push-button war" in the early fifties. An August 1953 *New York Times* article written by George Barrett described the typical soldier returning from Korea in these terms: "Raised as sixth-graders to family tales of the mechanized fighting of World War II, mechanically conditioned then and later to the push-button concept of living and the cosmic-ray concept of fighting, sent very young with other very young soldiers to a country they had never heard about to fight a war they did not understand, the new veterans are disquieting, machine-like products of their special time, and products particularly of the impersonalized low-pressure but deadly war that they have been waging."[3]

Veterans and policymakers regularly debate the value assigned to the military combat experience. At the root of legislative battles between figures like Olin Teague and Ralph Yarborough, who were attempting to grant a literal dollar value to military service through a new GI Bill, was a fundamental disagreement over how to interpret divergent types of combat experiences in World War II and the Cold War conflicts that followed. Military women have inherited a well-worn discourse that now struggles to reflect both gender and the complexities of contemporary counterinsurgency operations.

It is important to remember that these examples pertain to a narrative largely occurring *between* veterans. The inflection point is even more pronounced when it considers the diverse veterans' community and the vast majority of civilians who have, according to one author, a "reverent but disengaged attitude toward the military."[4] Often, as is the case with academic programs in American universities, it is a discussion that tries to be well informed and has good intentions but fails to establish a workable rapport between veterans and their civilian counterparts.

There are points where the results of misunderstandings are relatively benign. For a regular civilian consumer, the term "military grade" is a hallmark of quality. For a veteran, it is a fairly common joke, part of a soldier's cynical banter about something produced by the lowest bidder.

Other disconnects cut more deeply. The growth of educational support for veterans is a positive trend. But new entrants to higher academe sometimes need help navigating the thicket of campus policies and culture that are alien to many veterans. The same is true for individuals suffering from traumatic brain injury, military sexual trauma, and post-traumatic stress disorder. They need help adapting to the intellectual rigors of college, and although most can access treatment through Veterans Affairs (VA), they still need assistance bridging the many smaller gaps that appear on the way to matriculation. And not every veteran has a disability. Unfortunately, too many well-intentioned staff, faculty, and even students assume a protective role in an effort to mitigate the effects of military experience. In many cases, this approach is timely and useful. However, for more than a few veterans, it reeks of misinformed condescension, driving a wedge more deeply between themselves and the outside world.

FINAL DEPARTURES?

A point exists in the veteran's experience where compromise might be impossible. Many men and women realize that there are no ways to close the unbridgeable gaps between their experience and an outsider's. In his book *Fields of Fire*, James Webb perfectly captures this understanding: "Fuck 'em. Just fuck 'em. Fuck everybody who doesn't come out here and do this."[5] What is interesting and often overlooked by authors citing the passage is that Lieutenant Hodges, Webb's fictional proxy in the novel, is actually referring to other Marines in Vietnam.

Webb's characterization again speaks to the gradations between military combatants dictated by proximity to the enemy, but a larger significance is at work. At certain points in their experience, a number of veterans, like Lieutenant Hodges, make a conscious decision to embrace their separateness at the exclusion of "everybody who doesn't come out here and do this." However, rather than passively wait to be defined by an ignorant mass of civilian interlopers, many veterans engage in a deliberate process of subjectification so as to deliberately segregate their own identities.[6]

To what end? A 2010 issue of the *Journal of Higher Education* defined this effort as "identity renegotiation," where veterans essentially reconstruct themselves to cope with an existence that is neither purely military nor civilian. In effect, what they do is a compromise, not a rejection. One veteran noted: "Normalcy would be a return to a prior condition. This is impossible. Once you've been affected by a life-altering experience such as deployment, it is impossible and counter-productive to make an attempt at 'normalcy.'"[7] In this context, veterans want to be part of the civilian world without accumulating positive or negative stereotypes. They take charge of their identities to move forward with their own lives on their own terms.

Other motives are more crass. Perhaps one of the best examples is Mat Best, a veteran who has very shrewdly crafted a public identity designed to support a variety of marketing platforms. Best, and a cohort of others just like him, have carefully constructed their public personas, combining humor, machismo, patriotism, and approachability, largely for the sake of profit. As a result, the world is oversaturated with former Navy SEALs hawking everything from home security to motivational speaking. Veterans rightly rail against stolen valor, but the wide-scale practice of commodifying military service has become another way to cheapen it. Subjectification can also mean self-exploitation.

A better, more productive example of "identity renegotiation" may be the latest generation of veterans' nonprofits. Organizations like the Student Veterans of America (SVA) and the Servicewomen's Action Network (SWAN) are the natural successors to the American Veterans Committee or the Vietnam Veterans of America. They are intent on moving past the gatekeepers of the status quo—such as the American Legion, the Veterans of Foreign Wars, and the VA—to define the boundaries of both their unique needs and potential solutions. Organizations like SWAN represent the significantly growing diversity within the veterans' community and the desire to transcend decades of faulty official policy and public inattention that has repeatedly failed new constituencies of women, students, and minorities. Veteran members of these nonprofits are idealists who also understand the pragmatic value of training, education, and integrated networking and are willing to leverage their status to win corporate sponsorship and funding as well as recognition of their service through market affiliations.

New veterans' nonprofits are good examples of the historical topic "splitting" along lines considered throughout this book. Their point of origin illustrates the increasing inclusion of race, gender, education, and class apparent within the veterans' community since Vietnam.[8] In 2014, 22.6 percent of veterans were from minority groups. By 2040, minorities are projected to comprise one-third of veterans. The fact that nonprofits exist as advocates also highlights the profound gaps and lack of continuity evident in official institutions charged with the care and reassimilation of veterans. The same is true of the distances present between civil society and these separate subgroups of veterans. As much as the average person wants to understand and support contemporary veterans, they are hamstrung by a lack of basic experience and cognizance. There are fault lines to be found everywhere in this narrative.

If there is one quality that unites veterans today, it is their realization that identity renegotiation can take the form of self-advocacy. There is no single process in this effort. Advocacy might pursue disability benefits stemming from a particular war or facilities for the care and treatment of women veterans. It may involve more transparency about legitimate educational opportunities or a consistent understanding of what constitutes transfer credits from military training. It may manifest in simple interpersonal relations.

Whether there will be a point in time that will see a new confluence of veteran, public, and official institutional interests remains to be seen. Our current wars are in the process of winding down. Military deployments at the time of this writing are a fraction of what they were during the respective "surges" in Iraq and Afghanistan. Although U.S. Defense Department spending is a formidable part of the federal budget, overall numbers of personnel are declining.[9] The possibility exists that an appropriate degree of self-awareness for all parties may result in a relationship defined by quality instead of quantity. Time and a constant exercise of informed good faith will tell.

NOTES

INTRODUCTION

1. Peter D. Feaver and Richard H. Kohn, "The Gap: Soldiers, Civilians, and Their Mutual Misunderstanding," *National Interest* 61 (Fall 2000): 33.
2. For an excellent, more recent history, see Guy de la Bédoyère, *Praetorian: The Rise and Fall of Rome's Imperial Bodyguard* (New Haven, CT: Yale University Press, 2017), 30–56.
3. Colin S. Gray, "The American Way of War: Critique and Implications," in *Rethinking the Principles of War*, ed. Anthony D. McIvor (Annapolis, MD: Naval Institute Press, 2005), 18–20.
4. Phillip Carter, "What America Owes Its Veterans: A Better System of Care and Support," *Foreign Affairs* 96 (September/October 2017): 115–27.
5. Kathryn H. Anderson and Jean M. Mitchell, "Effects of Military Experience on Mental Health Problems and Work Behavior," *Medical Care* 30 (June 1992): 556.
6. The number of women who were veterans was small in the years immediately after Vietnam. In 1976, 5.5 percent of veterans were female. See Department of Defense, Office of the Assistant Secretary of Defense (Manpower, Reserve Affairs, and Logistics), *America's Volunteers: A Report on the All-Volunteer Armed Forces* (Washington, DC: Department of Defense, December 31, 1978), 70.
7. Bruce Drake, "On Memorial Day, Public Pride in Veterans, but at a Distance," *Pew Research Center*, May 24, 2013, https://www.pewresearch.org/fact-tank/2013/05/24/on-memorial-day-public-pride-in-veterans-but-at-a-distance-2/.
8. Gallup, "Confidence in Institutions," https://news.gallup.com/poll/1597/confidence-institutions.aspx.
9. Morris Janowitz, "The All-Volunteer Military as a 'Sociopolitical' Problem," *Social Problems* 22 (February 1975): 432; Sebastian Junger, *Tribe: On Homecoming and Belonging* (New York: Twelve, 2016).
10. John Lewis Gaddis, *Strategies of Containment: A Critical Appraisal of Postwar American National Security Policy* (New York: Oxford University Press, 1982), vii. The terms originally come from Jack H. Hexter, *On Historians* (Cambridge, MA: Harvard University Press, 1979), 241–43.
11. See Russell F. Weigley, *The American Way of War: A History of United States Military Strategy and Policy* (New York: Macmillan, 1973).

CHAPTER ONE:
A BRIEF HISTORY OF THE AMERICAN VETERAN TO THE VIETNAM WAR

1. Allan R. Millett and Peter Maslowski, *For the Common Defense: A Military History of the United States of America* (New York: Free Press, 1994), 1–13.
2. Peter Karsten, "The US Citizen-Soldier's Past, Present, and Likely Future," *Parameters* 31 (Summer 2001): 62.
3. The classic work remains Russell F. Weigley, *The American Way of War: A History of United States Military Strategy and Policy* (New York: Macmillan, 1973).
4. See Eleanor L. Hannah, *Manhood, Citizenship, and the National Guard, 1870–1917* (Columbus: Ohio State University Press, 2007).

5. George B. Tindall and David E. Shi, *America: A Narrative History*, 5th ed. (New York: W. W. Norton, 2000), 313.
6. William S. McFeeley, *Grant: A Biography* (New York: W. W. Norton, 1982), 276–77.
7. Edmund Morris, *The Rise of Theodore Roosevelt* (New York: Ballantine Books, 1979), 662–87.
8. William H. Glasson, *History of Military Pension Legislation in the United States* (New York: Columbia University Press, 1900), 12–19.
9. Glasson, *Military Pension Legislation*, 17.
10. Glasson, 42.
11. Glasson, 73–76, 78, 90, 104; William H. Glasson, *Federal Military Pensions in the United States* (New York: Oxford University Press, 1918), 123–30.
12. Patrick J. Kelly, *Creating a National Home: Building the Veterans' Welfare State, 1860–1900* (Cambridge, MA: Harvard University Press, 1997), 55–57.
13. Zachary R. New, "Ending Citizenship for Service in the Forever War," *Yale Law Journal* 129 (February 11, 2020), https://www.yalelawjournal.org/forum/ending-citizenship-for-service-in-the-forever-wars; see also the excellent work by Nancy Gentile Ford, *Americans All! Foreign-Born Soldiers in World War I* (College Station: Texas A&M University Press, 2001).
14. Aline Barros, "US Court Clears Path for Fast-Track Citizenship for Foreign-Born Military Service Members," *Voice of America*, September 3, 2020, https://www.voanews.com/usa/immigration/us-court-clears-path-fast-track-citizenship-foreign-born-military-service-members.
15. Millett and Maslowski, *For the Common Defense*, 681.
16. David M. Kennedy, *Over Here: The First World War and American Society* (New York: Oxford University Press, 1980), 45–92.
17. William P. Dillingham, *Federal Aid to Veterans, 1917–1941* (Gainesville: University of Florida Press, 1952), 54, 58–59.
18. J. M. Stephen Peeps, "A B.A. for the GI . . . Why?" *History of Education Quarterly* 24 (Winter 1984): 513–25.
19. Dillingham, *Federal Aid to Veterans*, 14–15.
20. Dillingham, 131–32, 141, 224. Congress awarded veterans certificates of $1,000 in 1924. Although redeemable in 1945, veterans wanted earlier payment because of the Great Depression.
21. Willard Waller, *The Veteran Comes Back* (New York: Dryden, 1944).
22. Omar N. Bradley, *Collected Writings: Articles, Broadcasts, and Statements, 1945–1967*, vol. 3 (Washington, DC: Government Printing Office, 1967), 217.
23. Michael D. Gambone, *The Greatest Generation Comes Home: The Veteran in American Society* (College Station: Texas A&M University Press, 2005), 34–35.
24. Gambone, *Greatest Generation Comes Home*, 83.
25. David P. Smole and Shannon S. Loane, *A Brief History of Veterans' Education Benefits and Their Value*, RL34549 (Washington, DC: Congressional Research Service, June 25, 2008), 3.
26. See Mark Boulton, *Failing Our Veterans: The G.I. Bill and the Vietnam Generation* (New York: New York University Press, 2014).
27. Bill Mauldin, *Back Home* (New York: Bantam, 1948), 68, 72–73.
28. Peter D. Hoefer, "A David against Goliath: The American Veterans Committee's Challenge to the American Legion in the 50s" (PhD diss., University of Maryland, 2010), 13, 29, 73, 76, 111. The AVC's membership rose to about one hundred thousand by 1947 and plummeted to approximately thirty-five thousand only three years later, where it remained for the rest of the fifties. In contrast, the American Legion had 2.8 million members in 1956. The Veterans of Foreign Wars could count 1.6 million members in 1955.

29. "Veterans Protest College Fees," *New York Times*, December 3, 1945, 19; "37 Hurt, 13 Seized in Coast Movie Riot," *New York Times*, October 2, 1946, 3.
30. Wendy Plotkin, "'Hemmed In': The Struggle against Racial Restrictive Covenants and Deed Restrictions in Post–World War II Chicago," *Journal of the Illinois State Historical Society* 94 (Spring 2001): 67; Robert L. Tyler, "The American Veterans Committee: Out of a Hot War and into the Cold," *American Quarterly* 18 (Autumn 1966): 422.
31. Lance Hill, *The Deacons for Defense: Armed Resistance and the Civil Rights Movement* (Chapel Hill: University of North Carolina Press, 2004), 26, 42.
32. Art Goldberg, "Vietnam Vets: The Anti-War Army," *Ramparts* 10 (July 1971): 12–14; see also Vietnam Veterans Against the War, *The Winter Soldier Investigation: An Inquiry into American War Crimes* (Boston: Beacon Press, 1972).
33. Jerry Lembcke, *The Spitting Image: Myth, Memory, and the Legacy of Vietnam* (New York: New York University Press, 1998), 49–51.
34. Memo, Special Agent in Charge (Albany) to Director (FBI), "Counterintelligence Program, Black Nationalist—Hate Groups, Internal Security," August 25, 1967, 3, 100-HQ-448006-01, and Memo, Special Agent in Charge (Chicago) to the Director (FBI), "Counterintelligence Program, Black Nationalist–Hate Groups, Racial Intelligence," October 29, 1968, 179, 100-HQ-448006-02, https://archive.org/details/FBI-COINTELPRO-BLACK.
35. Memo, Special Agent in Charge (SAC), New York, to Director, FBI, "Winter Soldier Investigation," November 24, 1970, https://archive.org. See also *Hearings before the Select Committee to Study Governmental Operations with Respect to Intelligence Activities of the United States Senate*, 94th Cong., 1st sess., vol. 6 (Washington, DC: Government Printing Office, 1976).
36. Stephen E. Ambrose, *Nixon: The Triumph of a Politician, 1962–1972*, vol. 2 (New York: Simon & Schuster, 1989), 265.

CHAPTER TWO: JOINING UP

1. David H. Hackworth, *About Face: The Odyssey of an American Warrior* (New York: Simon & Schuster, 1989), 32.
2. E. B. Sledge, *With the Old Breed: At Peleliu and Okinawa* (New York: Presidio Press, 1981), 5.
3. Ironically, John Wayne was exempted from World War II service. He was classified 3-A, which was a hardship deferment for an individual with family obligations.
4. Anthony Swofford, "First Chapter: 'Jarhead,'" *New York Times*, March 2, 2003, https://www.nytimes.com/2003/03/02/books/chapters/jarhead.html.
5. Paul Fussell, *Wartime: Understanding and Behavior in the Second World War* (New York: Oxford University Press, 1989), 132–35.
6. Phil Klay, *Redeployment* (New York: Penguin Press, 2014), 119.
7. Richard M. Nixon, The All-Volunteer Armed Force: A Radio Address by the Republican Presidential Nominee, Washington, DC: Republican National Committee, October 17, 1968, Speech File (PPS 208), box 97, Richard Nixon Presidential Library and Museum, Yorba Linda, CA.
8. Stephen E. Ambrose, *Nixon: The Triumph of a Politician, 1962–1972* (New York: Simon & Schuster, 1989), 124–25; Tanya Harmer, *Allende's Chile and the Inter-American Cold War* (Chapel Hill: University of North Carolina Press, 2011), 41.
9. Louis G. Yuengert, "America's All-Volunteer Force: A Success?," *Parameters* 45 (Winter 2015–16): 54.
10. Beth Bailey, "Soldiering as Work: The All-Volunteer Force in the United States," in *Fighting for a Living: A Comparative History of Military Labour, 1500–2000*, ed. Erik-Jan Zürcher (Amsterdam: Amsterdam University Press, 2013), 586–87.

11. Thomas W. Evans, "The All-Volunteer Army after Twenty Years: Recruiting in the Modern Era," *Army History* 27 (Summer 1993): 40–41.
12. Bailey, "Soldiering as Work," 587.
13. Bailey, 588.
14. G. Kurt Piehler, ed., *Encyclopedia of Military Science* (Los Angeles: SAGE Reference, 2013), 12.
15. Courtney Mabeus, "Inside Big Navy's War on Beards," *Navy Times*, October 13, 2019, https://www.navytimes.com/news/your-navy/2019/10/14/inside-big-navys-war-on-beards/.
16. Tom Evans, "All We Could Be: How an Advertising Campaign Helped Remake the Army," *On Point* 12 (Summer 2006): 13.
17. Between 1940 and 1971, the number of military "dependents" increased from only sixty-seven thousand to five hundred thousand. See E. James Lieberman, "American Families and the Vietnam War," *Journal of Marriage and Family* 33 (November 1971): 712.
18. Bailey, "Soldiering as Work," 589.
19. William Schneider, "Personnel Recruitment and Retention: Problems and Prospects for the United States," *Annals of the Academy of Political and Social Science* 457 (September 1981): 165.
20. Herbert R. Northrup, Steven M. DiAntonio, John A. Brinker, and Dale F. Daniel, *Black and Other Minority Participation in the All-Volunteer Navy and Marine Corps* (Philadelphia: University of Pennsylvania Press, 1979), 46–47.
21. Bailey, "Soldiering as Work," 594.
22. Current data on race is more comprehensive. According to a 2018 report, 43 percent of male enlisted personnel and 56 percent of female enlisted personnel were a racial minority. See George M. Reynolds and Amanda Shendruk, "Demographics of the U.S. Military," *Council on Foreign Relations*, April 24, 2018, https://www.cfr.org/article/demographics-us-military.
23. Morris Janowitz, "The All-Volunteer Military as a 'Sociopolitical' Problem," *Social Problems* 22 (February 1975): 447.
24. Kristy N. Kamarck, *Women in Combat: Issues for Congress*, R42075 (Washington, DC: Congressional Research Service, December 13, 2016), 2. The same law limited women to 10 percent of the officer corps.
25. Nancy Goldman, "The Changing Role of Women in the Armed Forces," *American Journal of Sociology* 78 (January 1973): 892.
26. Bailey, "Soldiering as Work," 595.
27. Robert L. Nichols, Alfred R. Saeger Jr., Hans S. Driessnack, LeRoy House, and Richard G. Reid, "The Officer Corps in an All-Volunteer Force: Will College Men Serve?," *Naval War College Review* 23 (January 1971): 34.
28. Nichols et al., "Officer Corps," 37. There were approximately ninety thousand cadets enrolled in ROTC basic courses in 1961.
29. Colin L. Powell, *My American Journey* (New York: Ballantine Books, 1995), 182; Janowitz, "All-Volunteer Military," 437.
30. Janowitz, "All-Volunteer Military," 445.
31. Constance Holden, "Doubts Mounting about All-Volunteer Force," *Science* 209 (September 5, 1980): 1095.
32. Holden, "Doubts Mounting," 1095; James F. Dunnigan and Raymond M. Macedonia, *Getting It Right: American Military Reforms after Vietnam to the Persian Gulf and Beyond* (New York: William Morrow, 1993), 146.
33. Holden, "Doubts Mounting," 1096, 1099.
34. Timothy W. Cooke and Aline O. Quester, "What Characterizes Successful Enlistees in the All-Volunteer Force: A Study of Male Recruits in the U.S. Navy," *Social Science Quarterly* 73 (June 1992): 241.

35. Cooke and Quester, "Successful Enlistees," 241.
36. Cooke and Quester, 241.
37. Richard Halloran, "Army Rates Six of Ten Divisions Unready to Fight," *New York Times*, September 9, 1980, A17.
38. Michael A. Urquhart and Marillyn A. Hewson, "Unemployment Continued to Rise in 1982 and Recession Deepened," *Monthly Labor Review* 106 (February 1983): 3; HSH Associates, Prime Rate, 1980–1989, https://www.hsh.com/indices/prime80s.html.
39. Andrew Feickert and Stephen Daggett, *A Historical Perspective on "Hollow Forces,"* R42334 (Washington, DC: Congressional Research Service, February 9, 2012), 4. An E-4 holds the rank of corporal or specialist.
40. James L. Lacy, "Whither the All-Volunteer Force?," *Yale Law and Policy Review* 5 (Fall–Winter 1986): 47–48.
41. Public Law 94-502 created the Veterans Educational Assistance Program in 1976. It offered federal matching funds for payroll deductions up to $2,700 during a term of service. The program lapsed in 1985. See Cassandria Dortch, *G.I. Bills Enacted Prior to 2008 and Related Veterans' Educational Assistance Programs: A Primer*, R42785 (Washington, DC: Congressional Research Service, October 6, 2017), 24–26.
42. "House Panel Narrowly Votes a Limited G.I. Education Bill," *New York Times*, April 29, 1982, B11.
43. Richard Halloran, "G.I. Bill, Once a Reward, Is Now a Lure," *New York Times*, December 5, 1986, A32.
44. Jacob V. Lamar, "The Pentagon Goes Hollywood: Filmmakers and the Military Enjoy a Profitable Partnership," *Time*, November 24, 1986, 30–31.
45. David Sirota, "25 Years Later, How Top Gun Made America Love War," *Washington Post*, August 26, 2011, https://www.washingtonpost.com/opinions/25-years-later-remembering-how-top-gun-changed-americas-feelings-about-war/2011/08/15/gIQAU6qJgJ_story.html.
46. Mark Evje, "'Top Gun' Boosting Service Sign-Ups," *Los Angeles Times*, July 5, 1986, https://www.latimes.com/archives/la-xpm-1986-07-05-ca-20403-story.html.
47. Lacy, "Whither the All-Volunteer Force?," 46.
48. Lawrence Kapp, *Recruiting and Retention in the Active Component Military: Are There Problems?*, RL31297 (Washington, DC: Congressional Research Service, February 25, 2002), 19–22.
49. John W. Ellwood, "The Politics of the Enactment and Implementation of Gramm-Rudman-Hollings: Why Congress Cannot Address the Deficit Dilemma," *Harvard Journal on Legislation* 25 (Summer 1988): 553–76.
50. Feickert and Daggett, *Historical Perspective on "Hollow Forces,"* 9.
51. Feickert and Daggett, 10.
52. Alan R. Millett, Peter Maslowski, and William B. Feis, *For the Common Defense: A Military History of the United States from 1607 to 2012* (New York: Free Press, 2012), 684.
53. James A. Knowles, Greg H. Parlier, Gregory C. Hoscheit, Rick Ayer, Kevin Lyman, and Robert Fancher, "Reinventing Army Recruiting," *Interfaces* 32 (January–February 2002): 78–92.
54. James T. Patterson, *Restless Giant: The United States from Watergate to Bush v. Gore* (New York: Oxford University Press, 2005), 350.
55. M. Thomas Davis, "Operation Dire Straits: Here's Why the Military Is Failing to Attract the Right Recruits," *Washington Post*, January 16, 2000, B1.
56. Peter D. Feaver and Richard H. Kohn, "The Gap: Soldiers, Civilians, and Their Mutual Misunderstanding," *National Interest*, Fall 2000, 29–37.

57. Feaver and Kohn, "The Gap," 33; Don M. Snider, "America's Postmodern Military," *World Policy Journal* 17 (Spring 2000): 47.
58. Kapp, *Recruiting and Retention*, 17, 7.
59. David R. Segal, Jerald G. Bachman, Peter Freedman-Doan, and Patrick M. O'Malley, "Propensity to Serve in the U.S. Military: Temporal Trends and Subgroup Differences," *Armed Forces & Society* 25 (Spring 1999): 419–20.
60. Kapp, *Recruiting and Retention*, 10; Feickert and Daggett, *Historical Perspective on "Hollow Forces,"* 3.
61. Kapp, *Recruiting and Retention*, 2–5.
62. RAND, *Research Brief: The Evolution of the All-Volunteer Force*, RB 9195-RC (Santa Monica, CA: RAND, 2006), 2.
63. Christopher J. Coyne, Abigail R. Hall, Patrick A. McLaughlin, and Ann Zerkle, "A Hidden Cost of War: The Impact of Mobilizing Reserve Troops on Emergency Response Times," *Public Choice* 161 (December 2014): 289–90.
64. Congressional Budget Office, *Recruiting, Retention, and Future Levels of Military Personnel*, Pub. No. 2777 (Washington, DC: CBO, October 2006), 1.
65. Congressional Budget Office, *Contractors' Support of U.S. Operations in Iraq*, Pub No. 3053 (Washington, DC: CBO, August 2008), 8–11. There were 190,000 contractors of all types as opposed to 160,000 U.S. military forces in 2007.
66. Lawrence J. Korb and Sean E. Duggan, "An All-Volunteer Army? Recruitment and Its Problems," *PS: Political Science and Problems* 40 (July 2007): 468–69. By 2009, the number had declined to twelve thousand personnel. See Charles A. Henning, *U.S. Military Stop Loss Program: Key Questions and Answers*, R40121 (Washington, DC: Congressional Research Service, July 10, 2009), 1.
67. Lawrence J. Korb, "Fixing the Mix: How to Update the Army's Reserves," *Foreign Affairs* 83 (March–April 2004): 5.
68. For an excellent study, see Adam J. Berinsky, *In Time of War: Understanding American Public Opinion from World War II to Iraq* (Chicago: University of Chicago Press, 2009).
69. Richard Fry, "Millennials Overtake Baby Boomers as America's Largest Generation," *Pew Research Center*, April 28, 2020, https://www.pewresearch.org/fact-tank/2020/04/28/millennials-overtake-baby-boomers-as-americas-largest-generation/.
70. Congressional Budget Office, *Future Levels of Military Personnel*, 25–26.
71. Congressional Budget Office, xii–xiii.
72. Department of Defense, Defense Manpower Data Center, *Historical Reports: FY 1994–2012*, https://www.dmdc.osd.mil/appj/dwp/dwp_reports.jsp.
73. See https://www.americasarmy.com. Versions of the game are still available and in use today.
74. Congressional Budget Office, *Future Levels of Military Personnel*, 8.
75. Congressional Budget Office, 6
76. Tim Kane, *Who Are the Recruits? The Demographic Characteristics of U.S. Military Enlistments, 2003–2005* (Washington, DC: Heritage Foundation, 2006), 5–6. The rate increased from 0.53 percent of 2003 enlistees to 2.15 percent of enlistees in 2005.
77. Korb and Duggan, "An All-Volunteer Army?," 468.
78. Lawrence Kapp, *Recruiting and Retention: An Overview of FY2013 and FY2014 Results for Active and Reserve Component Enlisted Personnel*, RL32965 (Washington, DC: Congressional Research Service, June 26, 2015), 4; Korb and Duggan, "An All-Volunteer Army?," 468–69; Shawn Snow, "Top Marine Says Most Marine Recruits Require a Drug Waiver: But Does the Marine Corps Have a Drug Problem?," *Marine Corps Times*, July 18, 2019, https://www.marinecorpstimes.com/news/your-marine-corps/2019/07/18/top-marine-says

79. -most-marine-recruits-require-a-drug-waiver-but-does-the-marine-corps-have-a-drug-problem/; General David H. Berger, *Commandant's Planning Guidance: 38th Commandant of the Marine Corps* (Quantico, VA: USMC, 2019), 21.
79. Justin Rohrlich, "How the Army Recruits Straight Out of Prisons," *Daily Beast*, April 23, 2018, https://www.thedailybeast.com/how-the-army-recruits-straight-out-of-prisons; Gustav Eyler, "Gangs in the Military," *Yale Law Journal* 118 (January 2009): 696–742.
80. Bryan Bender, "Almost 12% of U.S. Army Recruits Required Waivers for Criminal Records," *New York Times*, July 13, 2007, https://www.nytimes.com/2007/07/13/world/americas/13iht-13recruits.6652316.html.
81. Eyler, "Gangs in the Military," 696–742.
82. Christopher J. McMahon and Colin J. Bernard, "Storm Clouds on the Horizon," *Naval War College Review* 72 (Summer 2019): 90. The National Center for Education Statistics reported a 2014–15 public high school graduation rate of 83 percent.
83. Glen H. Elder Jr., Lin Wang, Naomi J. Spence, Daniel E. Adkins, and Tyson H. Brown, "Pathways to the All-Volunteer Military," *Social Science Quarterly* 91 (June 2010): 458–59, 467.
84. Meghann Myers, "America's Obesity Is Threatening National Security, According to This Study," *Army Times*, October 10, 2018, https://www.armytimes.com/news/your-army/2018/10/10/americas-obesity-is-threatening-national-security-according-to-this-study/. Almost 8 percent of active duty service members were overweight according to height/weight standards. See also Council for a Strong America, *Unhealthy and Unprepared* (Washington, DC: Council for a Strong America, October 2018).
85. McMahon and Bernard, "Storm Clouds on the Horizon," 85.
86. The other is the so-called Generation Z (1997–2012).
87. Robert D. Putnam, *Bowling Alone: The Collapse and Revival of American Community* (New York: Simon & Schuster, 2000); Kim Parker, Nikki Graf, and Ruth Ingielnik, "Generation Z Looks a Lot Like Millennials on Key Social and Political Issues," *Pew Research Center*, January 17, 2019.
88. McMahon and Bernard, "Storm Clouds on the Horizon," 89, 92.
89. McMahon and Bernard, 93.
90. Evan Wright, *Generation Kill: Devil Dogs, Iceman, Captain America, and the New Face of American War* (New York: Berkeley Publishing Group, 2004), 24.
91. Janowitz, "All-Volunteer Military," 439.
92. Janowitz, 432; Elder et al., "Pathways to the All-Volunteer Military," 455.

CHAPTER THREE: THE NATURE OF THE BEAST

1. Russell F. Weigley, *The American Way of War: A History of United States Military Strategy and Policy* (New York: Macmillan, 1973), xx.
2. Samuel P. Huntington, *The Soldier and the State: The Theory and Politics of Civil-Military Relations* (Cambridge, MA: Belknap Press of Harvard University Press, 1957). Otherwise, the scholarship on this topic is voluminous. Some recent examples include Brian McAllister Linn, "The American Way of War," *OAH Magazine of History* 22 (October 2008): 19–23; Marc Milner, "In Search of the American Way of War: The Search for a Wider National and International Context," *Journal of American History* 93 (March 2007): 1151–53; Roger Spiller, "Military History and Its Fictions," *Journal of Military History* 70 (October 2006): 1081–97; Max Boot, "The New American Way of War," *Foreign Affairs* 82 (July–August 2003): 41–58; and Edward M. Coffman, "The Duality of the American Military Tradition: A Commentary," *Journal of Military History* 64 (October 2000): 967–80.

3. Colin S. Gray, "The American Way of War: Critique and Implications," in *Rethinking the Principles of War*, ed. Anthony D. McIvor (Annapolis, MD: Naval Institute Press, 2005), 21.
4. Victoria I. Young, Joyce Y. Brown, Theresa I. Jefferson, Cindy H. Kapinos, Kurt A. Kladivko, Patrick G. Potter, Douglas P. Schultz, *Evolution of the U.S. Army Force Structure*, vol. 1 (Bethesda, MD: United States Army Concepts Analysis Agency, 1989), ES-16. A study conducted by the Pentagon in 1955 placed the percentage of combatants at 38.8 percent. See "Enlisted Occupational Groupings for President's Commission on Veterans' Pensions," n.d., 7, U.S. President's Commission on Veterans' Pensions (Bradley Commission): Records, 1954–1958, box 59, Dwight D. Eisenhower Presidential Library and Museum, Abilene, KS.
5. Young et al., *U.S. Army Force Structure*, ES-16.
6. John J. McGrath, *The Other End of the Spear: The Tooth-to-Tail Ratio (T3R) in Modern Military Operations*, Long War Series Occasional Paper 23 (Ft. Leavenworth, KS: Combat Studies Institute Press, 2007), 53.
7. See U.S. Military MOS Database, http://www.mosdb.com.
8. John M. Broder, "Commandos Rescue Soldier; She Was Held since Ambush," *New York Times*, April 2, 2003, A1.
9. "Is Infantry a Good Career Choice?," September 13, 2019, https://www.quora.com/Is-infantry-a-good-career-choice.
10. Sezgin Ozcan, *Casualty Profile of the United States Army in Afghanistan and Iraq* (Monterrey, CA: Naval Postgraduate School, June 2012), 18.
11. Gray, "American Way of War," 29–30.
12. See Adam J. Berinsky, *In Time of War: Understanding American Public Opinion from World War II to Iraq* (Chicago: University of Chicago Press, 2009).
13. An old classic covers this idea at length. See Walter Millis, *Arms and Men: A Study in American Military History* (New York: Putnam, 1956).
14. An excellent study may be found in Antoine Bousquet, *The Eye of War: Military Perception from the Telescope to the Drone* (Minneapolis: University of Minnesota Press, 2018).
15. See Doug Atkinson, *Crusade: The Untold Story of the Persian Gulf War* (New York: Houghton Mifflin, 1993).
16. Colonel David H. Petraeus, Major Damien P. Carr, and Captain John C. Abercrombie, "Why We Need FISTs—Never Send a Man When You Can Send a Bullet," *Field Artillery* 2 (May–June 1997), 3–5.
17. Anthony H. Cordesman, *The Lessons of Afghanistan: War Fighting, Intelligence, and Force Transformation* (Washington, DC: Center for Strategic and International Studies Press, 2002), 19.
18. See Todd R. Phinney, *Airpower versus Terrorism: Three Case Studies* (Maxwell AFB, AL: Air University Press, March 2007).
19. Cordesman, *Lessons of Afghanistan*, 64.
20. See David Kilcullen, *Blood Year: The Unraveling of Western Counterterrorism* (New York: Oxford University Press, 2016).
21. An excellent study of some of the modern trends may be found in Mary Roach, *Grunt: The Curious Science of Humans at War* (New York: W. W. Norton, 2016), 18–39.
22. David H. Petraeus, "Multinational Force-Iraq Commander's Counterinsurgency Guidance," *Military Review* 88 (September–October 2008): 2.
23. Michael Hastings, *The Operators: The Wild and Terrifying Inside Story of America's War in Afghanistan* (New York: Penguin Group, 2012), 232.
24. Dale R. Herspring, *Rumsfeld's Wars: The Arrogance of American Power* (Lawrence: University Press of Kansas, 2008), 81–83.

25. T. Grady Gallant, *On Valor's Side* (New York: Avon Books, 1966), 209.
26. Sebastian Junger, *War* (New York: Twelve, 2010), 14–15.
27. Gary Riccio, Randall Sullivan, Gerald Klein, Margaret Salter, and Henry Kinnison, *Warrior Ethos: Analysis of the Concept and Initial Development of Applications*, Research Report 1827, U.S. Army Research Institute for the Behavioral and Social Sciences (Arlington, VA: U.S. Army Research Institute for Behavioral and Social Sciences, September 2004), 2.
28. The Combat Action Ribbon was created in 1969 and made retroactive to 1941.
29. See, for example, James Jones, *WWII* (New York: Ballantine Books, 1976), 61.
30. Headquarters, Department of the Army, AR 600-8-22, Personnel-General: Military Awards, March 5, 2019, 110, https://carson.armymwr.com/application/files/1015/6512/4389/Updated_MOVSM_AR_600_8_22.pdf.
31. James Clark, "Army Swears Expert Action Badge Isn't a Participation Trophy," *Task & Purpose*, May 16, 2017, https://taskandpurpose.com/news/army-defends-expert-action-badge-ncos-think-easy-earn.
32. Hope Hodge Seck, "No CAR, No Respect: The Push to End the Ribbon Rack Divide," *Marine Corps Times*, March 30, 2015, https://www.marinecorpstimes.com/news/your-marine-corps/2015/03/30/0-car-no-respect-the-push-to-end-the-ribbon-rack-divide/.
33. Jeff Schogol, "Marine Who Pissed on Taliban Wins in Court," *Marine Corps Times*, November 9, 2017, https://www.marinecorpstimes.com/news/your-marine-corps/2017/11/09/marine-who-urinated-on-dead-taliban-wins-in-court/; "Did Marines Urinate on Dead Bodies?," January 11, 2012, https://www.youtube.com/watch?v=fDub_zV68hI; Dan Lamothe, "Marine Who Urinated on Dead Taliban Has Conviction Thrown Out due to General's Meddling," *Washington Post*, November 9, 2017, https://www.washingtonpost.com/news/checkpoint/wp/2017/11/09/marine-who-urinated-on-dead-taliban-has-conviction-thrown-out-due-to-generals-meddling/; Lee Ferran, "Marine Who Urinated on Taliban Dead Says He'd Do It Again," *ABC News*, July 17, 2013, https://abcnews.go.com/Blotter/marine-urinated-taliban-dead-hed/story?id=19687916.
34. Bugliosi quoted in James T. Patterson, *Restless Giant: The United States from Watergate to Bush v. Gore* (New York: Oxford University Press, 2005), 418.
35. Gallup, Presidential Approval Ratings—George W. Bush, https://news.gallup.com/poll/116500/presidential-approval-ratings-george-bush.aspx. Joseph Schumpeter theorized at length about the influence of public "atavism" in foreign policy. See Wolfgang J. Mommsen, *Theories of Imperialism* (Chicago: University of Chicago Press, 1980), 18–28.
36. Gallup, Confidence in Institutions, https://news.gallup.com/poll/1597/confidence-institutions.aspx.
37. Thomas Ruyle, "What Is 'Stolen Valor,'" *Stars and Stripes*, June 16, 2010, https://www.stripes.com/news/veterans/what-is-stolen-valor-1.107359.
38. Brian Mockenhaupt, "The Stolen-Valor Detective," *Atlantic*, December 2016, 20–22.
39. Todd South, "Army Veteran Faces Federal Prison, Fines for Stolen Valor and Lying about PTSD," *Army Times*, January 14, 2020, https://www.armytimes.com/news/your-army/2020/01/14/army-veteran-faces-federal-prison-time-fines-for-stolen-valor-and-lying-about-ptsd/.
40. Department of Justice, U.S. Attorney's Office, District of Kansas, "Co-owner of Construction Company Sentenced for Defrauding Service-Disabled Veteran-Owned Small Business Program," November 12, 2015, https://www.justice.gov/usao-ks/pr/co-owner-construction-company-sentenced-defrauding-service-disabled-veteran-owned-small.

41. Peter Hermann, "Teacher Who Faked Military Service Sentenced to 21 Months," *Baltimore Sun*, August 30, 2011, https://www.baltimoresun.com/maryland/bs-md-hillar-sentenced-20110830-story.html.
42. Mockenhaupt, "Stolen-Valor Detective," 20–22.
43. Public Law 113–12, June 3, 2013.
44. Congressional Budget Office, *Contractors' Support of U.S. Operations in Iraq* (Washington, DC: CBO, August 2008), 8–11.
45. The author was a "site security specialist" under U.S. Army contract in Mosul, Iraq, in 2006.
46. For an overview of this particular history, see John H. Riley and Michael D. Gambone, "Men with Guns: The Private Military Corporation and International Law," *Wisconsin International Law Journal* 28 (2010): 39–73.
47. Riley and Gambone, "Men with Guns."
48. John Riley and Michael D. Gambone, "Old Wounds, New Warriors: The Problem of Contractor Medical Care during and after Contingency Operations," *Armed Forces & Society* 42 (April 2016): 1–18.
49. Ahmed Azam, "Afghan Interpreters for the U.S. Are Left Stranded and at Risk," *New York Times*, April 15, 2013, A1; T. A. Frail, "The Tragic Fate of the Afghan Interpreters the U.S. Left Behind," *Smithsonian Magazine*, November 2016, https://www.smithsonianmag.com/history/tragic-fate-afghan-interpreters-left-behind-180960785/; Spencer S. Hsu, "Judge Orders U.S. to End Visa Delays for Afghans, Iraqis Who Worked for U.S. Forces," *Washington Post*, February 6, 2020, https://www.washingtonpost.com/local/legal-issues/judge-orders-us-to-end-visa-delays-for-afghans-iraqis-who-worked-for-us-forces/2020/02/06/b0f02328-4915-11ea-9164-d3154ad8a5cd_story.html.
50. Max Boot, *The Savage Wars of Peace: Small Wars and the Rise of American Power* (New York: Basic Books, 2002).

CHAPTER FOUR: COMING HOME

1. Michael D. Gambone, *The Greatest Generation Comes Home: The Veteran in American Society* (College Park: Texas A&M University Press, 2005), 15.
2. David Finkel, *The Good Soldiers* (New York: Farrar, Straus and Giroux, 2009), 22.
3. Alair MacLean, "The Things They Carry: Combat, Disability, and Unemployment among U.S. Men," *American Sociological Review* 75 (August 2010): 563–85; Alair MacLean and Glen H. Elder, "Military Service in the Life Course," *Annual Review of Sociology* 33 (March 2007): 175–96; H. Stuart Hughes, "Emotional Disturbance and American Social Change," in U.S. Department of Veterans Affairs, Department of Medicine and Surgery, *The Vietnam Veterans in Contemporary Society: Collected Materials Pertaining to the Young Veterans* (Washington, DC: Veterans Administration, May 1972), II-2.
4. Edward W. McCranie and Leon A. Hyer, "Posttraumatic Stress Disorder Symptoms in Korean Conflict and World War II Combat Veterans Seeking Outpatient Treatment," *Journal of Traumatic Stress* 13 (2000): 437.
5. See Jerry Lembcke, *The Spitting Image: Myth, Memory, and the Legacy of Vietnam* (New York: New York University Press, 1998).
6. Eric T. Dean, "The Myth of the Troubled and Scorned Vietnam Veteran," *Journal of American Studies* 26 (April 1992): 60; emphasis in original.
7. Lyle Pirnie, "Letter to the Editor: A Vietnam Vet's Recollection of Returning," *Sun Chronicle*, November 26, 2018, https://www.thesunchronicle.com/opinion/letters_to_editor/letter-to-the-editor-a-vietnam-vets-recollection-of-returning/article_15de2f12-1316-5b51-8b23-914e1bd87325.html; Bob Feist, "Disrespect for

Vietnam Vets Is Fact, Not Fiction," *Star Tribune*, June 26, 2012, https://www.startribune.com/disrespect-for-vietnam-vets-is-fact-not-fiction/160444095/; Sandy Goodman, "Invisible Veterans," *Nation*, June 3, 1968, 724; June A. Willenz, "The Returning Vietnam Veterans: A Challenge to the Nation's Conscience," *Vital Issues*, October 1972, 1, American Veterans Committee Records, box 15, Gelman Library, Washington, DC.

8. Leslie H. Gelb, with Richard K. Betts, *The Irony of Vietnam: The System Worked* (Washington, DC: Brookings Institution, 1979), 130.
9. Marilyn B. Young, *The Vietnam Wars, 1945–1990* (New York: Harper Perennial, 1991), 220–21.
10. Stanley Karnow, *Vietnam: A History* (New York: Viking Press, 1983), 548. Karnow makes the point that Walter Cronkite's famous February 27, 1968, editorial after Tet was simply reflecting, rather than shaping, existing public opinion.
11. Seymour M. Hersh, "Lieutenant Accused of Murdering 109 Civilians," *St. Louis Post-Dispatch*, November 13, 1969, 1.
12. See Vietnam Veterans Against the War, *The Winter Soldier Investigation: An Inquiry into American War Crimes* (Boston: Beacon Press, 1972).
13. Neil Sheehan, "Conversations with Americans: Book Review," *New York Times*, December 27, 1970, 165.
14. David K. Shipler, "Another View of Vietnam Veterans," *New Yorker*, May 2, 2015, https://www.newyorker.com/news/news-desk/another-view-of-vietnam-veterans.
15. There is an excellent study of these features from World War II to the current wars in Adam J. Berinsky, *In Time of War: Understanding American Public Opinion from World War II to Iraq* (Chicago: University of Chicago Press, 2009).
16. Victoria I. Young, Joyce Y. Brown, Theresa I. Jefferson, Cindy H. Kapinos, Kurt A. Kladivko, Patrick G. Potter, Douglas P. Schultz, *Evolution of the U.S. Army Force Structure*, vol. 1 (Bethesda, MD: United States Army Concepts Analysis Agency, 1989), ES-16.
17. Louis Harris and Associates, Inc., *A Study of the Problems Facing Vietnam Era Veterans: Their Readjustment to Civilian Life* (New York: Louis Harris and Associates, 1971), 10.
18. Jan Barry, "Why Veterans March against the War," *New York Times*, April 23, 1971, 37.
19. "A Hero's Welcome: The American Public and Attitudes toward Veterans," *Roper Center for Public Opinion Research*, n.d., https://ropercenter.cornell.edu/heros-welcome-american-public-and-attitudes-toward-veterans.
20. Lance Morrow, "Vietnam: A Bloody Rite of Passage," *Time*, April 15, 1985, 20–30.
21. D. Keith Mano, "The Vietnam Veterans' Parade," *National Review*, July 26, 1985, 52; David Fitzgerald, "Support the Troops: Gulf War Homecomings and a New Politics of Military Celebration," *Modern American History* 2 (March 2019): 6.
22. Gallup, "Confidence in Institutions," https://news.gallup.com/poll/1597/confidence-institutions.aspx.
23. Phillip Carter, "What America Owes Its Veterans: A Better System of Care and Support," *Foreign Affairs* 96 (September/October 2017): 115–27.
24. "Transcript of President Reagan's News Conference on the Attack in Beirut," *New York Times*, October 25, 1983, A10.
25. David Shribman, "Poll Shows Support for Presence of U.S. Troops in Lebanon and Grenada," *New York Times*, October 29, 1983, 9.
26. Richard A. Melanson, *American Foreign Policy since the Vietnam War: The Search for Consensus from Richard Nixon to George W. Bush*, 4th ed. (New York: Routledge, 2005), 179.
27. Adam Clymer, "A Poll Finds 77% in U.S. Approve Raid on Libya," *New York Times*, April 17, 1986, A23.

28. David K. Shipler, "Poll Finds Americans Divided on Reply to Terror," *New York Times*, February 9, 1986, 14.
29. John T. Correll, "The Weinberger Doctrine," *Air Force Magazine* 97 (March 2014): 62–67.
30. Anthony H. Cordesman, *Iraq's Military Forces, 1988–1993* (Washington, DC: Center for International Studies, September 1994), 77.
31. Eric Schmitt, "Fighting the Iraqis: Four Scenarios, All Disputed," *New York Times*, November 19, 1990, A1; "Potential War Casualties Put at 100,000," *Los Angeles Times*, September 5, 1990, https://www.latimes.com/archives/la-xpm -1990-09-05-mn-776-story.html.
32. Allan R. Millet, Peter Maslowski, and William B. Feis, *For the Common Defense: A Military History of the United States from 1607 to 2012* (New York: Free Press, 2012), 682. The term "hundred-hour war" appears frequently in scholarship and media. See Daniel S. Zazworsky, "The 100-Hour War with Iraq: Could It Have Been Longer?" (Newport, RI: Naval War College, November 13, 1993); "The Hundred-Hour War," *Newsweek*, March 14, 1999, https://www.newsweek.com /hundred-hour-war-163936.
33. Jim Hoagland, "Schwarzkopf Exorcised the Demon of Vietnam," *South Florida Sun Sentinel*, February 28, 1991, https://www.sun-sentinel.com/news/fl-xpm -1991-02-28-9101110038-story.html; Tom Wicker, "Ghosts of Vietnam," *New York Times*, January 26, 1991, 29; John D. Morrocco, "From Vietnam to Desert Storm," *Air Force Magazine* 75 (January 1, 1992), https://www.airforcemag.com/article /0192storm/; S. W. Cloud, "Exorcising an Old Demon," *Time*, March 11, 1991, 52–53.
34. Alessandra Stanley, "New York Prepares Embrace for Troops," *New York Times*, June 10, 1991, A1.
35. Fitzgerald, "Support the Troops," 2.
36. Elsa Brenner, "Besieged, Stores Run Out of Flags," *New York Times*, February 3, 1991, WC10.
37. Enloe quoted in Linda Pershing and Margaret R. Yocom, "The Yellow Ribboning of the USA: Contested Meanings in the Construction of a Political Symbol," *Western Folklore* 55 (Winter 1996): 41.
38. Tom Wicker, "Yellow Fever," *New York Times*, February 27, 1991, A27.
39. "A Father's Pride, a Yellow Ribbon," *New York Times*, January 9, 1991, A8.
40. Roger Stahl, "Why We 'Support the Troops': Rhetorical Evolutions," *Rhetoric and Public Affairs* 12 (Winter 2009): 533–34.
41. Shuh quoted in Alessandra Stanley, "War's Ribbons Are Yellow with Meaning of Many Hues," *New York Times*, February 3, 1991, 1. See also Katharine M. Millar, "'They Need Our Help': Non-Governmental Organizations and the Subjectifying Dynamics of the Military as Social Cause," *Media, War & Conflict* 9 (April 2016): 13–14.
42. Stahl, "Why We 'Support the Troops,'" 535; David Flores, "Politicization beyond Politics: Narratives and Mechanisms of Iraq War Veterans' Activism," *Armed Forces & Society* 43 (January 2017): 167; Patrick G. Coy, Lynne M. Woehrle, and Gregory M. Maney, "Discursive Legacies: The U.S. Peace Movement and 'Support the Troops,'" *Social Problems* 55 (May 2008): 161–89.
43. Andrew J. Bacevich, *The New American Militarism: How Americans Are Seduced by War* (New York: Oxford University Press, 2005), 108.
44. Richard Parker, "Centrism, Populist Style," *Nation*, October 7, 1996, 19.
45. See Richard M. Swain, *"Lucky War": Third Army in Desert Storm* (Fort Leavenworth, KS: Command and General Staff College, 1994); Timothy M. Karcher, "The Victory Disease," *Military Review* 83 (July–August 2002): 9–17. See

also Timothy M. Karcher, *Understanding the "Victory Disease": From Little Bighorn to Mogadishu* (Fort Leavenworth, KS: Combat Studies Institute Press, 2004).

46. Headquarters, Task Force Eagle, "Operational Guidance D+60 thru D+180," February 27, 1996, Task Force Eagle Papers, 1995–1996, box 1, Army Heritage and Education Center (hereafter AHEC), Carlisle, PA.
47. "Beyond D+120: Tasks We Don't Want, May Get," n.d., Melissa E. Patrick Papers, 1995–1996, box 1, AHEC.
48. Headquarters, U.S. Army Europe, Office of the Chief of Public Affairs, *A Soldier's Guide to Bosnia-Herzegovina*, 12, n.d., Task Force Eagle Papers, 1995–1996, box 1, AHEC.
49. Gallup, Confidence in Institutions, https://news.gallup.com/poll/1597/confidence-institutions.aspx.
50. See, for example, "The 2000 Presidential Election—A Mid-Year Gallup Report," June 22, 2000, https://news.gallup.com/poll/9898/2000-presidential-election-midyear-gallup-report.aspx.
51. Government Accountability Office, GAO-06-794R, *VA and DOD Health Care: Efforts to Provide Seamless Transition of Care for OEF and OIF Servicemembers and Veterans* (Washington, DC: GAO, June 30, 2006), 1.
52. Tim Hefferman, "Ten Numbers on the State of Iraq War Veterans," *Esquire*, March 2006, 212–13.
53. Department of Defense, Office of the Secretary of Defense, Defense Science Board, *Final Report of the Defense Science Board Task Force on Deployment of Members of the National Guard and Reserve in the Global War on Terrorism* (Washington, DC: Department of Defense, 2007), 9.
54. Al Hemingway, "Gray-Haired Warriors: Vietnam Veterans in Iraq," *Veterans of Foreign Wars Magazine*, April 2005, 22; Hefferman, "State of Iraq War Veterans," 212–13.
55. Department of Defense, Office of the Deputy Undersecretary of Defense (Military Community and Family Policy), *Demographics 2010: Profile of the Military Community* (Washington, DC: Department of Defense, 2010), 15.
56. Frank Newport, "Seventy-Two Percent of Americans Support War against Iraq," Gallup News Service, March 24, 2003, https://news.gallup.com/poll/8038/seventytwo-percent-americans-support-war-against-iraq.aspx.
57. "Most Americans Still Upset about Iraq Invasion," *Angus Reid Global Monitor*, March 8, 2008, http://www.angus-reid.com (no longer available).
58. Lydia Saad, "Republicans and Democrats Disagree on War, but Support Troops," Gallup News Service, September 2006, https://news.gallup.com/poll/24760/republicans-democrats-disagree-iraq-war-support-troops.aspx.
59. Laura McDaniel, "Students and Veterans—Can They Connect on Campus?," *Veterans of Foreign Wars Magazine*, September 2004, 20.
60. James F. Kelly, "Draft Debate Resurfaces," *U.S. Naval Institute Proceedings* 133 (January 2007): 12; Beth Bailey, "The Army in the Marketplace: Recruiting an All-Volunteer Force," *Journal of American History* 94 (June 2007): 47–74; "Two-Thirds of Americans Reject Military Draft," *Angus Reid Global Monitor*, October 3, 2007, http://www.angus-reid.com (no longer available).
61. Grant Gallicho, "Torture's Enablers," *Commonweal Magazine* 134 (November 9, 2007): 5; Nat Hentoff, "Waterboarding the White House," *Village Voice*, January 9–15, 2008, 18; "Americans Reject Torture during Interrogations," *Angus Reid Global Monitor*, December 3, 2007, http://www.angus-reid.com (no longer available).
62. Chris Hedges and Laila al-Arian, "The Other War," *Nation*, July 30–August 6, 2007, 11–31. See also Kayla Williams, *Love My Rifle More Than You: Young and Female in the U.S. Army* (New York: W. W. Norton, 2006).

63. "Troops Committed War Crimes, Say Americans," *Angus Reid Global Monitor*, June 18, 2006, http://www.angus-reid.com (no longer available).
64. Alex Vernon, "The Gulf War and Postmodern Memory," *Wilson Quarterly*, Winter 2001, 73.
65. See, for example, the Multi-National Force—Iraq site at https://www.youtube.com/results?search_query=combat+in+iraq.
66. In part, this development is of the military's own making. See Lev Grossman, "The Army's Killer App," *Time*, February 28, 2005, 43–44, and William Lugo, "Violent Video Games to Recruit American Youth," *Reclaiming Children and Youth* 15 (Spring 2006): 11–14.
67. Sara Corbett, "The Permanent Scars of Iraq," *New York Times Magazine*, February 15, 2004, 37.
68. Ben Fountain, *Billy Lynn's Long Halftime Walk* (New York: Ecco, 2012), 1–2.
69. Colby Buzzell, "The Best Years of Our Lives," *Esquire*, March 2006, 206–15.
70. Gambone, *Greatest Generation Comes Home*, 32–33.
71. Paul Fussell, *Wartime: Understanding and Behavior in the Second World War* (New York: Oxford University Press, 1989), 65. Originally quoted in Don M. Wolfe, ed., *The Purple Testament* (Garden City, NY: Doubleday, 1947), xxvi.

CHAPTER FIVE: HEALING NEW WOUNDS

1. Lois M. Davis, Susan D. Hosek, Michael G. Tate, Mark Perry, Gerard Hepler, and Paul S. Steinberg, *Army Medical Support for Peace Operations and Humanitarian Assistance* (Santa Monica, CA: RAND, 1996), 5–10.
2. Douglas R. Bey and Walter E. Smith, "Organizational Consultation in a Combat Unit," *American Journal of Psychiatry* 128 (October 1971): 401–6; Sandra L. Huppenbauer, "A Portrait of a Problem," *American Journal of Nursing* 82 (November 1982): 1700; U.S. Department of Veterans Affairs, Department of Medicine and Surgery, Edward M. Colbach, and Matthew D. Parrish, "Army Mental Health Activities in Vietnam, 1965–1970," in *The Vietnam Veterans in Contemporary Society: Collected Materials Pertaining to the Young Veterans* (Washington, DC: Veterans Administration, May 1972), III-39.
3. Michael D. Gambone, *The Greatest Generation Comes Home: The Veteran in American Society* (College Park: Texas A&M University Press, 2005), 38–62.
4. Herbert Mitgang, "The Double Wounds of War," *New York Times*, October 19, 1970, 39; Charles Childs, "From Vietnam to a VA Hospital: Assignment to Neglect," *Life*, May 22, 1970, 26.
5. Alfonso O. Narvaez, "McCarthy Tours Bronx Wards: Says Veterans' Care Is Poor," *New York Times*, June 13, 1970, 18; James M. Naughton, "McGovern Stresses Help for Veterans in Visit to Hospital," *New York Times*, October 24, 1972, 89.
6. Dana Priest and Anne Hull, "Soldiers Face Neglect at Army's Top Medical Facility," *Washington Post*, February 18, 2007, A1. See also Tom Bowman, "Walter Reed Was the Army's Wake-Up Call in 2007," *National Public Radio*, August 31, 2011, https://www.npr.org/transcripts/139641856, and Michael Winerip, "And This Was Called Care? The Walter Reed Story," *New York Times*, September 30, 2013, https://www.nytimes.com/2013/09/30/booming/and-this-was-called-care-the-walter-reed-story.html.
7. Gerald Nicosia, *Home to War: A History of the Vietnam Veterans' Movement* (New York: Crown, 2001), 159.
8. See, for example, U.S. Department of Veterans Affairs, Office of Research and Development, VA Research on Traumatic Brain Injury, https://www.research.va.gov/topics/tbi.cfm. According to the VA, the Defense and Veterans Brain Injury Center reported 414,000 TBI of all types between 2000 and 2019.

9. President's Commission on Veterans' Pensions, *Veterans' Benefits in the United States: A Report to the President by the President's Commission on Veterans' Pensions* (Washington, DC: Government Printing Office, April 1956), 112–13.
10. "Excerpts from President Eisenhower's 1956 Budget Message," n.d., Bradley Commission, box 3, Dwight David Eisenhower Presidential Library and Museum (hereafter DDE), Abilene, KS.
11. President's Commission on Veterans' Pensions, *Veterans' Benefits*, 4, 24.
12. Memorandum, "Reaction to the Commission's Report, May 10, 1956, 1, Bradley Commission, box 7, DDE; "Statement of Omar B. Ketchum, Director, National Legislative Service, Veterans of Foreign Wars of the U.S. before the House Committee on Veterans Affairs," May 11, 1956, 2, Bradley Commission, box 104, DDE.
13. U.S. Bureau of the Census, *The Statistical History of the United States: From Colonial Times to the Present* (New York: Basic Books, 1976), 1146.
14. "A Close Look at the Cold War GI Bill," *American Legion Magazine*, September 1966, 26. The number of months of funding was based on "one month of aid for each month, or fraction, of service on active duty after January 31, 1955."
15. Mark Boulton, *Failing Our Veterans: The G.I. Bill and the Vietnam Generation* (New York: New York University Press, 2014), 72, 96–97.
16. Boulton, *Failing Our Veterans*, 126.
17. Mitgang, "The Double Wounds of War," 39; Kirsten J. Colello and Sidath Viranga Panangala, *Long-Term Care Services for Veterans*, R44697 (Washington, DC: Congressional Research Service, February 14, 2017), 3.
18. "Nader Report Says V.A. Is Failing Vietnam Veterans: Safeguards on Discharges," *New York Times*, March 4, 1973, 50.
19. Carol M. Ashton, Thomas W. Weiss, Nancy J. Petersen, Nelda P. Wray, Terri J. Menke, and Robin C. Sickles, "Changes in VA Hospital Use, 1980–1990," *Medical Care* 32 (May 1994): 454.
20. Department of Veterans Affairs, National Center for Veterans Analysis and Statistics, *VA Utilization Profile: FY2017* (Washington, DC: Department of Veterans Affairs, May 2020), 3, 6.
21. Department of Veterans Affairs, *VA Utilization Profile*, 11; Department of Veterans Affairs, Office of Policy and Planning, *Analysis of Unique Veterans Utilization of VA Benefits & Services* (Washington, DC: Department of Veterans Affairs, April 29, 2009), 5–6. Health care (33%) had the highest utilization. Veterans over the age of 65 were the largest constituency, comprising 3.75 million of 8.5 million veterans receiving benefits in 2009.
22. Department of Veterans Affairs, National Center for Veteran Analysis and Statistics, *Trend Data: Fiscal Years 1970–1995* (Washington, DC: Department of Veterans Affairs, June 1996), 39; Department of Veterans Affairs, *Annual Report of the Secretary of Veterans Affairs: Fiscal Year 1998* (Washington, DC: Department of Veterans Affairs, December 1999), 7.
23. Department of Veterans Affairs, *VA Pandemic Influenza Plan* (Washington, DC: Department of Veterans Affairs, March 2006), 60.
24. Department of Veterans Affairs, Veterans Health Administration, *Analysis of Health Care Utilization among Operation Enduring Freedom (OEF), Operation Iraqi Freedom (OIF), and Operation New Dawn (OND) Veterans* (Washington, DC: Department of Veterans Affairs, January 2017), 6.
25. Guenter Levy, *America in Vietnam* (New York: Oxford University Press, 1978), 262–63. Recent studies estimate that as many as 4.8 million Vietnamese were affected by the defoliants. See Richard Stone, "Agent Orange's Bitter Harvest," *Science* 315 (January 12, 2007): 177.
26. Michael G. Palmer, "The Case of Agent Orange," *Contemporary Southeast Asia* 29 (April 2007): 174.

27. U.S. District Court for the Eastern District of New York, *In Re Agent Orange Product Liability Litigation*, 597 F. Supp. 740 (E.D.N.Y. 1984), September 25, 1984, https://www.benefits.va.gov/compensation/claims-postservice-agent_orange-settlement-settlementFund.asp.
28. Fred Milano, "Gulf War Syndrome: The 'Agent Orange' of the Nineties," *International Social Science Review* 75 (2000): 18; Department of Veterans Affairs, Agent Orange Settlement Fund, https://www.benefits.va.gov/compensation/claims-postservice-agent_orange-settlement-settlementFund.asp.
29. Department of Veterans Affairs, Agent Orange Settlement Fund. See also Department of Veterans Affairs, "Additional Regulations Published for Women Veterans' Children with Certain Birth Defects," *Agent Orange Review*, July 2003, 9–10.
30. Patricia Kime, "Agent Orange Delay Draws Criticism," *Military Times*, February 12, 2020, https://www.militarytimes.com/news/pentagon-congress/2020/02/12/agent-orange-decision-delay-draws-criticism/. The specific diseases under discussion were Parkinson's, bladder cancer, hypertension, and hyperthyroidism.
31. Wilbur J. Scott, "PTSD in DSM-III: A Case in the Politics of Diagnosis and Disease," *Social Problems* 37 (August 1990): 298.
32. Nicosia, *Home to War*, 158–209.
33. For the initial definition of PTSD, see Robert L. Spitzer, ed., *DSM-III: Diagnostic and Statistical Manual of Mental Disorders*, 3rd ed. (Washington, DC: American Psychiatric Press, 1980), 236.
34. Spitzer, *DSM-III*, 236–37.
35. Kathryn H. Andersen and Jean M. Mitchell, "Effects of Military Experience on Mental Health Problems and Work Behavior," *Medical Care* 30 (June 1992): 554. Interestingly, the percentage corresponds almost exactly with estimates of Vietnam-era combatants.
36. Janet S. Pierson and Raymond F. Pierson. "Posttraumatic Stress Disorder or Midlife Crisis in Vietnam Veterans?," *Social Work* 39 (May 1994): 328.
37. Andersen and Mitchell, "Effects of Military Experience," 557.
38. See, for example, Donald W. Black, Caroline P. Carney, Paul M. Peloso, Robert F. Woolson, David A. Schwartz, Margaret D. Voelker, Drue H. Barrett, and Bradley N. Doebbeling, "Gulf War Veterans with Anxiety: Prevalence, Comorbidity, and Risk Factors," *Epidemiology* 15 (March 2004): 135–42; Maureen Murdoch, James Hodges, Carolyn Hunt, Diane Cowper, Nancy Kressin, and Nancy O'Brien, "Gender Differences in Service Connection for PTSD," *Medical Care* 41 (August 2003): 950–61.
39. Robert H. Stretch, David H. Marlowe, and Kathleen M. Wright, "Post-Traumatic Stress Disorder Symptoms among Gulf War Veterans," *Military Medicine* 161 (July 1996): 407.
40. Drew A. Helmer, Mindy E. Flanagan, Robert F. Woolson, and Bradley N. Doebbeling, "Health Services Use among Gulf War Veterans and Gulf War–Era Nondeployed Veterans: A Large Population-Based Survey," *American Journal of Public Health* 97 (December 2007): 2145; Gozde Ozakinci, William K. Hallman, and Howard M. Kipen, "Persistence of Symptoms in Veterans of the First Gulf War: 5-Year Follow-up," *Environmental Health Perspectives* 114 (October 2006): 1553.
41. Milano, "Gulf War Syndrome," 21.
42. Milano, 20.
43. Hollie V. Thomas, Nicola J. Stimpson, Alison L. Weightman, Frank Dunstan, and Glyn Lewis, "Systematic Review of Multi-Symptom Conditions in Gulf War Veterans," *Psychological Medicine* 36 (January 26, 2006): 736.
44. Debora MacKenzie, "The Disease That Never Was?," *New Scientist* 184 (November 6–12, 2004): 8–10.

45. Dennis Bernstein and Thea Kelley, "The Gulf War Comes Home: Sickness Spreads, but the Pentagon Denies All," *Progressive*, March 1995, 30; William K. Hallman, Howard M. Kipen, Michael Diefenbach, Kendal Boyd, Han Kang, Howard Leventhal, and Daniel Wartenbert, "Symptom Patterns among Gulf War Registry Veterans," *American Journal of Public Health* 93 (April 2003): 624–30.
46. Bernstein and Kelley, "Gulf War Comes Home," 30
47. Tim A. Bullman, Clare M. Mahan, Han K. Kang, and William F. Page, "Mortality in US Army Gulf War Veterans Exposed to 1991 Khamisiyah Chemical Munitions Destruction," *American Journal of Public Health* 95 (August 2005): 1382–88.
48. Amy Waldman, "Credibility Gulf: The Military's Battle over Whether to Protect Its Image or Its Troops," *Washington Monthly*, December 1996, 32.
49. Milano, "Gulf War Syndrome," 20.
50. Gil High, "Illness Probe Widened," *Soldiers*, February 1997, 6–7.
51. Tim Dyhouse, "Pentagon Updates Gulf War Vets," *Veterans of Foreign Wars Magazine*, May 2006, 12.
52. Nikki Wentling, "VA Extends Deadline for Seeking Gulf War Illness Benefits to 2021," *Stars and Stripes*, October 17, 2016, https://www.stripes.com/news/va-extends-deadline-for-seeking-gulf-war-illness-benefits-to-2021-1.434547.
53. Nikki Wentling, "Report: VA Claims for Gulf War Illness Denied 80 Percent of the Time," *Stars and Stripes*, July 10, 2017, https://www.stripes.com/news/pacific/report-va-claims-for-gulf-war-illness-denied-80-percent-of-the-time-1.477436.
54. Department of Defense, *Casualty Status*, June 8, 2020. These are daily announcements that appear on this website https://www.defense.gov/Newsroom/Casualty-Status/%EF%BB%BF/. The Department of Labor tracks contractor casualties. As of April 2019, these amounted to 3,413 killed and 39,953 wounded. See Christopher T. Mann, *U.S. War Costs, Casualties, and Personnel Levels since 9/11*, IF11182 (Washington, DC: Congressional Research Service, April 18, 2019), 2.
55. Matthew S. Goldberg, "Death and Injury Rates of U.S. Military Personnel in Iraq," *Military Medicine* 175 (April 2010): 220. The Army Surgeon General claimed a 92 percent survival rate for Iraq and Afghanistan by 2016. See David Vergun, "Survival Rates Improving for Soldiers Wounded in Combat, Says Army Surgeon General," *Army Times*, August 24, 2016, https://www.army.mil/article/173808/survival_rates_improving_for_soldiers_wounded_in_combat_says_army_surgeon_general. See also Mary Roach, *Grunt: The Curious Science of Humans at War* (New York: W. W. Norton, 2016), 18–39. Roach addresses the ongoing problem of uniform fabric that could protect soldiers from heat and not pose a risk of infection when it became embedded in tissue as the result of an explosion.
56. Department of Veterans Affairs, National Center for Veterans Analysis and Statistics, Benefits Programs, *Summary of Veterans Benefits: FY 2000 to FY 2016*. The total number of VA benefits recipients increased from 2,321,103 in 2001 to 4,356,443 in 2016, https://www.va.gov/vetdata/Utilization.asp.
57. Department of Veterans Affairs, *VA Priority Groups*, https://www.va.gov/health-care/eligibility/priority-groups; Department of Veterans Affairs, National Center for Veterans Analysis and Statistics, *Number of Veteran Patients by Healthcare Priority Group: FY2000 to FY2017*, https://www.va.gov/vetdata/docs/Utilization/Number_of_Veteran_Patients_by_HC_Priority_Groups_2000_2017.pdf.
58. Department of Veterans Affairs, National Center for Veterans Analysis and Statistics, *Service-Connected Disabled Veterans by Disability Rating Group: FY1986 to FY2016* (Washington, DC: Department of Veterans Affairs, August 2018), https://www.data.va.gov/dataset/Service-Connected-Disability-SCD-Veterans-by-Disab/vne6-2zez.
59. Department of Veterans Affairs, National Center for Veterans Analysis and Statistics, *Profile of Post-9/11 Veterans: 2016* (Washington, DC: Department of Veterans Affairs, March 2016), 10.

60. Hannah Fischer, *A Guide to U.S. Military Casualty Statistics: Operation Freedom's Sentinel, Operation Inherent Resolve, Operation New Dawn, Operation Iraqi Freedom, and Operation Enduring Freedom*, RS22452 (Washington, DC: Congressional Research Service, August 7, 2015), 3–7.
61. Fischer, *U.S. Military Casualty Statistics*, 2.
62. Department of Veterans Affairs, National Center for Analysis and Statistics, *Profile of Post-9/11 Veterans: 2016* (Washington, DC: Department of Veterans Affairs, March 2018), 2; Department of Veterans Affairs, PTSD: National Center for PTSD, *How Common Is PTSD in Veterans?*, https://www.ptsd.va.gov/understand/common/common_veterans.asp.
63. Terri Tanielian and Lisa H. Jaycox, eds., *Invisible Wounds of War: Psychological and Cognitive Injuries, Their Consequences, and Services to Assist Recovery* (Santa Monica, CA: RAND, 2008), 100–112; James O. E. Pittman, "Latino Veterans with PTSD: A Systematic Review," *Behavioral Sciences* 4 (September 2014): 321.
64. Carri-Ann Gibson, "Review of Posttraumatic Stress Disorder and Chronic Pain: The Path to Integrated Care," *Journal of Rehabilitation Research and Development* 49 (2012): 756.
65. Richard J. McNally, "Psychiatric Casualties of War," *Science* 313 (August 18, 2006): 923–24.
66. David Dobbs, "The Post-Traumatic Stress Trap," *Scientific American*, April 2009, 64–65.
67. Pittman, "Latino Veterans with PTSD," 322. This appears to be an ongoing problem. See Lawrence G. Flores, "Perceptions of Veterans Administration Health Care Services by Hispanic Veterans" (PhD diss., University of Southern California, 1982), 51.
68. Anne L. LeFevre, "Sociocultural Mechanisms Associated with Posttraumatic Stress Disorder: An Analysis of Latino Veterans" (PhD diss., University of Maryland, 2011), 24–26; Antonio F. Garcia, "Moral Injury Themes in Latino Combat Veterans: A Qualitative Investigation" (PhD diss., University of Texas, 2018), 77.
69. Studies of mixed-race mental group therapy seem promising. A 2018 study found no differences in outcomes based on race following this format. See Jennifer A. Coleman, John R. Lynch, Kathleen M. Ingram, Christina M. Sheerin, Lance M. Rappaport, and Stephen K. Trapp, "Examination of Racial Differences in Posttraumatic Stress Disorder Group Therapy Program for Veterans," *Group Dynamics* 22 (September 2018): 12.
70. Art Levine, "How the VA Fueled the National Opioid Crisis and Is Killing Thousands of Veterans," *Newsweek*, October 12, 2017, https://www.newsweek.com/2017/10/20/va-fueled-opioid-crisis-killing-veterans-681552.html.
71. Aaron Glantz, "VA's Opiate Overload Feeds Veterans' Addictions, Overdose Deaths," *Center for Investigative Reporting*, September 28, 2013, https://oklahomawatch.org/2013/10/31/vas-opiate-overload-feeds-veterans-addictions-overdose-deaths/; Karen H. Seal, Ying Shi, Gregory Cohen, Beth E. Cohen, Shira Maguen, Erin E. Krebs, and Thomas C. Neylan, "Association of Mental Health Disorders with Prescription Opioids and High-Risk Opioid Use in US Veterans of Iraq and Afghanistan," *Journal of the American Medical Association* 307 (March 7, 2012): 940–47.
72. Karen H. Seal et al., "Association of Mental Health Disorders," 944; Levine, "VA Fueled the National Opioid Crisis."
73. Department of Veterans Affairs, Office of Mental Health and Suicide Prevention, *National Veteran Suicide Prevention Annual Report* (Washington, DC: Department of Veterans Affairs, September 2019), 8.

74. Department of Veterans Affairs, *National Veteran Suicide Prevention*, 9. The adjusted rate was 18.5 per 100,000 in 2005 and 27.7 per 100,000 by 2017; House Committee on Oversight and Reform, "Veterans and Active-Duty Military Suicides," May 8, 2019, https://oversight.house.gov/legislation/hearings/veteran-and-active-duty-military-suicides.
75. Levine, "VA Fueled the National Opioid Crisis."
76. Veterans Overmedication Prevention Act of 2017, S. 992, 115th Cong. (May 1, 2017), https://www.congress.gov/bill/115th-congress/senate-bill/992.
77. "'Buddy Check on 22!' Veterans Use Social Media to Combat Suicide," *New York Times*, April 24, 2016, 19; James Dao, "Voice on Phone Is Lifeline for Suicidal Veterans," *New York Times*, July 31, 2010, A1.
78. Michael Weisskopf, "The Meaning of Walter Reed," *Time*, March 19, 2007, 100; Alicia Mundy, "The VA Isn't Broken, Yet," *Washington Monthly*, March–May 2016, 25–34.
79. Estafanía Ponti, "Military Citizenship in the Post-9/11 Homefront" (PhD diss., City University of New York, 2018), 12.
80. Ashish K. Jha, Jonathan B. Perlin, Kenneth W. Kizer, and R. Adams Dudley, "Effect of the Transformation of the Veterans Affairs Health Care System on the Quality of Care," *New England Journal of Medicine* 348 (May 29, 2003): 2218–27.
81. Mundy, "VA Isn't Broken, Yet," 27–28.
82. Richard A. Oppel and Abby Goodnough, "Doctor Shortage Is Cited in Delays at V.A. Hospitals," *New York Times*, May 29, 2014, A1.
83. German Lopez, "The VA Scandal of 2014, Explained," *Vox*, May 13, 2015, https://www.vox.com/2014/9/26/18080592/va-scandal-explained.
84. Statement of Joseph A. Violante, DAV National Legislative Director, before the Committee on Veterans' Affairs, United States Senate, May 15, 2014, 5, https://www.veterans.senate.gov/imo/media/doc/DAV%20Violante%20Testmony%2005.15.15.pdf; Oppel and Goodnough, "Doctor Shortage," A1.
85. Cameron Brenchley, "President Obama Signs Bill to Give the VA the Resources It Needs," Whitehouse.gov (August 7, 2014), https://obamawhitehouse.archives.gov/blog/2014/08/07/president-obama-signs-bill-give-va-resources-it-needs.
86. Department of Veterans Affairs, Office of Public Affairs and Media Relations, Fact Sheet: Veterans Access, Choice, and Accountability Act of 2014 ("Choice Act"), n.d., https://www.va.gov/opa/choiceact/documents/Choice-Program-Fact-Sheet-Final.pdf.
87. Suzanne Gordon, "The VA Privatizing Veterans' Health Care while Launching a Campaign to Deny It," *American Prospect*, March 11, 2019, https://prospect.org/health/va-privatizing-veterans-health-care-launching-campaign-deny/.
88. "Trump Meets with Health Care Leaders, Considers Privatizing Veterans' Health Care," *Modern Healthcare*, January 2, 2017, 2.
89. Leo Shane III, "Vet Groups and Lawmakers Say They're Against It—But What Does 'Privatization' of Veterans Affairs Really Mean?," *Military Times*, April 10, 2018, https://www.militarytimes.com/veterans/2018/04/11/vets-groups-and-lawmakers-say-theyre-against-it-but-what-does-privatization-of-veterans-affairs-really-mean/; Lori Short, "Privatizing the Veterans Healthcare System," *Journal of Healthcare Contracting*, June 2, 2020, https://www.jhconline.com/privatizing-the-veterans-healthcare-system.html.
90. Gillums quoted in Shane, "Vet Groups and Lawmakers."
91. Terri Taniellan, Carrie M. Farmer, Rachel M. Burns, Erin Lindsey Duffy, and Claude Messan Setodji, *Ready or Not? Assessing the Capacity of New York State Health Care Providers to Meet the Needs of Veterans* (Santa Monica, CA: RAND, 2018).

92. Jennifer Steinhauer and Dave Philipps, "V.A. Seeks to Direct Billions of Dollars into Private Care," *New York Times*, January 12, 2019, https://www.nytimes.com/2019/01/12/us/politics/veterans-administration-health-care-privatization.html.
93. See Disabled American Veterans, "Independent Budget Statement on VA's FY 2020 Budget Request," March 13, 2019, https://www.dav.org/learn-more/news/2019/independent-budget-statement-on-vas-fy-2020-budget-request/. The FY 2020 VA funding request was $51.4 billion.
94. "RNs and Veterans Expose Privatization of Health Care," *National Nurse*, April/May/June 2019, 12.
95. Joe Davidson, "Whistleblower Says There's a Secret VA Wait List for Care," *Washington Post*, June 3, 2019, https://www.washingtonpost.com/politics/whistleblower-says-theres-a-secret-va-wait-list-for-care-the-department-says-thats-not-true/2019/06/01/197e59a2-83df-11e9-bce7-40b4105f7ca0_story.html.
96. See, for example, Brian H. Chermol, "Wounds without Scars: Treatment of Battle Fatigue in the U.S. Armed Forces in the Second World War," *Military Affairs* 49 (January 1985): 9–11.
97. Stephen E. Ambrose, *Band of Brothers: E Company, 506th Regiment, 101st Airborne from Normandy to Hitler's Eagle's Nest* (New York: Simon & Schuster, 1992).
98. Sebastian Junger, *Tribe: On Homecoming and Belonging* (New York: Twelve, 2016), 55, 88, 97.
99. Omar N. Bradley, Speech before the Army Air Force Conference on Community Centers, Mitchell Field, New York, December 5, 1945, Records of the NAACP, Branch Files, 1940–1955, box A657, Library of Congress, Washington, DC.
100. There are multiple instances of fraud. See, for example, Dorothy Mills-Gregg, "Granting VA Disability Claims by Remote Questionnaire Led to Fraud, Report Shows," Military.com, February 20, 2020, https://www.military.com/daily-news/2020/02/20/granting-va-disability-claims-remote-questionnaire-led-fraud-report-shows.html; Office of the Inspector General, Social Security Administration, "Montana Man Pleads Guilty to Social Security Fraud and Veterans Affairs Fraud," December 14, 2018, https://oig.ssa.gov/audits-and-investigations/investigations/dec14-montana-fraud.
101. Junger, *Tribe*, 89. See also Department of Veterans Affairs, Office of Inspector General, *Veterans Benefits Administration: Follow-Up Audit of 100 Percent Disability Evaluations*, 14-01686-185 (Washington, DC: Department of Veterans Affairs, June 6, 2014).
102. McNally, "Psychiatric Casualties of War," 923.
103. Iron Warriors, https://iron-warriors.org; for Soldier Sanctuary, see https://www.facebook.com/SoldierSanctuary.
104. Wounded Warrior Project, https://www.woundedwarriorproject.org/programs/wwp-resource-center. According to Charity Navigator, the Wounded Warrior Project's top three expenses as of September 2019, besides overhead, were mental health and wellness ($62.7 million), "connection" ($45.8 million), and "financial wellness" ($31.5 million); see https://www.charitynavigator.org/index.cfm?bay=search.programs&orgid=12842.
105. Dave Philipps, "Wounded Warrior Projects Spends Lavishly on Itself, Insiders Say," *New York Times*, January 27, 2016, https://www.nytimes.com/2016/01/28/us/wounded-warrior-project-spends-lavishly-on-itself-ex-employees-say.html.

CHAPTER SIX: THE ECONOMICS OF THE VETERAN

1. C. Wright Mills, *The Power Elite* (New York: Oxford University Press, 1956), 214.
2. William M. McClenahan and William H. Becker, *Eisenhower and the Cold War*

Economy (Baltimore, MD: Johns Hopkins University Press, 2011), 43–47, 85–96, 102–3.
3. William E. Leuchtenburg, *A Troubled Feast: American Society since 1945* (Boston: Little, Brown, 1983), 38; World Bank, Data, United States, https://data.world bank.org/country/united-states?most_recent_year_desc=true.
4. Judith Stein, *Pivotal Decade: How the United States Traded Factories for Finance in the Seventies* (New Haven, CT: Yale University Press, 2010), 5–6. See also Paul Kennedy, *The Rise and Fall of the Great Powers: Economic Change and Military Conflict from 1500 to 2000* (New York: Random House, 1987), 436, and Diane B. Kunz, *Butter and Guns: America's Cold War Economic Diplomacy* (New York: Free Press, 1997).
5. James T. Patterson, *Restless Giant: The United States from Watergate to Bush v. Gore* (New York: Oxford University Press, 2005), 62, 738. As foreign competition improved, the U.S. economy suffered from declining productivity, averaging 3 percent annually from 1947 to 1965, 2.4 percent from 1965 to 1970, and 1.2 percent from 1973 to 1979.
6. Michael A. Urquhart and Marillyn A. Hewson, "Unemployment Continued to Rise in 1982 and Recession Deepened," *Monthly Labor Review* 105 (February 1983): 3; HSH Associates, Prime Rate, 1980–1989, https://www.hsh.com/indices/prime80s.html.
7. "Unemployment Still Hurts," *New York Times*, May 16, 1982, E22.
8. Patterson, *Restless Giant*, 60.
9. Drew Desilver, "For Most U.S. Workers, Real Wages Have Barely Budged in Decades," Pew Research Center, August 7, 2018, https://www.pewresearch.org/fact-tank/2018/08/07/for-most-us-workers-real-wages-have-barely-budged-for-decades/.
10. "Twenty Years after Black Monday," *International Economy Magazine*, Fall 2007, 32.
11. On April 12, 1991, Disney stock was valued at $9.33 a share. U.S. Steel stock on the same date was valued at $22.75 a share. By December 15, 2000, their respective standing was reversed, with Disney at $28.06 and U.S. Steel at $15.88. As of this writing in March 2020, Disney stock is worth more than ten times as much as U.S. Steel.
12. Patterson, *Restless Giant*, 350–51.
13. Doron P. Levin, "General Motors to Cut 70,000 Jobs; 21 Plants to Shut," *New York Times*, December 19, 1991, A1.
14. Edmund L. Andrews, "Job Cuts at AT&T Will Total 40,000, 13% of Its Staff," *New York Times*, January 3, 1996, A1.
15. Congressional Budget Office, *The Budget and Economic Outlook, 2016–2026* (Washington, DC: CBO, January 2016), 124.
16. Harlan Jacobson, "A Leader of the Left Meets a Follower of the Left Behind: Michael and Me," *Film Comment*, November 1989, 17.
17. "Islam Is Peace" Says President, Remarks by the President at Islamic Center of Washington, DC," September 17, 2001, https://georgewbush-whitehouse.archives.gov/news/releases/2001/09/20010917-11.html.
18. Congressional Budget Office, "Changes in CBO's Baseline Projections since January 2001," June 7, 2012. https://www.cbo.gov/publication/41463.
19. Neta C. Crawford, *United States Budgetary Costs and Obligations of Post-9/11 Wars through FY2020: $6.4 Trillion* (Providence, RI: Watson Institute of International and Public Affairs, November 13, 2019).
20. Renae Merle, "A Guide to the Financial Crisis—10 Years Later," *Washington Post*, September 10, 2018, https://www.washingtonpost.com/business/economy/a-guide-to-the-financial-crisis--10-years-later/2018/09/10/114b76ba-af10-11e8-a20b-5f4f84429666_story.html.

21. John Irons, *Economic Scarring: The Long-Term Impacts of the Recession*, EPI Briefing Paper No. 243 (Washington, DC: Economic Policy Institute, September 30, 2009), 2. The number of businesses filing for bankruptcy in 2006 was 19,700.
22. Matt Taibbi, *The Divide: American Injustice in the Age of the Wealth Gap* (New York: Spiegel & Grau, 2014), 3–4.
23. Barbara Brotman, "Surviving the Recession: One Family's Story," *Chicago Tribune*, May 15, 2009, https://www.chicagotribune.com/business/success/chi-051909-recession-lead-story.html.
24. Department of the Treasury, Initiatives, Financial Stability, TARP Programs, https://www.treasury.gov/initiatives/financial-stability/TARP-Programs/Pages/default.aspx#. The initial outlay was for $700 billion in 2008. It was later reduced to $475 billion under the Dodd-Frank Wall Street Reform and Consumer Protection Act.
25. Barbara Klein and Klaas Staal, "Was the American Recovery and Reinvestment Act an Economic Stimulus?," *International Advances in Economic Research* 23 (2017): 395–404.
26. Annie Lowrey, "The Great Recession Is Still with Us," *Atlantic*, December 1, 2017, https://www.theatlantic.com/business/archive/2017/12/great-recession-still-with-us/547268/.
27. Veterans Administration, Office of Information Management and Statistics, *Data on Vietnam Era Veterans* (Washington, DC: Veterans Administration, April 1985), 20.
28. Michelotti Kopp and Kathyrn R. Gover, "The Employment Situation of Vietnam Era Veterans," *Monthly Labor Review* 95 (December 1972): 9.
29. June A. Willenz, "The Returning Vietnam Veterans: A Challenge to the Nation's Conscience," *Vital Issues* 22 (October 1972): 3, American Veterans Committee (hereafter AVC) Papers, box 15, Estelle and Melvin Gelman Library, Washington, DC; Paul Starr, *The Discarded Army: Veterans after Vietnam* (New York: Charterhouse, 1973), 134–36. A total of 88,408 discharges occurred under such terms.
30. Public Law 89-358, *Veterans' Readjustment Benefits Act of 1966*, March 3, 1966, chap. 34, sec. 1652, 13; Statement of Dr. F. J. Pepper, National Vice Chairman, American Veterans Committee before the Subcommittee on Health and Hospitals of the Committee on Veterans Affairs and Subcommittee on Alcoholism and Narcotics of the Committee on Labor and Public Welfare—Meeting Jointly, 23 June 1971, NAACP Records, box V:2839, Library of Congress (hereafter LOC), Washington, DC.
31. Letter, June A. Willenz [Director, AVC] to IBM, Director of Public Relations, September 17, 1968, AVC Papers, box 7, Gelman Library, Washington, DC; "The Plight of Viet Nam Era Vets," *Time*, December 27, 1971, 57.
32. Letter, Headquarters, First United States Army, to Charles Eason (Acting Director, Eastern Regional Office, National Urban League), June 13, 1972, National Urban League Records, 1900–1988, Part III: Economic Development, 1961–1977, Military and Veterans Affairs Division, 1967–1976, box III:156, LOC.
33. Veterans Administration, *Two Years of Outreach, 1968–1970: A Report from the Administrator of Veterans Affairs*, n.d., 14–15, RG 15, entry 69, box 4, National Archives and Records Administration, Washington, DC.
34. Veterans Administration, *Two Years of Outreach*, 29. Memorandum, Henry A. Talbert (Army Officers' Procurement) to Thomas Brady (Acting Director, Economic Development), "Monthly Report—March 1972," 1, National Urban League Records, 1900–1988, Part III: Economic Development, 1961–1977, Military and Veterans Affairs Division, 1967–1976, box III:156, LOC.
35. Starr, *Discarded Army*, 211.

36. Starr, 210.
37. Louis Harris Associates, Inc., *A Study of the Problems Facing Vietnam Era Veterans: Their Readjustment to Civilian Life* (New York: Louis Harris and Associates, 1971), 72. "Word of mouth" (48%), "from family" (35%), and "newspaper ads" (16%) accounted for most placements, according to the poll. "Public employment service" (13%) and "job marts/job fairs for veterans" (1%) were very last on the list. Percentages refer to multiple methods by veteran job applicants.
38. Willenz, "Returning Vietnam Veterans," 3; Starr, *Discarded Army*, 201.
39. Memorandum, William H. Edward to Thomas Brady (Director, Military and Veterans Affairs Division) to George Northcroft, May 22, 1974, 4, National Urban League Papers, Part III: Economic Development, 1961–1977, Military and Veterans Affairs Division, 1967–1976, box III:157, LOC.
40. Testimony of Lewis C. Olive Jr., Director of Military and Veterans Affairs, National Urban League, on Unemployment Problems of Returning Minority Veterans, before the Committee on Veterans Affairs, United States Senate, April 28, 1972, NAACP Papers, box V:2716, LOC.
41. Starr, *Discarded Army*, 210.
42. "Returning Heroes Get the Cold Shoulder," *Business Week*, July 31, 1971, 46.
43. House Committee on Veterans' Affairs, *Legacies of Vietnam: Comparative Adjustment of Veterans and Their Peers* (Washington, DC: Government Printing Office, March 9, 1981), 197, 199.
44. U.S. Department of Labor, *Thirty-Fifth Annual Report of the Secretary of Labor for the Fiscal Year Ended June 30, 1947* (Washington, DC: Government Printing Office, 1948), 104.
45. Gina M. Scuteri, "Casualties of War and Research: A Case Study of U.S. Women Veterans of Vietnam" (PhD diss., Purdue University, 1993), 81.
46. Mark C. Berger and Barry T. Hirsch, "The Civilian Earnings Experience of Vietnam-Era Veterans," *Journal of Human Resources* 18 (Autumn 1983): 461.
47. Saul Schwartz, "The Relative Earnings of Vietnam and Korea-Era Veterans," *Industrial and Labor Relations Review* 39 (July 1986): 568. Family income for Korea veterans was $10,020 versus $9,930 for civilians. Family income for Vietnam veterans was $23,030 versus $23,170 for civilians, according to the author. See also Berger and Hirsch, "Civilian Earnings Experience," 477.
48. Barry T. Hirsch and Stephen L. Mehay, "Evaluating the Labor Market Performance of Veterans Using a Matched Group Design," *Journal of Human Resources* 38 (Summer 2003): 693–95.
49. Hirsch and Mehay, "Labor Market Performance of Veterans," 693–95.
50. Stephen Drachler, "Penn State Tuition Hike Likely," *Morning Call*, February 26, 1986. Annual Penn State tuition for residents was $2,760. For a broader study of state colleges and universities, see Meredith Ludwig and Heidi Wassan, *Student Charges at Public Institutions: Annual Survey, 1987–1988* (Washington, DC: American Association of State Colleges and Universities, 1988), 2–3.
51. House Committee on Veterans Affairs, *Final Report: Evaluation of the Emergency Veterans' Job Training Program* (Washington, DC: Government Printing Office, 1986), 1–9. Salaries for veterans completing the program were 7.5 percent higher than for those who did not.
52. P. W. Singer, *Corporate Warriors: The Rise of the Privatized Military Industry* (Ithaca, NY: Cornell University Press, 2003), 53.
53. David Evans, "Thousands Leave the Army with Early-Out Bonuses," *Chicago Tribune*, May 14, 1992, 36.
54. Maria C. Lytell, Kenneth Kuhn, Abigail Haddad, Jefferson P. Marquis, Nelson Lim, Kimberly Curry Hall, Robert Stewart, and Jennie W. Wenger, *Force Drawdowns and Demographic Diversity: Investigating the Impact of Force*

Reductions on the Demographic Diversity of the U.S. Military (Santa Monica, CA: RAND, 2015), 1.
55. Robin Wright, "The Good Soldier: As the Military Downsizes, the War-Hardened Vietnam Generation Is Retiring, including Army Legend Alfred Baker," *Los Angeles Times*, August 21, 1994, https://www.latimes.com/archives/la-xpm-1994-08-21-tm-29399-story.html; Charles Moskos, "The New Army: Loving It and Leaving It," *Chicago Tribune*, April 13, 1994, https://www.chicagotribune.com/news/ct-xpm-1994-04-13-9404130195-story.html.
56. "The Human Peace Dividend," editorial, *New York Times*, February 24, 1992, A18.
57. Claudia H. Deutsch, "Soldiers Return to the Workplace," *New York Times*, October 20, 1991, F27.
58. Eric Schmitt, "Peace Dividend: Troops Turn to Teaching," *New York Times*, November 30, 1994, A1.
59. Deutsch, "Soldiers Return to the Workplace," F27.
60. Department of Defense, press release, "Defense and Justice Departments Announce 'Troops to Cops' Program," Release No. 233-95, May 2, 1995, http://www.defense.gov/releases/release.aspx?releaseid=475.
61. Deutsch, "Soldiers Return to the Workplace," F27.
62. Department of Veterans Affairs, *Employment Situation for Vietnam-Era Veterans* (Washington, DC; Veterans Administration, June 1998), 7.
63. Christopher J. Coyne, Abigail R. Hall, Patrick A. McLaughlin, and Ann Zerkle, "A Hidden Cost of War: The Impact of Mobilizing Reserve Troops on Emergency Response Times," *Public Choice* 161 (December 2014): 289–90.
64. Congressional Budget Office, *The Effects of Reserve Call-Ups on Civilian Employers* (Washington, DC: CBO, May 2005), 9.
65. Coyne et al., "Hidden Cost of War," 290; Congressional Budget Office, *Effects of Reserve Call-Ups*, 6–7.
66. Timothy W. Maier, "Pink Slips Greet Returning Soldiers," *Insight on the News* 20 (January 6, 2004): 26.
67. Alexandra Zavis, "National Guard Soldiers and Airmen Face Unemployment Crisis," *Los Angeles Times*, November 23, 2012, https://www.latimes.com/world/la-xpm-2012-nov-23-la-me-national-guard-employment-20121124-story.html.
68. United States Department of Justice, Uniformed Services Employment and Reemployment Rights Act of 1994, https://www.justice.gov/crt-military/uniformed-services-employment-and-reemployment-rights-act-1994.
69. Congressional Budget Office, *Effects of Reserve Call-Ups*, 13, 16–17.
70. Alexandra Zavis, "Betrayed? Citizen Soldiers Lose Jobs: U.S. Government Biggest Offender," *Los Angeles Times*, May 5, 2013, https://www.latimes.com/local/la-xpm-2013-may-05-la-me-citizen-soldiers-20130506-story.html.
71. Congressional Budget Office, *Effects of Reserve Call-Ups*, 15; Zavis, "Betrayed?"
72. Maier, "Pink Slips Greet Returning Soldiers," 26.
73. Libby Denkmann, "Fired after Military Deployment, Reservist Seeks His Day in Court," American Homefront Project, October 20, 2017, https://americanhomefront.wunc.org/post/fired-after-military-deployment-reservist-seeks-his-day-court.
74. Bureau of Labor Statistics, "Employment Situation of Veterans—2018," USDL-19-0451, March 21, 2019, https://www.bls.gov/news.release/archives/vet_03212019.pdf.
75. James A. Walker, "Employment and Earnings of Recent Veterans: Data from the CPS," *Monthly Labor Review* 133 (July 2010): 5. In 2008, women veterans experienced a 9.1 percent unemployment rate; the comparable percentage for civilian women was 5.5 percent. In 2009, the respective percentages were 11.3 percent and 8.3 percent.

76. David S. Loughran, *Why Is Veteran Unemployment So High?* (Santa Monica, CA: RAND, 2014), 1; Bureau of Labor Statistics, Civilian Unemployment Rate, https://www.bls.gov/charts/employment-situation/civilian-unemployment-rate.htm.
77. Loughran, *Veteran Unemployment*, ix.
78. Department of Veterans Affairs, National Center for Veterans Analysis and Statistics, *Minority Veterans Report: Military Service History and Benefits Utilization Statistics* (Washington, DC: Department of Veterans Affairs, March 2017), 33; Sharon Y. Murphy, "Employment Experiences of Black and White Veterans with Service-Connected Disabilities" (PhD diss., Wayne State University, 2014), 3.
79. Loughran, *Veteran Unemployment*, 13.
80. Loughran, 17.
81. Sebastian Junger, *Tribe: On Homecoming and Belonging* (New York: Twelve, 2016), 78–88; Bureau of Labor Statistics, *Employment Situation of Veterans—2018*, USDL-19-0451, news release, March 21, 2019, 1; Sharon R. Cohany, "Employment and Unemployment among Vietnam-Era Veterans," *Monthly Labor Review* 113 (April 1990): 23.
82. Kristy N. Kamarck and Eva G. McKinsey, *DoD's Troops to Teachers Program (TTT)*, IF10850 (Washington, DC: Congressional Research Service, March 15, 2018), 1–3.
83. Kristy N. Kamarck, *Military Transition Assistance Program (TAP): An Overview*, IF10347 (Washington, DC: Congressional Research Service, July 12, 2018), 1–3.
84. Benjamin Collins, *Veterans' Benefits: The Vocational Rehabilitation and Employment Program*, RL34627 (Washington, DC: Congressional Research Service, February 21, 2018), 1.
85. Kamarck, *Military Transition Assistance Program*, 1–3.
86. Memorandum from John Berry (Director, Office of Personnel and Management) to Chief Human Capital Officers, "VOW (Veterans Opportunity to Work) to Hire Heroes Act of 2011," June 15, 2012, https://www.chcoc.gov/content/vow-veterans-opportunity-work-hire-heroes-act-2011; Loughran, *Veteran Unemployment*, 2, 7.
87. Jack Sher, "Why Hire Disabled Vets?," *American Legion Magazine*, October 1947, 22–23.
88. Benjamin Collins, *Veterans' Employment*, IF10490 (Washington, DC: Congressional Research Service, April 24, 2018), 2.
89. Department of Labor, My Next Move: For Veterans, https://www.mynextmove.org/vets/.
90. Collins, *Veterans' Employment*, 1.
91. Department of Labor, Bureau of Labor Statistics, Table A-5, Employment status of the civilian population 18 years and over by veteran status, period of service, and sex, not seasonally adjusted, https://www.bls.gov/news.release/empsit.t05.htm.
92. Francesco Renna and Amanda Weinstein, "The Veterans Wage Differential," *Applied Economics* 51 (2019): 1286.
93. Joel B. McKelvey, "War and Welfare: The Later Life Consequences of Military Service" (PhD diss., Florida State University, 2011), 32–33; Renna and Weinstein, "Veterans Wage Differential," 1288–89. See also Barry T. Hirsch and Stephen L. Mehay, "Evaluating the Labor Market Performance of Veterans Using a Matched Comparison Group Design," *Journal of Human Resources* 38 (Summer 2003): 686.
94. Department of Veterans Affairs, *Minority Veterans Report*, 36; Department of Veterans Affairs, National Center for Veterans Analysis and Statistics, *Minority Veterans: 2011* (Washington, DC: Department of Veterans Affairs, May 2013), 16.
95. William Gibson, *Zero History* (New York: G. P. Putnam's Sons, 2010), 213.

96. Simon van Zuylen-Wood, "The Heavily Armed Millennials of Instagram," *Washington Post Magazine*, March 4, 2019, https://www.washingtonpost.com/news/magazine/wp/2019/03/04/feature/the-heavily-armed-millennials-of-instagram/.
97. Theodore Ropp, *War in the Modern World* (Durham, NC: Duke University Press, 1962), 53. Ropp quotes Maurice de Saxe's *Reveries on the Art of War* (1757).
98. Beth Bailey, "The Army in the Marketplace: Recruiting an All-Volunteer Force," *Journal of American History* 94 (June 2007): 47–74; quotation on 68.
99. Lee A. Daniels, "With Military Set to Thin Ranks, Blacks Fear They'll Be Hurt the Most," *New York Times*, August 7, 1991, D5.
100. John Morton Bloom, *V Was for Victory: Politics and American Culture during World War II* (New York: Harcourt Brace, 1976), 108–10.
101. *Shell . . . Soldier and Civilian* (New York: Shell Union Oil Corporation, 1945), 3, Imprints, Hagley Museum and Library, Wilmington, DE.
102. Sandi Gohn, "12 Must-See Photos of Troops and NFL Players through the Decades," February 5, 2021, USO, https://www.uso.org/stories/2609-12-must-see-photos-of-troops-and-nfl-players-through-the-decades.
103. Adam Kilgore, "For Decades, the NFL Wrapped Itself in the Flag: Now That's Made Business Uneasy," *Washington Post*, September 6, 2018, https://www.washingtonpost.com/sports/for-decades-the-nfl-wrapped-itself-in-the-flag-now-thats-made-business-uneasy/2018/09/06/bc9aab64-b05d-11e8-9a6a-565d92a3585d_story.html.
104. Michael Janofsky, "Biggest Game: The Bill Runs to $9 Million," *New York Times*, January 13, 1985, S1.
105. Ben Fountain, *Billy Lynn's Long Halftime Walk* (New York: HarperCollins, 2012).
106. Janofsky, "Biggest Game," S1; Andrew Mach, "Report: Defense Dept. Paid Millions of Taxpayer Dollars to Salute Troops," *PBS NewsHour Weekend*, May 10, 2015, https://www.pbs.org/newshour/nation/defense-department-paid-5-4-million-nfl-honor-troops.
107. Stephen R. Patnode, "Labor's Lost Love: The Influence of Gender, Race, and Class on the Workplace in Postwar America" (PhD diss., SUNY Stonybrook, 2008), 98, 105.
108. Pentagon Revolving Door Database, POGO, January 15, 2021, https://www.pogo.org/database/pentagon-revolving-door/. The total list of former military and civilian officials moving to the private sector is enormous.
109. Mark L. Rockefeller, "The Top 25 Veteran-Founded Startups in America," *Forbes*, November 11, 2016, https://www.forbes.com/sites/marklrockefeller/2016/11/11/the-top-25-veteran-startups-in-america/?sh=1d17a37a6e84.
110. Daniel Cebul, "Tech Firm Looks to Revolutionize How Recruits Keep in Touch with Family," *Marine Corps Times*, May 24, 2018, https://www.marinecorpstimes.com/news/your-military/2018/05/25/tech-firm-looks-to-revolutionize-how-recruits-keep-in-touch-with-family/.
111. See https://www.sandboxx.us.
112. James Bradley, with Ron Powers, *Flags of Our Fathers* (New York: Bantam Books, 2000), 311–12.
113. "How to Be an Operator" recorded over four million hits as of May 2021, for example. See https://www.youtube.com/watch?v=yfoR7no2owM.
114. James Barber, "Mat Best's 'Not Your Typical Military Book' Hits the Top of the Charts," Military.com, September 4, 2019, https://www.military.com/off-duty/2019/09/05/mat-bests-not-your-typical-military-book-hits-top-charts.html.
115. Jeffrey Cimmino, "Review: 'Thank You for My Service,'" *Washington Free Beacon*, August 25, 2019, https://freebeacon.com/culture/review-thank-you-for-my-service/.

116. Mat Best, with Ross Patterson and Nils Park, *Thank You for My Service* (New York: Bantam Books, 2019), 187. Best's emphasis in original.
117. Michelle Miller and Vidya Singh, "Black Rifle Coffee: Behind the Company Selling Beans with a Message," *CBS News*, February 3, 2018, https://www.cbsnews.com/news/black-rifle-coffee-company-veterans-culture-conservative-approach/.
118. Mark L. Rockefeller, "How This Veteran Entrepreneur Brewed $30 Million from Coffee and Passion," *Forbes*, April 5, 2018, https://www.forbes.com/sites/marklrockefeller/2018/04/05/making-30-million-on-coffee-and-passion/#398003556aef.
119. Rockefeller, "Veteran Entrepreneur"; Frank Connor, "Green Beret Turns Battlefield Coffee into an $80M Business," Fox Business, November 11, 2019, https://www.foxbusiness.com/lifestyle/green-beret-battlefield-coffee-business.
120. Van Zuylen-Wood, "Heavily Armed Millennials of Instagram."
121. Harry Lever and Joseph Young, *Wartime Racketeers* (New York: G. P. Putnam's Sons, 1945), 75–85.
122. Karina Hernandez, "Why These Veterans Regret Their For-Profit College Degrees—and Debt," *PBS Newshour*, October 23, 2018, https://www.pbs.org/newshour/education/why-these-veterans-regret-their-for-profit-college-degrees-and-debt.
123. Aaron Glantz, "University of Phoenix Sidesteps Obama Order on Recruiting Veterans," Reveal, June 30, 2015, https://revealnews.org/article/university-of-phoenix-sidesteps-obama-order-on-recruiting-veterans/.
124. Danielle Douglas-Gabriel, "Why the Defense Department Is Kicking the University of Phoenix Off Military Bases," *Washington Post*, October 9, 2015, https://www.washingtonpost.com/news/grade-point/wp/2015/10/09/why-the-defense-department-is-kicking-the-university-of-phoenix-off-military-bases/.
125. U. S. Senate, Health, Education, Labor, and Pensions Committee, *Is the New G.I. Bill Working?: For-Profit Colleges Increasing Veteran Enrollment and Federal Funds*, Majority Committee Staff Report (Washington, DC: Government Printing Office, July 30, 2014), 5.
126. Samantha Allen, "Death of a Diploma Mill: University of Phoenix Going Down in Flames?," *Daily Beast*, April 14, 2017, https://www.thedailybeast.com/death-of-a-diploma-mill-university-of-phoenix-going-down-in-flames. The 2008 graduation rate for online students was 5.0%. See Mamie Lynch, Jennifer Engle, and José L. Cruz, *Subprime Opportunity: The Unfulfilled Promise of For-Profit Colleges and Universities* (Washington, DC: Education Trust, 2010), 5.
127. Douglas-Gabriel, "University of Phoenix Off Military Bases"; Allen, "Death of a Diploma Mill; Rachel Leingang, "VA Plans to Suspend New GI Bill Enrollments at the University of Phoenix," *Arizona Republic*, March 9, 2020, https://www.azcentral.com/story/news/local/arizona-education/2020/03 . . . plans-suspend-new-gi-bill-enrollments-university-phoenix/5002668002/.
128. "Statement of Commissioner Rohit Chopra in the Matter of University of Phoenix," Commission File Number 1523231, December 10, 2019, https://vetsedsuccess.org/letter-of-support-from-veterans-groups-for-rohit-chopra-to-head-consumer-financial-protection-bureau/; Danielle Douglas-Gabriel, "FTC Reaches $191 Million Settlement with University of Phoenix in Deceptive-Ad Probe," *Philadelphia Inquirer*, December 10, 2019, https://www.inquirer.com/business/university-phoenix-ads-college-debt-fraud-ftc-20191210.html.
129. Leingang, "VA Plans to Suspend New G.I. Bill Enrollments."
130. Viqtory Media, "Why Military Friendly®?," https://www.militaryfriendly.com/about-us/. Victory Media made its name change to Viqtory Media after the 2017 FTC report on the company became public.

131. See 2021 Military Friendly Employers, https://www.militaryfriendly.com/employers/.
132. Viqtory Media, https://www.militaryfriendly.com.
133. Veterans Education Success, *Understanding Misleading Websites and "Lead Generators": A Case Study: Victory Media's "Military Friendly Schools,"* February 2017, 2, 17, 23, https://vetsedsuccess.org/misleading-websites-lead-generators-case-study-victory-media-military-friendly-schools/.
134. Andrew Kreighbaum, "Crackdown on 'Pay to Play' for 'Military Friendly' Colleges," *Inside Higher Ed*, October 20, 2017, https://www.insidehighered.com/news/2017/10/20/ftc-settlement-says-rankings-military-friendly-colleges-were-deceptive-promotions.
135. Patterson, *Restless Giant*, 360–61.
136. See, for example, Department of Veterans Affairs, *Minority Veterans Report*.

CHAPTER SEVEN: LOST ON CAMPUS

1. Alexis de Tocqueville, *Democracy in America: In Relation to Political Institutions* (New York: Edward Walker, 1850), 320.
2. Daniel J. Boorstin, *The Americans: The Colonial Experience* (New York: Vintage Books, 1958), 150.
3. Milton Greenberg, *The GI Bill: The Law That Changed America* (New York: Lickle, 1997), 35; Michael C. Behnke, "Five Decades on Campus: Snapshots of College Life in America," *College Board Review* 157 (Fall 1990): 6; Thomas N. Bonner, "The Unintended Revolution in America's Colleges since 1940," *Change*, September/October 1986, 44.
4. Michael D. Gambone, *The Greatest Generation Comes Home: The Veteran in American Society* (College Station: Texas A&M University Press, 2005), 65.
5. Gambone, *Greatest Generation Comes Home*, 66–69. In 1947, for example, 6.6 million veterans applied for educational benefits and 1.1 million enrolled in college.
6. Department of Commerce, *Historical Statistics of the United States from Colonial Times to 1970* (Washington, DC: Government Printing Office, 1974), 142–44.
7. Greenberg, *The GI Bill*, 36; Rufus D. Smith and Ray F. Harvey, "College Population Trends," *School and Society* 66 (July 5, 1947): 1–5.
8. Corey B. Rumann and Florence A. Hamrick, "Student Veterans in Transition: Re-Enrolling after War Zone Deployments," *Journal of Higher Education* 81 (July/August 2010): 431.
9. Rumann and Hamrick, "Student Veterans in Transition," 382; Veterans Administration, *Annual Report, 1985* (Washington, DC: Department of Veterans Affairs, 1985), 82.
10. Robert L. Eaton, "The Sorry State of Vietnam Vets' Education," *American Legion Magazine*, June 1974, 8.
11. Memorandum for the AVC National Office, "GI Bill in Trouble—Veto Promised," November 22, 1974, Gelman Library, American Veterans Committee Papers, box 7, Gelman Library, Washington, DC; Mark Boulton, *Failing Our Veterans: The G.I. Bill and the Vietnam Generation* (New York: New York University Press, 2014), 190–95.
12. Railey quoted in Mark Boulton, "How the G.I. Bill Failed African-American Vietnam War Veterans," *Journal of Blacks in Higher Education* 58 (Winter 2007/2008): 57.
13. Boulton, "G.I. Bill Failed."
14. Charles Moskos, "The All-Volunteer Force," *Wilson Quarterly* 3 (Spring 1979): 134. By 1979, African Americans comprised 19 percent of military personnel.

15. Veterans Administration, *Annual Report, 1985*, 82. In 1976, total college enrollment was 10.9 million. See National Center for Education Statistics, *Digest of Education Statistics*, https://nces.ed.gov/programs/digest/d17/tables/dt17_306.10.asp.
16. Max Kutner, "What It's Like to Go from War to a Liberal Arts College," *Newsweek*, May 29, 2017, https://www.newsweek.com/2017/06/16/veterans-college-campuses-vassar-posse-615839.html.
17. Cassandria Dortch, *GI Bills Enacted Prior to 2008 and Related Veterans' Educational Assistance Programs: A Primer*, R42785 (Washington, DC: Congressional Research Service, October 6, 2017), 45.
18. Barry T. Hirsch and Stephen L. Mehay, "Evaluating the Labor Market Performance of Veterans Using a Matched Group Design," *Journal of Human Resources* 38 (Summer 2003): 693–95.
19. According to the National Center for Education Statistics, in-state annual costs for four-year public universities averaged $3,859 in 1985–86. However, if private institutions are included, the cost rose to $9,228. See National Center for Education Statistics, https://nces.ed.gov/programs/digest/d07/tables/dt07_320.asp; see also Stephen Drachler, "Penn State Tuition Hike Likely," *Morning Call*, February 26, 1986, https://www.mcall.com/news/mc-xpm-1986-02-26-2510596-story.html. Annual Penn State tuition for residents was $2,760. For a broader study of state college and university costs, see Meredith Ludwig and Heidi Wassan, *Student Charges at Public Institutions: Annual Survey, 1987–1988* (Washington, DC: American Association of State Colleges and Universities, 1988), 2–3.
20. Lesley McBain, Young M. Kim, Bryan J. Cook, and Kathy M. Snead, *From Soldier to Student II: Assessing Campus Programs for Veterans and Service Members* (Washington, DC: American Council on Education, July 2012), 5. Between 2008 and 2012, five hundred thousand veterans or family members had used their educational benefits.
21. Department of Veterans Affairs, *Education and Training, Post-9/11 GI Bill (Chapter 33) Payment Rates for 2019 Academic Year* (August 1, 2019–July 31, 2020), https://benefits.va.gov/GIBILL/resources/benefits_resources/rates/ch33/ch33rates080119.asp.
22. Cassandria Dortch, *The Post-9/11 GI Bill: A Primer*, R42755 (Washington, DC: Congressional Research Service, August 1, 2018), 1, 11.
23. Tim Dyhouse, "167,000 GI Claims Filed in 2009," *VFW Magazine*, April 2010, 13.
24. Natalie Gross, "Senate Stalls on Bill to Help Student Vets, Even as GI Bill Processing Delays Spike," *Military Times*, October 25, 2018, https://rebootcamp.militarytimes.com/news/education/2018/10/25/senate-stalls-on-a-bill-to-help-student-vets-even-as-gi-bill-processing-delays-spike/.
25. Douglas Herrmann, "College Is for Veterans, Too," *Chronicle of Higher Education* 55 (November 21, 2018): A33.
26. Aaron Glantz, "The Soldier and the Student," *Nation*, November 27, 2007, https://www.thenation.com/article/archive/soldier-and-student/.
27. Congressional Budget Office, *The Post-9/11 GI Bill: Beneficiaries, Choices, and Cost* (Washington, DC: CBO, May 2019), 1.
28. "Let's Enroll!," *Mother Jones*, September/October 2011, 11; Hanover Research, *Veterans Marketing Research* (Washington, DC: Hanover Research, 2012), 4, 20.
29. Catherine Morris, "For Profits Under Fire," *Diverse Issues in Higher Education* 31 (November 6, 2014): 16–18, https://diverseeducation.com/article/67984/.
30. "Let's Enroll!," 11.
31. Congressional Budget Office, *Post-9/11 GI Bill*, 20.
32. The 2008 graduation rate for online students was just 5.0 percent. See Mamie Lynch, Jennifer Engle, and José L. Cruz, *Subprime Opportunity: The Unfulfilled*

Promise of For-Profit Colleges and Universities (Washington, DC: Education Trust, 2010), 4–5.
33. 140 Cong. Rec. H14065 (daily ed. June 22, 1994) (extensions of remarks, GI Bill 50th Anniversary, William D. Ford); Gambone, *Greatest Generation Comes Home*, 29.
34. I had the honor of attending courses with two of these individuals, Dr. Robert Murray at Penn State and Dr. Arthur Mann at the University of Chicago.
35. Hanson W. Baldwin, "Reserve Program: Arguments Weighed," *New York Times*, June 19, 1955, E7.
36. Congressional Budget Office, *The All-Volunteer Military: Issues and Performance*, Pub. No. 2960 (Washington, DC: Congressional Budget Office, July 2007), 5; Department of Veterans Affairs, Office of Research and Development, *VA Research on Vietnam Veterans*, https://www.research.va.gov/topics/vietnam.cfm.
37. Robert Timberg, *The Nightingale's Song* (New York: Simon & Schuster, 1995), 15–16.
38. Timberg, *Nightingale's Song*, 14.
39. When I entered the University of Chicago doctoral program in 1988, there were sixty-four other graduate students in my cohort. Two of us were veterans. Department of Veterans Affairs, *Annual Report of the Secretary of Veterans Affairs—1997* (Washington, DC: Department of Veterans Affairs, 1997), 123.
40. In 2015–16, 870,500 veterans attended college. See Laura Holian and Tara Adam, *Veterans' Education Benefits: A Profile of Military Students Who Received Federal Veterans' Education Benefits, 2015–16* (Washington, DC: National Center for Educational Statistics, 2020), 2; Mary E. Falkey, "An Emerging Population: Student Veterans in Higher Education in the 21st Century," *Journal of Academic Administration in Higher Education* 12 (Spring 2016): 29.
41. D. Alexis Hart and Roger Thompson, "Veterans in the Writing Classroom: Three Programmatic Approaches to Facilitate the Transition from the Military to Higher Education," *College Composition and Communication* 68 (December 2016): 354.
42. Young M. Kim and James S. Cole, *Student Veterans/Service Members' Engagement in College and University Life and Education* (Washington, DC: American Council on Education, December 2013), 1–2, 4. According to the study, 78.9 percent were 25 or older.
43. Rumann and Hamrick, "Student Veterans in Transition," 441.
44. Hart and Thompson, "Veterans in the Writing Classroom," 351. See also Thomas E. Ricks, "The Widening Gap between the Military and Society," *Atlantic Monthly*, July 1997, 66–78.
45. Margaret Bellafiore, "From Combat to Campus," *Knowledge and Technology* 98 (September–October 2012): 35.
46. Janis Newby Parham and Stephen P. Gordon, "Military Veterans Bring Many Positives—and Some Needs—into Teaching," *Phi Delta Kappan*, April 2016, 44.
47. Jennifer L. Steele, Nicholas Salcedo, and James Coley, *Service Members in School: Military Veterans' Experiences Using the Post-9/11 GI Bill and Pursuing Postsecondary Education* (Santa Monica, CA: RAND, November 2010), 33–35.
48. Steele, Salcedo, and Coley, *Service Members in School*, 33–36.
49. Dymilah Luwanna Hewitt, "The Experiences and Academic Successes of African American Post-9/11 Veterans at Martin R. Delany State University (Pseudonym of an Actual Historically Black University)" (PhD diss., University of North Carolina, 2017), 3.
50. Heather Marie Reyes, "Minority Veteran Educational Outcomes in the All-Volunteer Era" (master's thesis, University of Washington, 2015), 4, 17, 29. Reyes examined minority veterans from 1982 to 2014.

51. Roberto Cancio, "Examining the Effect of Military Service on Education: The Unique Case of Hispanic Veterans," *Hispanic Journal of Behavioral Sciences* 40 (March 2018): 150–57.
52. Cancio, "Effect of Military Service on Education," 167; "ACE Report Suggests New GI Bill Will Change Attendance Trends," *Hispanic Outlook in Higher Education* 20 (November 2, 2009): 31.
53. Hart and Thompson. "Veterans in the Writing Classroom," 346
54. Kim and Cole, *Engagement in College*, 2, 9.
55. Alisa Roost and Noah Roost, "Supporting Veterans in the Classroom," *Academe*, May–June 2014, 31–34.
56. Hart and Thompson. "Veterans in the Writing Classroom," 353.
57. There is extensive recent literature on the topic. See Laura C. Hart, "Why 'Separate' May Be Better: Exploring Single-Sex Learning as a Remedy for Social Anxieties in Female Middle School Students," *Middle School Journal* 47 (January 2016): 32–40, and Wayne Martino, Martin Mills, and Bob Lingard, "Interrogating Single-Sex Classes as a Strategy for Addressing Boys' Educational and Social Needs," *Oxford Review of Education* 31 (June 2005): 237–54.
58. Veterans Writing Project, "What We Do," https://veteranswriting.org.
59. For examples of each, see Ron Capps, *Writing War: A Guide to Telling Your Own Story* (Washington, DC: Veterans Writing Project, 2014).
60. Capps, *Writing War*, 8, 1.
61. McBain, Kim, Cook, and Snead, *From Soldier to Student II*, 7, 17.
62. Colleen Murphy, "How Traditional Colleges Can Compete to Enroll Veterans," *Chronicle of Higher Education*, July 24, 2015, A15.
63. University of Oklahoma Veteran Support Alliance, https://www.ou.edu/veterans/green-zone/green_zone_training; Purdue University, Veterans Success Center, https://www.purdue.edu/veterans/resources/greenzonetraining.php.
64. Falkey, "An Emerging Population," 33–34; Press Release, "UNC System Establishes Partnership with PsychArmor Institute," July 12, 2019, University of North Carolina System, https://dev.northcarolina.edu/news/unc-system-establishes-partnership-with-psycharmor-institute/.
65. Media Bias/Fact Check, *Military Times*, https://mediabiasfactcheck.com/military-times/; MilitaryTimes.com, https://www.militarytimes.com/about-us/. The publication originally appeared as *Army Times* in 1940.
66. George Altman, "Methodology: Best for Vets Colleges 2020," MilitaryTimes.com, October 28, 2019, https://www.militarytimes.com/education-transition/2019/10/28/methodology-best-for-vets-colleges-2020.
67. See, for example, the author's home institution: "Kutztown University Named Best for Vets by Military Times Sixth-Straight Year," November 6, 2019, https://www.kutztown.edu/news-and-media/news-releases/november-2019/kutztown-university-named-best-for-vets-by-military-times-for-sixth-straight-year.html.
68. Charity Navigator notes that PsychArmor lacks seven years of IRS Form 990 documentation for a complete review of its nonprofit status. However, the watchdog group did recognize PsychArmor's overall transparency. See https://www.charitynavigator.org/index.cfm?bay=search.profile&ein=465124059.
69. Veterans Education Success, *Understanding Misleading Websites and "Lead Generators": A Case Study: Victory Media's "Military Friendly Schools*," February 2017, 2, 17, 23.
70. McBain, Kim, Cook, and Snead, *From Soldier to Student II*, 14–15.
71. Kim and Cole, *Engagement in College*, 7.
72. Chris Andrew Cate, Jared S. Lyon, James Schmeling, and Barrett Y. Bogue, *National Veteran Education Success Tracker: A Report on the Academic Success of*

Student Veterans Using the Post-9/11 GI Bill (Washington, DC: Student Veterans of America, 2017), 14, https://www.luminafoundation.org/files/resources/veteran-success-tracker.pdf.

73. Lyon et al., *Veterans Education Success Tracker*, 10; Jon Marcus, "Despite Family and Work Commitments, Student Veterans Outpace Classmates," *Hechinger Report*, February 24, 2017, https://hechingerreport.org/despite-family-work-commitments-student-veterans-outpace-classmates/.
74. Kelly Gibson, "From 'Boots to Books': Adapting to College Life," *VFW Magazine*, August 2011, 19.
75. Student Veterans of America, "About SVA," https://studentveterans.org/about/.
76. Dave Spiva, "Student Veterans Helping Student Veterans," *VFW Magazine*, February 2019, 17.
77. National Association for Black Veterans, https://nabvets.com.
78. Iraq Veterans Against the War, "Winter Soldier," http://www.ivaw.org/wintersoldier. The IVAW website is no longer active.
79. Ruth Igielnik and Kim Parker, "Majorities of U.S. Veterans, Public Say the Wars in Iraq and Afghanistan Were Not Worth Fighting," Pew Research Center, "FactTank," July 10, 2019, https://www.pewresearch.org/fact-tank/2019/07/10/majorities-of-u-s-veterans-public-say-the-wars-in-iraq-and-afghanistan-were-not-worth-fighting/. Ironically, 64 percent of surveyed veterans believed the war in Iraq was not worth fighting. Fifty-eight percent of surveyed veterans believed the same about Afghanistan. The IVAW website is no longer active.
80. Spiva, "Student Veterans Helping Student Veterans," 20.
81. David Flores, "Politicization beyond Politics: Narratives and Mechanisms of Iraq War Veterans' Activism," *Armed Forces & Society* 43 (January 2017): 169.
82. Stephanie Marken, "Returning Vets Don't Feel Their College Understood Their Needs," Gallup, November 11, 2015, https://news.gallup.com/poll/186548/returning-vets-don-feel-college-understood-needs.aspx.
83. "Vets Score Well in College Survey," *VFW Magazine*, February 2016, 8.

CHAPTER EIGHT: THE VETERAN IN POLITICS

1. Edmund Morris, *The Rise of Theodore Roosevelt* (New York: Coward, McCann & Geoghegan, 1979), 704.
2. Morris, *Rise of Theodore Roosevelt*, 717–21.
3. Michael D. Gambone, *The Greatest Generation Comes Home: The Veteran in American Society* (College Park: Texas A&M University Press, 2005), 82–83.
4. A. W. Geiger, Kristin Bialik, and John Gramlick, "The Changing Face of Congress in 6 Charts," "FactTank," Pew Research Center, March 10, 2021, https://www.pewresearch.org/fact-tank/2019/02/15/the-changing-face-of-congress/.
5. John Lewis Gaddis, *The United States and the End of the Cold War: Implications, Reconsiderations, Provocations* (New York: Oxford University Press, 1992), 214–15.
6. Bob Dreyfuss, "Taking Aim at the Pentagon Budget," *Nation*, March 23, 2011, https://www.thenation.com/article/archive/taking-aim-pentagon-budget/.
7. Michael D. Gambone, *Long Journeys Home: American Veterans of World War II, Korea, and Vietnam* (College Station: Texas A&M University Press, 2017), 129–30; Henry Jepson Latham, Biographical Directory of the United States Congress, 1784–present, https://bioguideretro.congress.gov/Home/MemberDetails?memIndex=L000108.
8. Gambone, *Greatest Generation Comes Home*, 57–60.
9. Gambone, *Long Journeys Home*, 115–16.
10. Refer to Chapter Five.

11. Mark Boulton, *Failing Our Veterans: The G.I. Bill and the Vietnam Generation* (New York: New York University Press, 2014), 51.
12. Boulton, *Failing Our Veterans*, 85.
13. Boulton, 54, 82–83.
14. Gambone, *Long Journeys Home*, 120, 123.
15. Boulton, *Failing Our Veterans*, 126.
16. John P. Murtha Congressional Papers Website, University of Pittsburgh University Library System, http://murtha.pitt.edu/jack.html.
17. James T. Wooten, "Democrat a Narrow Victor for House," *New York Times*, February 6, 1974, 19.
18. Dennis B. Roddy, "Obituary: John P. Murtha/Powerful Johnston Congressman," *Pittsburgh Post-Gazette*, February 9, 2010, https://www.post-gazette.com/news/nation/2010/02/09/Obituary-John-P-Murtha-Powerful-Johnstown-congressman/stories/201002090275.
19. Ronald Sullivan, "Veterans for Peace Simulate the War," *New York Times*, September 5, 1970, 6; David Mikkelson, "John Kerry: Does a Photograph Show Senator John Kerry at a 1970 Antiwar Rally?," Snopes, February 12, 2004, https://www.snopes.com/fact-check/john-kerry/; "User Clip: John Kerry on the *Dick Cavett Show*," C-SPAN, June 30, 1971, https://www.c-span.org/video/?c4464379/user-clip-john-kerry-dick-cavett-show. Kerry also appeared on the show on May 7, 1970.
20. *Complete Testimony of Lt. John Kerry to Senate Foreign Relations Committee on Behalf of the Vietnam Veterans Against the War*, 92nd Cong., 1st sess., April 22, 1971, 182.
21. *Complete Testimony of Lt. John Kerry*, 210–11.
22. Dan Payne, "How Kerry Wins," *Salon*, April 14, 2004, https://www.salon.com/test2/2004/04/13/kerry_27/.
23. Neil Sheehan, "Conversations with Americans: Book Review," *New York Times*, December 27, 1970, 165.
24. Brian C. Mooney, "First Campaign Ends in Defeat," *Boston Globe*, June 18, 2003, http://archive.boston.com/globe/nation/packages/kerry/061803.shtml; MA District 5, https://www.ourcampaigns.com/RaceDetail.html?RaceID=54220&ShowAllMUPoll=Y.
25. George B. Merry, "Shannon Senate Bid Gets Key Endorsement," *Christian Science Monitor*, June 11, 1984, https://www.csmonitor.com/1984/0611/061134.html.
26. Katherine Q. Seelye, "After 19 Years Voting in Senate, the Kerry of Today Is Far from the Kerry of 1985," *New York Times*, March 20, 2004, A10.
27. Congress, Members of Congress, Sen. John Kerry, Govtrack, https://www.govtrack.us/congress/members/john_kerry/300060.
28. Robert Timberg, *The Nightingale's Song* (New York: Simon & Schuster, 1995), 302–3.
29. Timberg, *Nightingale's Song*, 303–4.
30. Scholarship on this topic is voluminous. See, for example, Heonik Kwon, "Rethinking Traumas of War," *Southeast Asia Research* 20 (June 2012): 227–37; Robert J. McMahon, "Contested Memory: The Vietnam War and American Society, 1975–2001," *Diplomatic History* 26 (Spring 2002): 159–84; Robin Wager-Pacifici and Barry Schwartz, "The Vietnam Veteran's Memorial: Commemorating a Difficult Past," *American Journal of Sociology* 97 (September 1991): 376–420.
31. Lance Morrow, Joseph J. Kane, John F. Stacks, and Elizabeth Taylor, "A Bloody Rite of Passage: Vietnam Cost America Its Innocence and Still Haunts Its Conscience," *Time*, April 15, 1985, 20.

32. David K. Shipler, "The Vietnam Experience and the Congressman of the 1980's," *New York Times*, May 28, 1987, B6.
33. Timberg, *Nightingale's Song*, 392; Douglas Frantz, "Powerful Publisher Put McCain on a Political Path," *New York Times*, February 21, 2000, A14.
34. Shipler, "Vietnam Experience and the Congressman," B6.
35. Steven V. Robert, "Foreign Policy: Lots of Table Thumping Going On," *New York Times*, May 29, 1985, A16; Nikolas Kozloff, "McCain Roughing Up Sandinista: Smoking Gun in Campaign '08?," *North American Congress on Latin America*, August 3, 2008, https://nacla.org/news/mccain-roughing-sandinista-smoking-gun-campaign-'08.
36. Timberg, *Nightingale's Song*, 393–94.
37. Timberg, 458; Tom Fitzpatrick, "McCain: The Most Reprehensible of the Keating Five," *Phoenix New Times*, November 29, 1989, https://www.phoenixnewtimes.com/news/mccain-the-most-reprehensible-of-the-keating-five-6431838.
38. James Ring Adams, "How to Win Friends and Influence Regulators," *National Review*, March 19, 1990, 36.
39. W. Black, "Control Fraud as an Explanation for White-Collar Crime Waves: The Case of the Savings and Loan Debacle," *Crime, Law and Social Change* 43 (February 2005): 10.
40. Weston Kosova, "Cranston Wiggling," *New Republic*, March 19, 1990, 24. See also C-SPAN, House Banking, Finance, and Urban Affairs Committee, Lincoln Savings and Loan Closing, Day 4, Part 1, November 14, 1989, https://www.c-span.org/video/?9907-1/lincoln-savings-loan-day-4-part-1.
41. Mac Johnson, "The Media Finally Treat John McCain Like a Republican Again," *Human Events*, February 25, 2008, 7.
42. R. W. Apple, "Fighting the Good Fight: North's View Is That a Band of Patriots Opposed by a Hostile and Unreliable World," *New York Times*, July 9, 1987, A1.
43. E. J. Dionne, "Many Are Found to Believe North, but According to a New Poll, Most See Reagan as Lying," *New York Times*, July 11, 1987, A1; Philip Shenon, "North, Poindexter and 2 Others Indicted on Iran-Contra Fraud and Theft Charges," *New York Times*, March 17, 1988, A1.
44. Timberg, *Nightingale's Song*, 473.
45. Bob Kemper, "Ex-Marines Fire Salvo at North," *Daily Press*, October 8, 1994, https://www.dailypress.com/news/dp-xpm-19941008-1994-10-08-9410080097-story.html.
46. David E. Sanger, "Kerry Says Focus on Iraq Endangers U.S.," *New York Times*, May 30, 2004, N12.
47. "Swift Veterans Letter to John Kerry," Swift Vets and POWs for Truth, May 4, 2004, https://web.archive.org/web/20050915133442/http://horse.he.net/~swiftpow/article.php?story=20040629220813790.
48. Jodi Wilgoren, "Kerry Backs Off Statements on Vietnam War," *New York Times*, April 19, 2004, A19.
49. See, for example, Brian McAllister Linn, *The Echo of Battle: The Army's Way of War* (Cambridge, MA: Harvard University Press, 2007), 197; Charles V. Mugno, "Maintaining the Quality of Our Military Awards System," *Marine Corps Gazette*, March 1994, 77–83.
50. Bill Wasik, "Our Friend the Smear," *Harper's Magazine*, November 2004, 81. See also Charles Musser, "War, Documentary and Iraq Dossier: Film Truth in the Age of George Bush," *Journal of Cinema and Media* 48 (Fall 2007): 19–22.
51. Michael Dobbs, "Swift Boat Accounts Incomplete," *Washington Post*, August 22, 2004, A1; Susan Milligan, "Veteran Claims Misquote on Kerry; Globe Stands by Its Story," Boston.com, August 7, 2004, http://archive.boston.com/news/nation/washington/articles/2004/08/07/veteran_claims_misquote_on_kerry_globe

_stands_by_its_story/; John Kerezy, "Rocking the Boat: What We Learned from the Swift Boat Campaign," *Public Relations Tactics* 11 (October 2004): 14, 21.
52. Maureen Balleza and Kate Zernike, "Memos on Bush Are Fake but Accurate, Typist Says," *New York Times*, September 15, 2004, A24.
53. Jeffrey M. Jones, "Americans Give GOP Slim Edge to Ensure Security, Prosperity," Gallup, September 26, 2018, https://news.gallup.com/poll/243038/americans-give-gop-slim-edge-ensure-security-prosperity.aspx.
54. James Dao and Adam Nagourney, "They Served, and Now They're Running," *New York Times*, February 19, 2006, C1; Joshua Green, "Company, Left," *Atlantic Monthly*, January/February 2006, 40.
55. Kathryn S. Olmstead, *Real Enemies: Conspiracy Theories and American Democracy, World War I to 9/11* (New York: Oxford University Press, 2009), 219–20.
56. Joshua Green, "The Fighting Democrats," *Rolling Stone*, October 19, 2006, 60.
57. Green, "Company, Left," 40.
58. Jeff Swicord, "Record Number of Iraq War Vets Running for Congress," Voice of America News, October 31, 2009, https://www.voanews.com/archive/record-number-iraq-war-vets-running-congress.
59. "Vets PAC Backs Seven Democratic Candidates," *Roll Call*, March 20, 2006, 1.
60. John Biemer, "Little Common Ground for Roskam, Duckworth," *Chicago Tribune*, September 23, 2006, https://www.chicagotribune.com/news/ct-xpm-2006-09-23-0609230204-story.html; "Kerry Salutes Iraq Vets; Asks Supporters to Help," *Roll Call*, March 2, 2006, 1.
61. Leo Shane, "9 Vets of Current Wars Win Seats on Capitol Hill," *Stars and Stripes*, November 3, 2010, https://www.stripes.com/news/9-vets-of-current-wars-win-seats-on-capitol-hill-1.124142.
62. Full Biography, Col. Paul Cook (ret.), http://caucus.militarytimes.com/speaker/paul-cook. Our Campaigns, CA-District 08, https://www.ourcampaigns.com/RaceDetail.html?RaceID=768683.
63. John McCormack, "The 9/11 Generation Runs for Office," *Weekly Standard*, September 19, 2016, 16–17.
64. David Halberstam, *The Best and the Brightest* (Greenwich, CT: Fawcett Publications, Inc., 1973), 51.
65. ABC UpNorthLive, Interview with Jack Bergman, 1st Congressional District Republican Candidate, July 26, 2016, https://upnorthlive.com/news/election/interview-with-jack-bergman-1st-congressional-dist-republican-candidate; Eleanor Hildebrandt, "Veterans Storm the Capitol," *Popular Mechanics*, November 2018, 12.
71 Hildebrandt, "Veterans Storm the Capitol," 12.
67. Matthew Kassel, "Fitness to Serve," *Men's Health*, October 2018, 110–11.
68. Nick Visser, "Dan Crenshaw Isn't Buying into 'Outrage Culture,' Urges Nation to Rediscover Civility," *HuffPost*, November 14, 2018, https://www.huffpost.com/entry/dan-crenshaw-washington-post-editorial-snl_n_5bebacc8e4bocaeec2bf37ea.
69. Dan Crenshaw, "SNL Mocked My Appearance. Here's Why I Didn't Demand an Apology," *Washington Post*, November 13, 2018, https://www.washingtonpost.com/opinions/i-made-amends-with-pete-davidson-on-snl-but-thats-only-the-beginning/2018/11/13/e7314fb0-e77e-11e8-b8dc-66cca409c180_story.html.
70. Quil Lawrence, "Why It's Notable That a Slew of New Members Elected to Congress Are Military Veterans," *All Things Considered*, November 9, 2018, https://www.npr.org/2018/11/09/666345074/why-its-notable-that-a-slew-of-new-members-elected-to-congress-are-military-vete.
71. Associated Press, Lisa Lerer and Jonathan Lemire, "Trump Attacks Speech by Father of Slain Muslim American Soldier," Military.com, July 30, 2016, https://

www.military.com/daily-news/2016/07/30/donald-trump-attacks-muslim-father-convention-speech.html.
72. Zachary R. New, "Ending Citizenship for Service in the Forever War," *Yale Law Journal* 129 (February 11, 2020), https://www.yalelawjournal.org/forum/ending-citizenship-for-service-in-the-forever-wars.
73. Richard Sisk, "The Naturalization Process Just Got Harder for Noncitizen Troops Stationed Overseas," Military.com, September 30, 2019, https://www.military.com/daily-news/2019/09/30/naturalization-process-just-got-harder-noncitizen-troops-stationed-overseas.html; New, "Ending Citizenship for Service."
74. Leo Shane, "Veterans in the 116th Congress by the Numbers," MilitaryTimes, updated December 18, 2018, https://www.militarytimes.com/news/pentagon-congress/2018/11/21/veterans-in-the-116th-congress-by-the-numbers/.
75. See, for example, Dan Crenshaw and Mike Gallagher, "Troops in the Mideast Keep Terrorism Away," Opinion, *Wall Street Journal*, February 24, 2019, https://www.wsj.com/articles/troops-in-the-mideast-keep-terror-away-11551045173.
76. "Political Waffler Alert," *Advocate*, September 26, 2006, 16
77. John Chase, "Duckworth's Record: Few Legislative Successes, Some Veterans Programs Spluttered," *Chicago Tribune*, October 19, 2016, https://www.chicagotribune.com/politics/ct-tammy-duckworth-veterans-affairs-met-20161018-story.html; Tammy Duckworth, "Tucker Carlson Doesn't Know What Patriotism Is," *New York Times*, July 9, 2020, https://www.nytimes.com/2020/07/09/opinion/tammy-duckworth-tucker-carlson.html.
78. Michael Levenson, "Tulsi Gabbard Votes 'Present' on Impeachment Articles," *New York Times*, December 18, 2019, https://www.nytimes.com/2019/12/18/us/elections/tulsi-gabbard-impeachment-vote.html; Michael Kruse, "The Town Hall That Impeachment Blew Up," *Politico*, press release, November 27, 2019, https://www.politico.com/news/magazine/2019/11/27/mikie-sherrill-impeachment-tearing-apart-her-district-074097; "Crenshaw Statement on the House Launching a Formal Impeachment Inquiry into President Trump," press release, September 25, 2019, https://crenshaw.house.gov/news/documentsingle.aspx?DocumentID=140#:~:text=Crenshaw%20Statement%20On%20The%20House%20Launching%20A%20Formal,launch%20a%20formal%20impeachment%20inquiry%20into%20the%20President%3A.

CHAPTER NINE: THE WOMEN PRAETORIANS

1. Nina Silber, "'A Woman's War': Gender and Civil War Studies," *OAH Magazine of History* 8 (Fall 1993): 11–13; Richard H. Hall, *Women on the Civil War Battlefront* (Lawrence: University Press of Kansas, 2006), 262.
2. Department of Veterans Affairs, National Center for Veterans Analysis and Statistics, *America's Women Veterans: Military Service History and VA Benefit Utilization Statistics* (Washington, DC: Department of Veterans Affairs, November 2011), 1; George Gallup, "Voters Back Draft of Single Women," *New York Times*, March 10, 1944, 32.
3. Janann Sherman, "'They Either Need These Women or They Do Not': Margaret Chase Smith and the Fight for Regular Status for Women in the Military," *Journal of Military History* 54 (January 1990): 58–59; D'Ann Campbell, *Women at War with America: Private Lives in a Patriotic Era* (Cambridge, MA: Harvard University Press, 1984), 22–26.
4. Department of Veterans Affairs, *America's Women Veterans*, 3, 5.
5. Maureen Murdoch, Arlene Bradley, Susan H. Mather, Robert E. Klein, Carole L. Turner, and Elizabeth M. Yano, "Women and War: What Physicians Should

Know," *Journal of General Internal Medicine* 21 (March 2006): S6, https://www.ncbi.nlm.nih.gov/pmc/articles/PMC1513175/.
6. Marine Corps Force Integration Plan—Summary, n.d., https://assets.documentcloud.org/documents/2394531/marine-corps-force-integration-plan-summary.pdf.
7. Louis Harris and Associates, *Survey of Female Veterans: A Study of the Needs, Attitudes, and Experiences of Women Veterans*, Study No. 843002 (New York: Louis Harris and Associates, 1985), 29.
8. Department of Defense, Office of the Assistant Secretary of Defense (Manpower and Reserve Affairs), Directorate for Manpower Research, *Recruiting of Women for the Military: Assessment of the Mental and Medical Standards and Their Present and Potential Effects on Recruiting Needs*, Report No. MR 75-4 (Alexandria, VA: Human Resources Research Organization, July 1975), 30. The study identified 9 percent of women in Category I versus 4.2 percent men and 76.5 percent of women in Category II versus 30.4 percent men. There were four categories, with Category IV being the lowest for acceptable recruits. Category V recruits were unfit for service.
9. Rodney R. Baker, Shirley W. Menard, and Louis A. Johns, "The Military Nurse Experience in Vietnam: Stress and Impact," *Journal of Clinical Psychology* 45 (September 1989): 738; Michael D. Gambone, *The Greatest Generation Comes Home: The Veteran in American Society* (College Park: Texas A&M University Press, 2005), 94.
10. Kathryn Marshall, *In the Combat Zone: An Oral History of American Women in Vietnam, 1966–1975* (Boston: Little, Brown, 1987), 116–17.
11. Judy Klemesrud, "For Women in the Military, New Attractions," *New York Times*, August 2, 1971, 28.
12. Department of Defense, *Recruiting of Women for the Military*, 1–8.
13. Kate A. Arbogast, "The Procurement of Women for the Armed Forces: An Analysis of Occupational Choice" (PhD diss., George Washington University, 1974), 134.
14. Department of Defense, Office of the Assistant Secretary of Defense (Manpower, Reserve Affairs, and Logistics), *America's Volunteers: A Report on the All-Volunteer Armed Forces* (Washington, DC: Department of Defense, December 31, 1978), 69–77. Conversely, the retention rate for women in mechanical and electrical repair specialties was lower.
15. Kate Germano, *Fight Like a Girl: The Truth behind How Female Marines Are Trained* (Amherst, NY: Prometheus Books, 2018), 35–36.
16. Interview, Georgia Jane Ford, March 27, 2004, Veterans History Project, Library of Congress, Washington, DC.
17. Interview, Constance Anderson, n.d., Veterans History Project, Library of Congress, Washington, DC.
18. Arbogast, "Procurement of Women for the Armed Forces," 128, 175.
19. Daniel H. Weinberg, "Earnings by Gender: Evidence from Census 2000," *Monthly Labor Review* 130 (July/August 2007): 29; Department of Defense, Defense Finance and Accounting Service, *Military Pay Charts—1949 to 2020*, https://www.dfas.mil/MilitaryMembers/payentitlements/Pay-Tables/PayTableArchives/.
20. There are numerous studies on this particular topic. See Congressional Budget Office, *Evaluating Military Compensation* (Washington, DC: CBO, June 2007), and James E. Grefer, *Comparing Military and Civilian Compensation Packages* (Alexandria, VA: CNA, March 2008).
21. Department of Defense, Office of the Undersecretary of Defense (Military Community and Family Policy), *Demographics 2018: Profile of the Military Community* (Washington, DC: Department of Defense, 2018), 19; Department

of Defense, Office of the Undersecretary of Defense (Military Community and Family Policy), *Demographics 2010: Profile of the Military Community* (Washington, DC: Department of Defense, 2010), 18; Kim Parker, Anthony Cilluffo, and Renee Stepler, "6 Facts about the U.S. Military and Its Changing Demographics," Pew Research Center, April 13, 2017, https://www.pewresearch.org/fact-tank/2017/04/13/6-facts-about-the-u-s-military-and-its-changing-demographics/; Department of Defense, *America's Volunteers*, 70.

22. Germano, *Fight Like a Girl*, 41. In 2018, the year Germano published her book, women represented 8.4 percent of all Marine Corps officers. The next lowest was the Navy at 23.3 percent.

23. Matthew S. Goldberg and John T. Warner, "Military Experience, Civilian Experience, and the Earnings of Veterans," *Journal of Human Resources* 22 (Winter 1987): 66–67.

24. Claudette Roulo, "Defense Department Expands Women's Combat Role," American Forces Press Service, January 24, 2013, https://web.archive.org/web/20140412193528/http://www.defense.gov/news/newsarticle.aspx?id=119098#; Kyle Rempfer, "Army 'Ahead of Schedule' in Integrating Women in Combat Arms, Outgoing SMA Says as He Departs," *Army Times*, August 16, 2019, https://www.armytimes.com/news/your-army/2019/08/16/army-ahead-of-schedule-in-integrating-women-in-combat-arms-outgoing-sma-says-as-he-departs/.

25. Eileen Patten and Kim Parker, "Women in the U.S. Military: Growing Share, Distinctive Profile," Pew Research Center, December 22, 2011, https://www.pewsocialtrends.org/2011/12/22/women-in-the-u-s-military-growing-share-distinctive-profile/.

26. Nese F. DeBruyne, *American War and Military Operations Casualties: Lists and Statistics*, RL32492 (Washington, DC: Congressional Research Service, April 26, 2017), 12, 14, 17, 19. During Operation Enduring Freedom (2001–14), women were 1.9 percent of wounded and 2.1 percent of combat deaths. During Operation Iraqi Freedom (2003–11), they were 1.9 percent of wounded and 2.4 percent of personnel killed in action.

27. Friedman quoted in Sara Corbett, "The Women's War," *New York Times Magazine*, March 18, 2007, 44.

28. Shelley Saywell, *Women in War: First-Hand Accounts from World War II to El Salvador* (Ontario, Canada: Penguin Books, 1985), 225.

29. Rodney R. Baker, Shirley W. Menard, and Louis A. Johns, "The Military Nurse Experience in Vietnam: Stress and Impact," *Journal of Clinical Psychology* 45 (September 1989): 737; Gina M. Scuteri, "Casualties of War and Research: A Case Study of U.S. Women Veterans of Vietnam," (PhD diss., Purdue University, 1993), 38.

30. Scuteri, "Casualties of War and Research," 45.

31. Government Accountability Office, *VA Health Care: Preliminary Findings on VA's Provision of Health Care Services to Women Veterans*, GAO-09-899T (Washington, DC: GAO, July 16, 2009), 1; Department of Veterans Affairs, National Center for PTSD, "How Common Is PTSD in Veterans?," n.d., https://www.ptsd.va.gov/understand/common/common_veterans.asp; Heidi M. Zinzow, Anouk L. Grusbaugh, Jeannine Monnier, Samantha Suffoletta-Maierle, and B. Christopher Frueh, "Trauma among Female Veterans: A Critical Review," *Trauma, Violence & Abuse* 8 (October 2007): 391.

32. Rachel Kimerling, Kristian Gima, Mark W. Smith, Amy Street, and Susan Frayne, "The Veterans Health Administration and Military Sexual Trauma," *American Journal of Public Health* 97 (December 2007): 2160.

33. Alina Suris and Lisa Lind, "Military Sexual Trauma: A Review of Prevalence and Associated Health Consequences in Veterans," *Trauma, Violence and Abuse* 9 (October 2009): 251, 253.

34. DeBruyne, *American War and Military Operations*, 14, 19.
35. Stephanie Gaskell, "VA Might Have Denied PTSD Claims Related to Military Sexual Trauma," *Veterans of Foreign Wars Magazine*, November/December 2018, 10. Original reference in Department of Veterans Affairs, Office of Inspector General, Office of Audits and Evaluations, *Denied Posttraumatic Stress Disorder Claims Related to Military Sexual Trauma*, Report No. 17-05248-241 (Washington, DC: Department of Veterans Affairs, August 21, 2018), ii, 1, 5, 14.
36. Kimerling et al., "Veterans Health Administration and Military Sexual Trauma," 2164.
37. See, for example, General Accounting Office, *Report to the Chairman, Subcommittee on Health, Committee of Veterans' Affairs, House of Representatives: VA Health Care for Women: Progress Made in Providing Services to Women Veterans*, GAO/HEHS-99-38 (Washington, DC: GAO, January 1999), 5.
38. Jane Hoppen, "Women in the Military: Who's Got Your Back?," *Off Our Backs* 36 (2006): 14.
39. Administrator of Veterans Affairs, *Annual Report, 1973* (Washington, DC: Veterans Administration, 1973), 2, RG 15, entry 53, box 1, National Archives and Records Administration (hereafter NARA), Washington, DC.
40. Department of Veterans Affairs, National Center for Veterans Analysis and Statistics, *Veteran Population Statistics at a Glance*, February 2020, 4, https://www.va.gov/vetdata/docs/Quickfacts/Homepage_slideshow_4_6_20.PDF.
41. Memorandum, P. H. Springsteen (Editorial Division) to Chief Medical Director, August 1, 1946, RG 15, entry 33, box 3, NARA.
42. Louis Harris Associates, *Survey of Female Veterans: A Study of the Needs, Attitudes, and Experiences of Women Veterans*, Study No. 843002 (New York: Louis Harris and Associates, 1985), 5.
43. Scuteri, "Casualties of War and Research," 52.
44. Rani A. Hoff and Robert A. Rosenheck, "The Use of VA and non-VA Mental Health Services by Female Veterans," *Medical Care* 36 (November 1998): 1524-33.
45. Government Accountability Office, *VA Health Care for Women: Despite Progress, Improvements Needed*. GAO/HRD-92-23 (Washington, DC: GAO, January 1992), 3; Jean Dunlavy, "A Band of Sisters: Vietnam Women Veterans' Organization for Rights and Recognition, 1965-1995" (PhD diss., Boston University, 2009), 146.
46. General Accounting Office, press release, "Statement of Robert A. Peterson, Senior Associate Director, Human Resources Division, before the Subcommittee on Hospitals and Healthcare, Committee on Veterans' Affairs," March 3, 1983, 2.
47. Elaine Sciolino, "Military Women Report Pattern of Sexual Abuse by Servicemen," *New York Times*, July 1, 1992, A16.
48. Franco quoted in Sciolino, "Sexual Abuse by Servicemen," A16.
49. Government Accountability Office, *Testimony before the Subcommittees on Disability Assistance and Memorial Affairs and Health, Committee on Veterans' Affairs, House of Representatives: Preliminary Findings on VA's Provision of Health Care Services to Women Veterans*, GAO-09-899T (Washington, DC: GAO, July 16, 2009), 8-9. The coordinator position did not become full-time until 2008.
50. General Accounting Office, *Report to the Chairman, Subcommittee on Health, Committee of Veterans' Affairs, House of Representatives: VA Health Care for Women: Progress Made in Providing Services to Women Veterans*, GAO/HEHS-99-38 (Washington, DC: GAO, January 1999), 2.
51. General Accounting Office, *Report to the Chairman*, 5-6.
52. General Accounting Office, *Testimony before the Subcommittee on Health, Committee on Veterans' Affairs, House of Representatives: Women Veterans' Health Care: VA Efforts to Respond to the Challenge of Providing Sexual Trauma Counseling*, GAO/T-HEHS-98-138 (Washington, DC: GAO, April 23, 1998), 2.

53. Rachel N. Lipari and Anita R. Lancaster, *Armed Forces 2002 Sexual Harassment Survey*, DMDC Report No. 2003–026 (Arlington, VA: Department Manpower Data Center, November 2003), iii.
54. Anne G. Sadler, Brenda M. Booth, Brian L. Cook, and Bradley N. Doebbeling, "Factors Associated with Women's Risk of Rape in the Military Environment," *American Journal of Industrial Medicine* 43 (March 2003): 266.
55. Rachel Kimerling, Amy E. Street, Joanne Pavao, Mark W. Smith, Ruth C. Cronkite, Tyson H. Holmes, and Susan M. Frayne, "Military-Related Sexual Trauma among Veterans Health Administration Patients Returning from Afghanistan and Iraq," *American Journal of Public Health* 100 (August 2010): 1409.
56. Kimerling et al., "Veterans Health Administration and Military Sexual Trauma," 2160.
57. Gaskell, "VA Might Have Denied PTSD Claims," 10.
58. Veterans Legal Services Clinic, Yale Law School, *Battle for Benefits: VA Discrimination against Survivors of Military Sexual Trauma* (Hartford: American Civil Liberties Union of Connecticut, November 2013), 1.
59. Government Accountability Office, *VA Health Care: Improved Monitoring Needed for Effective Oversight of Health Care for Women Veterans*, GAO-17-52 (Washington, DC: Government Accountability Office, December 2016), 1–3; Government Accountability Office, *Preliminary Findings on VA's Provision of Health Care Services to Women Veterans*, 14.
60. David Camelon, "I Saw the GI Bill Written," *American Legion Magazine*, November 1949, 45.
61. Letter, June A. Willenz (AVC, Executive Director) to Director of Public Relations (IBM), September 17, 1968, and American Veterans Committee, *A Sampling of Veterans' Cases Assisted by the American Veterans Committee (AVC)*, November 9, 1967, both in American Veterans Committee Records, box 7, Gelman Library, George Washington University, Washington, DC.
62. "Legion Admits All-Woman Post," *New York Times*, August 19, 1945, 37.
63. "WAC-Vets Philadelphia Chapter," *WAC Journal* 3 (December 1948): 7; June A. Willenz, *Women Veterans: America's Forgotten Heroines* (New York: Continuum, 1983); American Legion, "History," n.d., https://www.legion.org/history.
64. Women's Army Corps Veterans' Association—Army Women United, "About Us," n.d., https://www.armywomen.org/aboutUs.shtml.
65. Army Nurse Corps Association, "About Us," n.d., https://e-anca.org/About-Us.
66. Women Marines Association, https://womenmarines.wordpress.com.
67. Women's Army Corps Veterans' Association—Army Women United, for example, includes volunteering in VA hospitals, assisting in recruitment of women for the military, and ROTC scholarships among its member activities. Brochure, Women's Army Corps Veterans' Association—Army Women United, n.d. https://www.armywomen.org/pdf/Brochure%20WACVA.pdf.
68. Dunlavy, "Band of Sisters," 120–22, 139–41.
69. Department of Defense, *Conduct of the Persian Gulf War: Final Report to Congress, Appendix R: Role of Women in Theater of Operations* (Washington, DC: Department of Defense, 1992), R-1.
70. Thomas E. Shriver, Amy Chasteen Miller, and Sherry Cable, "Women's Work: Women's Involvement in the Gulf War Illness Movement," *Sociological Quarterly* 44 (Autumn 2003): 639–58.
71. Shriver, Miller, and Cable, "Women's Work," 644.
72. Shriver, Miller, and Cable, 649.
73. Megan H. MacKenzie, "Let Women Fight: Ending the U.S. Military's Female Combat Ban," *Foreign Affairs* 91 (November/December 2012): 35–36; Service Women's Action Network, "For Immediate Release: SWAN Statement on

Lawsuit against Department of Defense" press release, December 19, 2017, https://www.servicewomen.org/press-releases/for-immediate-release-swan-statement-on-lawsuit-against-department-of-defense/.

74. Service Women's Action Network, "What We Do," https://www.servicewomen.org/#what-we-do.

75. J. J. Montanaro, "Women Veterans Leadership and Diversity Conference," USAA Community, November 2018, https://communities.usaa.com/t5/Events/Women-Veterans-Leadership-and-Diversity-Conference/ba-p/192839.

76. Tom Schoenberg, "Booz Allen Investigated by U.S. Over Charging Practices," *Bloomberg*, June 15, 2017, https://www.bloomberg.com/news/articles/2017-06-15/booz-allen-investigated-by-u-s-over-charging-practices.

77. Service Women (SWAN)@Servicewomen, https://twitter.com/Servicewomen?ref_src=twsrc%5Egoogle%7Ctwcamp%5Eserp%7Ctwgr%5Eauthor.

78. Women Veterans Interactive, Operation Safety Net, http://womenveteransinteractive.org/operation-safety-net/; Service Women's Action Network, Weekly COVID 19 Resource Notice: Stay Connected, https://www.servicewomen.org/covid-19/.

79. Department of Veterans Affairs, National Center for Veterans Analysis and Statistics, *Women Veterans Report: The Past, Present, and Future of Women Veterans* (Washington, DC: Department of Veterans Affairs, February 2017), 11.

CHAPTER TEN: THE VETERAN IN POPULAR CULTURE

1. Siegfried Sassoon, "Trench Duty," 1919, https://poets.org/poem/trench-duty.
2. Ralph R. Donald, "Antiwar Themes in Narrative War Films: Soldiers' Experiences as Social Comment," *Studies in Popular Culture* 13 (1991): 77.
3. Donald, "Antiwar Themes," 78–90.
4. Figures are from IMDb. *Stop-Loss* (2008), https://www.imdb.com/title/tt0489281/?ref_=nv_sr_srsg_0; *Lone Survivor* (2013), https://www.imdb.com/title/tt1091191/?ref_=nv_sr_srsg_0.
5. Amy Mitchell, Jeffrey Gottfried, Michael Barthel, and Elisa Shearer, "The Modern News Consumer," Pew Research Center, July 7, 2016, https://www.journalism.org/2016/07/07/pathways-to-news/; Jeffrey Gottfried, Katerina Eva Matsu, and Michael Barthel, "As Jon Stewart Steps Down, 5 Facts about 'The Daily Show,'" Pew Research Center, August 6, 2015, *https://www.pewresearch.org/fact-tank/2015/08/06/5-facts-daily-show/*.
6. Ron Kovic, *Born on the Fourth of July* (New York: McGraw-Hill, 1976), 42–45; Philip Caputo, *A Rumor of War* (New York: Holt, Rinehart and Winston, 1977), 6.
7. Charles Musser, "War, Documentary and Iraq Dossier: Film Truth in the Age of George Bush," *Journal of Cinema and Media* 48 (Fall 2007): 11.
8. Samuel Vega Durán, "Hollywood and the Pentagon: The Propagandistic Cultural Production of the United States Defense Department," *Vivat Academia* 23 (March–June 2020): 81–102; "How to Do Better—American Military Tactics; America's Army," special report, *Economist* 377 (December 17, 2005): 22–24. See also Mark Harris, *Five Came Back: A Story of Hollywood and the Second World War* (New York: Penguin Books, 2015).
9. Donald, "Antiwar Themes," 84–85.
10. Julian Smith, "Between Vermont and Violence: Film Portraits of Vietnam Veterans," *Film Quarterly* 26 (Summer 1973): 12, 13–14; Peter McInerney, "Apocalypse Then: Hollywood Looks Back at Vietnam," *Film Quarterly* 33 (Winter 1979–80): 24.
11. Brian Turner, *Here, Bullet* (Farmington, ME: Alice James Books, 2005), 13.

12. Michael E. Birdwell, "'The Stunt Man': An Overlooked Commentary on Vietnam," *Literature/Film Quarterly* 20 (1992): 227.
13. Birdwell, "'The Stunt Man,'" 225.
14. J. Glenn Gray, *The Warriors: Reflections on Men in Battle* (New York: Harcourt, Brace, 1959), 26, 85; David Denby, "When Soldiers Return," *New Yorker*, April 7, 2008, 76–78.
15. Winkler cited in Lawrence Suid, "Hollywood and Vietnam," *Film Comment*, September/October 1979, 22.
16. McInerney, "Apocalypse Then," 24.
17. McInerney, 26–27.
18. Suid, "Hollywood and Vietnam," 24; J. Terry Frazier, "Vietnam War Stories: Looking at the Heart of Darkness," *Studies in Popular Culture* 5 (1982): 3.
19. Michael Selig, "From Play to Film: 'Strange Snow, Jacknife,' and Masculine Identity in the Hollywood Vietnam Film," *Literature/Film Quarterly* 20, no. 3 (July 1992): 178.
20. Trevor B. McCrisken and Andrew Pepper, *American History and Contemporary Hollywood Film* (Edinburgh: Edinburgh University Press, 2005), 136.
21. McCrisken and Pepper, *American History and Contemporary Hollywood Film*, 175; Ralph R. Donald, "Antiwar Themes in Narrative War Films: Soldiers' Experiences as Social Comment," *Studies in Popular Culture* 13 (1991): 85.
22. Chris Darke, "Dead Presidents," *Sight & Sound*, September 1996, 38–39.
23. Richard Brody, "Spike Lee's 'Da 5 Bloods' Reviewed: Vietnam and the Never-Ending War of Being Black in America," *Variety*, June 13, 2020, https://www.newyorker.com/culture/the-front-row/spike-lees-da-5-bloods-reviewed-vietnam-and-the-never-ending-war-of-being-black-in-america.
24. Samuel G. Freedman, "The War and the Arts," *New York Times*, March 31, 1985, SM50.
25. Maurizia Boscagli, "A Moving Story: Masculine Tears and the Humanity of Televised Emotions," *Discourse* 15 (Winter 1992–93): 76.
26. Mary Beth Haralovich, "'Champagne Tastes on a Beer Budget': Series Design and Popular Appeal of Magnum, P.I.," *Journal of Film and Video* 43 (Spring and Summer 1991): 123–34.
27. Neil Anderson, "Mythological Messages in 'The A-Team,'" *English Journal* 75 (February 1986): 30, 32.
28. Gina Marchetti, "Class, Ideology, and Commercial Television: An Analysis of *The A-Team*," *Journal of Film and Video* 39 (Spring 1987): 19–21.
29. David Everett Whitlock, "Defining the Fictive American Vietnam War Film: In Search of a Genre," *Literature/Film Quarterly* 16 (1988): 246–47.
30. Beverly Walker, "Billy Jack vs. Hollywood," *Film Comment*, July/August 1977, 24–30.
31. Joe Leydon, "Stop-Loss," *Variety*, March 24–March 30, 2008, 21.
32. Jessica Winter, "Stop-Loss," *Time Out*, April 22, 2008, https://www.timeout.com/en_gb/film/stop-loss.
33. Carol Fry, Christopher Kemp, and Carrol L. Fry, "Rambo Agonistes," *Literature/Film Quarterly* 24 (1996): 368–69.
34. John Morrell, *First Blood* (New York: Fawcett, 1982), 177.
35. Gaylyn Studlar and David Desser, "Never Having to Say You're Sorry: *Rambo's* Rewriting of the Vietnam War," *Film Quarterly* 42 (Autumn 1988): 11.
36. Studlar and Desser, "Never Having to Say You're Sorry," 13.
37. *Rambo III* earned $189,015,611 worldwide. See Rambo III (1988), Box Office Mojo.
38. Between 1981 and 1987, Stallone appeared in *Nighthawks* (1981), *Victory* (1981), *Rocky III* (1982), *First Blood* (1982), *Staying Alive* (1983), *Rhinestone* (1985), Rambo: First Blood Part II (1985), *Rocky IV* (1985), *Cobra* (1987), and *Over the Top* (1987).

39. Trevor Johnston, "The Messenger," *Sight & Sound*, June 2011, 70–71.
40. McCandlish Phillips, "'Sticks and Bones,' 'Verona' Win Tonys; Gorman, Sada Thompson Cited for Acting," *New York Times*, April 24, 1972, 40; Smith, "Between Vermont and Violence," 10.
41. Sylvia Shin Huey Chong, "Restaging the War: 'The Deer Hunter' and the Primal Scene of Violence," *Cinema Journal* 44 (Winter 2005): 100, 103.
42. Lance Morrow, Joseph J. Kane, John F. Stacks, and Elizabeth Taylor, "A Bloody Rite of Passage: Vietnam Cost America Its Innocence and Still Haunts Its Conscience," *Time*, April 15, 1985, 20.
43. Anna Froula, "What Keeps Me Up at Night: Media Studies Fifteen Years after 9/11," *Cinema Journal* 56 (Fall 2016): 114.
44. Lois Parshley, "In War Film, a Marine's Struggles in Afghanistan and at Home," *Atlantic*, October 14, 2011, https://www.theatlantic.com/international/archive/2011/10/in-war-film-a-marines-struggles-in-afghanistan-and-at-home/246679/.
45. Parshley, "In War Film."
46. Jesse Ellison, "'Hell and Back Again': PBS Airs Documentary on Wounded Marine," *Daily Beast*, May 27, 2012, https://www.thedailybeast.com/hell-and-back-again-pbs-airs-documentary-on-wounded-marine.
47. Susan L. Carruthers, "Bodies of Evidence: New Documentaries on Iraq War Veterans," *Cinéaste*, Winter 2008, 26.
48. Claudia Parsons, "'Lioness' Shows U.S. Women on Front Line in Iraq," Reuters, May 5, 2008, https://www.reuters.com/article/us-usa-military-lioness-idUSN2843902720080506.
49. Carruthers, "Bodies of Evidence," 26.
50. Ryan Gilbey, "Last Flag Flying," *Sight & Sound* 28 (February 2018): 66.
51. Ethan Brown, "The Dogs of War," *Mother Jones*, July/August 2008, 74.

CONCLUSIONS

1. Selective Service System, "Why Aren't Women Required to Register?," https://www.sss.gov/register/women/. The law as currently written refers only to "male persons" as liable for selective service.
2. Army Reserve, "Cyber Operations Officer (17A)," Overview, https://www.goarmy.com/reserve/jobs/browse/computers-and-technology/cyber-operations-officer.html.
3. George Barrett, "Portrait of the Korean War Veteran," *New York Times*, August 9, 1953, SM12.
4. James Fallows, "The Tragedy of the American Military," *Atlantic Monthly*, January/February 2015, 74.
5. James Webb, *Fields of Fire* (New York: Bantam Books, 1979), 160. Webb is often quoted elsewhere. See, for example, Robert Timberg, *The Nightingale's Song* (New York: Simon & Schuster, 1995), 15.
6. Katharine M. Millar, "'They Need Our Help': Non-Governmental Organizations and Their Subjectifying Dynamics of the Military as a Social Cause," *Media, War & Conflict* 9 (April 2016): 9–26; Deborah Cowen and Amy Siciliano, "Surplus Masculinities and Security," *Antipode* 43 (November 2011): 1534.
7. Corey B. Rumann and Florence A. Hamrick, "Student Veterans in Transition: Re-Enrolling after War Zone Deployments," *Journal of Higher Education* 81 (July/August 2010): 447, 448.
8. Department of Veterans Affairs, National Center for Veterans Analysis and Statistics, *Minority Veterans Report: Military Service History and Benefits Utilization Statistics* (Washington, DC: Department of Veterans Affairs, March

2017), vi; Department of Veterans Affairs, National Center for Veterans Analysis and Statistics, *Minority Veterans: 2011* (Washington, DC: Department of Veterans Affairs, May 2013), 3.
9. Defense Manpower Data Center, *DoD Personnel, Workforce Reports and Publications*, https://dwp.dmdc.osd.mil/dwp/app/dod-data-reports/workforce-reports. In 2010, there were 1.43 million military personnel. In July 2020, the number was 1.38 million. The requested defense budget for FY2021 was $705.4 billion. See Department of Defense, "DoD Releases Fiscal Year 2021 Budget Proposal," February 10, 2020, https://www.defense.gov/Newsroom/Releases/Release/Article/2079489/dod-releases-fiscal-year-2021-budget-proposal/.

INDEX

Abu Ghraib, 29
Afghanistan, 28, 35–39, 43–46, 56, 78, 96, 127, 129, 146, 164; casualties in, 65, 71; in film, 147, 155–57; Global War on Terrorism and, 81, 90, 105; politicians serving in, 130; student veterans and, 114, 116; women serving in; 57, 137–38, 141
African American veterans, 13; Deacons for Defense and Justice and, 15; discharges from military, 84; economic status of, 85, 90, 92; in film, 152; GI Bill benefits and, 13, 103; job training and, 86; participation in the military and, 32, 56–58, 93; recruiting and, 21, 27–28; women, 137
Agent Orange, 4–5, 62, 68–69
Agent Orange Act (1991), 66
Air Force, 14, 17, 51–52; military occupational specialties in, 35; NFL and, 94; recruiting and, 29; women serving in, 135–36
al-Qaeda, 2, 29, 38, 39, 137
Ambrose, Stephen E., 75
American Council on Education, 113
American Legion, 12–13, 43, 74, 141; Cold War service and, 120–21; conflicts with young veterans, 141–42, 163; response to Bradley Commission, 63–64; women and, 140
American Red Cross, 11, 98, 133
American Revolution, 4, 9, 135
American Sniper (2014), 7
Americans with Disabilities Act (1990), 110
American Veterans (AMVETS), 75
American Veterans Committee (AVC), 14, 48, 116, 141, 142, 163
Apocalypse Now (1979), 17, 147
Apollo Education Group, 98, 106, 107
Armed Forces Qualification Test (AFQT), 22, 27, 30
Army Air Corps College Training Program, 102
Army Criminal Investigation Division (CID), 30
Army Specialized Training Program, 102
The A-Team, 153–54

baby boomers, 103, 108, 147
Bacevich, Andrew J., 54
Bailey, Beth, 19, 20, 93
Barry, Jan, 50
Basic Training Naturalization Initiative, 131
Bates Advertising, 19–20
Beirut, 51
Berinsky, Adam J., 59
Best, Mat, 78, 96, 163
The Best Years of Our Lives (1946), 150–51, 157, 158
Bickerdyke, Mary Ann, 133
Billy Jack (1971), 154
Black Rifle Coffee, 96–97
Bonus March, 12
Boot, Max, 46
Born on the Fourth of July (1989), 151–52
Bradley, James, 95
Bradley, Omar N., 13, 119–20; Bradley Commission and, 63; female veterans and, 139; Veterans Administration reforms and, 61–62, 76
Bradley Commission, 63, 120
Bucci, Tom, 76
Bugliosi, Vincent, 42
Bush, George H.W., 10, 54, 55, 66, 117
Bush, George W., 28, 42–43, 56, 58, 73, 81, 126–27, 131

Caesar Augustus, 1
Calley, William L., Jr., 49
Capella University, 106
Capps, Ron, 111–12, 116
Caputo, Philip, 17, 111, 147
Carter, Jimmy, 10, 108, 117
Cassi, Emil, 10, 118
Centers for Disease Control and Prevention (CDC), 71–73
Cheney, Dick, 87
Cimino, Michael, 156, 159
Civil War, 9–10, 35, 117–18, 133, 141, 160
Clay, Henry, 9

INDEX

Cleland, Max, 124
Clinton, Bill, 26, 38, 54, 87, 126, 129
Cold War, 2, 3, 5, 13, 36, 52, 59, 78, 82, 108, 120–21, 124, 133, 148; corporations and, 45; end of, 55, 86; impact on force structure, 25, 27; media depictions of, 153–54; public opinion and, 49; recruiting and, 20; veterans' benefits and, 14, 83, 161
Cold War GI Bill. *See* Veterans' Readjustment Benefits Act (1966)
Combat Action Badge (CAB), 40–41
Combat Action Ribbon (CAR), 40, 173
Combat Infantry Badge (CIB), 40
Combat Medical Badge (CMB), 40
Coming Home (1978), 150–51, 155
Conant, James, 107
Congressional Budget Office, 81, 106
Congressional Research Service, 30, 71, 137
Congressional Veterans Caucus, 131
Contras, 124, 126
Cooper, John Sherman, 13
Coppola, Francis Ford, 147
Counterintelligence Program (COINTELPRO), 15
COVID-19, 30, 82, 144
Cranston, Alan, 125
Crenshaw, Dan, 130–32
Cronkite, Walter, 147

Da 5 Bloods (2020), 152
Deacons for Defense and Justice, 15
Dead Presidents (1995), 152
The Deer Hunter (1978), 156
Defense Intelligence Agency, 95
De Niro, Robert, 154, 156
Department of Defense, 24, 38, 45, 55, 68, 94, 119, 164; enlistment bonuses and, 29; film making and, 24–25; fraud committed against, 44; Gulf War syndrome and, 68–69; NFL and, 94; opioids and, 72; recruiting and, 93; survey of military rape, 140; veterans' education and, 98–99, 100, 104, 106–7, 112; veterans' employment and, 83, 87, 90–91; women and, 57, 135, 144
Department of Labor, 83, 89–92, 136
Department of Veterans Affairs, 13, 59, 63, 76, 83, 87–88, 91, 105, 119–20, 139, 145; education benefits and, 98, 113, 139; fraud committed against, 43–44; Gulf War syndrome and, 69–70; medical care and, 5, 65; minority veterans and, 92; opioids and, 72–73; outsourcing of functions, 73; scandals, 61–62, 73–74; women and, 139–41
Devry University, 98, 106
Diagnostic and Statistical Manual of Mental Disorders (DSM), 67, 72
discharge, 11, 85, 92, 122; other than honorable, 83–84; women and, 135, 144
draft. *See* selective service
Duckworth, Tammy, 6, 129, 132

Eastwood, Clint, 24, 149, 159
Eisenhower, Dwight D., 63, 117, 119–20
Erskine, Graves B., 59

Federal Bureau of Investigation (FBI), 15, 30
First Gulf War, 17, 37, 52–54, 59, 68–69
Ford, Gerald R., 10, 103, 117
Fort Bragg, 17, 46
Fort Indiantown Gap, 33
Fort Lewis, 33
Fountain, Ben, 58, 94
Freedom of Information Act (FOIA), 43
Friedman, Milton, 19, 20
Froula, Anna, 146, 147, 156, 159
Fulbright, J. William, 122
Fussell, Paul, 16, 60

Gallant, T. Grady, 39
Gallup, 43, 51, 57, 115, 128
Gates, Thomas, 19
Gates Commission. *See* President's Commission on an All-Volunteer Armed Force
General Pension Act of 1862, 10–11
Generation Z, 147
Germano, Kate, 133, 135, 136
GI Bill. *See* Serviceman's Readjustment Act (1944)
Gibson, William, 92
G.I. Joe, 19
Global War on Terrorism, 2, 32, 37, 45, 59, 81; Department of Veterans Affairs and, 65; impact on veterans'

education, 109; impact on veterans' employment, 89; medical care and, 69; nature of, 38; political candidates and, 128–29; reserves and, 29, 105; veterans of, 56, 88, 90; women veterans and, 137
Government Accountability Office, 91, 141
Grand Army of the Republic, 10, 117, 141
Grant, Ulysses S., 9, 24, 117
Gray, Colin S., 34, 37
Gray, J. Glenn, 149
Greenspan, Alan, 19
Green Zone Training, 112
Grumman Aircraft Engineering Corporation, 95, 119
Gulf of Tonkin, 49
Gulf War syndrome, 62, 68–69, 143

Hackworth, David, 16
Hafer, Evan, 96–97
Halberstam, David, 130
Harris, Ed, 151
Heartbreak Ridge (1986), 24
Hell and Back Again (2011), 157
Heroes (1977), 150–51
Hersh, Seymour M., 49
Hines, Frank T., 13, 61
Hispanic veterans, 28, 32, 71, 92, 137; education and, 110; mental health and, 72; recruiting and, 27
Huntington, Samuel P., 34
Hussein, Saddam, 26
Hutchins, Robert M., 107

improvised explosive device (IED), 36, 38, 57, 62, 71, 130
Iran-Contra scandal, 108, 124, 126, 155
Iraq, 37–39, 54, 78, 90, 96, 117, 127, 131–32, 164, 166; casualties, 65, 71, 137; chemical weapons and, 69; contractors in, 44; deployment to, 18, 35, 45, 56, 78; in fiction, 157–58; First Gulf War and, 52, 62, 68; invasion of, 28, 36; public support for war in, 57, 59; reserves and, 105; veterans of, 114, 116, 129–30; women veterans and, 138, 141
Iraq Veterans Against the War (IVAW), 114
iron triangles, 119

Islamic State of Iraq and Syria (ISIS), 38, 132, 137
ITT Technical Institute, 106

Jacknife (1989), 151
Jackson, Andrew, 9, 117
Janowitz, Morris, 3–4, 22, 32
Johnson, Lyndon B., 49, 64, 81, 117, 121
Joint Direct Attack Munitions (JDAMs), 37–38
Junger, Sebastian, 3–4, 39, 76, 90

Kansas Collegiate Veterans, 114
Keating, Charles, 125
Keating Five, 125
Kellogg Brown & Root (KBR), 45
Kennedy, John F., 10, 117, 118, 130
Kerrey, Bob, 124, 126
Kerry, John, 122–23, 126–28, 129
King Philip's War (1675–1678), 8
Klay, Phil, 18, 47
Korean War, 14, 23–24, 26, 28, 31, 39, 77, 105, 108, 118, 122, 128, 161; comparison with other conflicts, 67, 82, 85, 88, 113; psychological casualties in 61; reserves serving in, 45, 56; veterans' education and, 64, 102, 120–21; veterans' health care and, 63, 65; veterans' job training and, 86; women veterans and, 133–35
Kovic, Ron, 17, 147, 151–52

Last Flag Flying (2017), 158–59
Latinx veterans. *See* Hispanic veterans
Lembcke, Jeffrey, 48
Lethal Weapon (1987), 152
Lioness (2008), 157–58, 159
Lone Survivor (2013), 147
Lynch, Jessica, 36

Magnum P.I., 152–53
Mansfield, Joseph J., 13
Marine Corps, 20, 40, 41, 75, 106, 108, 130, 157; in contingency operations, 28; First Gulf War and, 17; minority service and, 21, 71; recruiting and, 22, 30; veterans' organizations 146; women and, 134–36
Mauldin, Bill, 14
McCain, John, 6, 26, 73, 94, 123–25, 128, 129, 131, 132

INDEX

McChrystal, Stanley, 39
McFarlane, Robert "Bud," 125
The Messenger (2009), 155
Meyer, Edward C., 23
military occupational specialty (MOS), 35, 36, 40, 84, 91, 104–5, 133, 136, 137, 161
military sexual trauma (MST), 5, 62, 110, 138, 141, 162
Military Times, 112–13
millennials, 31, 147
Mills, C. Wright, 79
Mine Resistant Ambush Protected (MRAP), 38–39
Mogadishu, 55
Montgomery GI Bill (1984), 24, 85–86, 88, 91, 93, 104, 113, 115
Moore, Michael, 80–81
Morgan, Shannon, 158
Murtha, John P., 121–22, 128
Mỹ Lai massacre, 49

Nader, Ralph, 64, 84
National Association for Black Veterans, 114
National Association for the Advancement of Colored People (NAACP), 19
National Center for PTSD, 71, 137
National Football League (NFL), 6, 94
National Guard, 27–29, 56, 68, 78, 88–89, 94, 97, 105, 111, 118, 119, 127, 128
National Home for Disabled Volunteer Soldiers, 11
National Urban League, 21, 84
National Vietnam Veterans Readjustment Study (NVVRS), 71–72
Navy V-12 Program, 102
Nicaragua, 51, 124, 126
Nixon, Richard M., 10, 13, 15, 18–19, 24, 64, 83–84, 87, 117, 121, 122
North, Oliver, 108, 125–26
North Vietnam, 49, 123
N. W. Ayer Advertising Agency, 20

Obama, Barack, 74, 82, 114, 129, 130, 131, 146
O'Neill, Thomas "Tip," 123
Operation Desert Shield (1990), 17, 52, 54, 68, 88, 143
Operation Desert Storm (1991), 25, 52, 54, 55, 68, 87, 88, 143

Operation Dewey Canyon III (1971), 15, 122, 127
Operation Enduring Freedom (2001), 38, 56, 65
Operation Infinite Reach (1998), 38
Operation Iraqi Freedom (2003), 56, 65
Operation Ranch Hand (1962–1971), 66
Operation RAW (Rapid American Withdrawal), 122
Operation Rolling Thunder (1965–1967), 49, 51–52
Operation Truth, 114
Operation Urgent Fury (1983), 52
Operation Welcome Home (1991), 53
Opinion Research Corporation, 57

Panetta, Leon, 41
Pelosi, Nancy, 129
Petraeus, David H., 37, 38, 39
Pew Research Center, 3, 31, 147
polling, 48, 59, 116, 126
Post-9/11 GI Bill, 104–6, 109, 110, 113, 115
post-traumatic stress disorder (PTSD), 5, 71–73, 75–76, 114, 162; classification of, 67; false claims of, 43; First Gulf War and, 68; Hispanic veterans and, 71, 110; post-9/11 veterans and, 90–91; representation in media, 153, 158; women and, 137–41, 143
post-Vietnam Syndrome, 62, 66
Powell, Colin, 21
Powhatan, 8
praetorians, 1–2
President's Commission on an All-Volunteer Armed Force, 19–20, 31

Rambo: First Blood (1982), 7, 154–55, 158
Rambo: First Blood Part II (1985), 155
RAND, 75, 90, 109
rapid decisive operations, 2
Reagan, Ronald, 10, 23, 24, 25, 51, 54, 56, 66, 79–80, 85, 94, 108, 123, 124–25
rear-echelon motherfucker (REMF), 35
recession, 11, 23, 54, 79, 84, 165; Great Recession (2007–2009), 30, 81–82, 90, 132
Reserve Officers' Training Corps (ROTC), 21, 104
Retired Army Nurse Corps Association, 142
Robb, Chuck, 124, 126
Rome, 1–2

INDEX

Roosevelt, Theodore, 10, 117
Rozelle, Pete, 94
Rumsfeld, Donald, 39

Sandboxx, 95
Sands of Iwo Jima (1949), 17
Sassoon, Siegfried, 111, 146
selective service, 3, 13, 15, 18, 19, 21–23, 26–28, 32–33, 50, 54, 56–57, 76, 83, 85, 93, 108, 119, 133, 135–36, 160
Selective Service College Qualification Test (SSCQT), 22, 108
Senate Committee on Veterans Affairs, 84
September 11 attacks, 3, 6, 27, 28, 29, 38, 42–43, 45, 54, 73, 81, 88, 89, 94, 105, 113, 114, 115, 128, 137, 144, 152, 156, 159
Serviceman's Readjustment Act (1944), 4, 13, 64, 89, 100–103, 121; creation of, 12–13; veterans' education and, 6, 86, 101, 108, 115
Service Women's Action Network (SWAN), 114, 144, 163
Sheehan, Neil, 49, 123
Shinseki, Eric, 74
Simcakoski, Jason, 72
Sledge, Eugene, 16, 17
Soldiers' and Sailors' Convention, 9
Soviet Union, 25, 55, 78, 86, 123, 124, 155
The Speed of Darkness (1989), 149
Stallone, Sylvester, 155
Stars and Stripes, 14, 43
Stewart, Jimmy, 13
stolen valor, 42–44, 163
stop-loss, 28, 114
Stop-Loss (2008), 147, 150, 154
Student Veterans of America (SVA), 113, 114, 163
Swift Boat Veterans for Truth (SBVT), 127
Swofford, Anthony, 17, 147

Tailhook, 140
Taliban, 2, 29, 38–39, 41, 137
Task Force Eagle, 55
Taxi Driver (1976), 7, 149, 154, 156
Teague, Olin E., 14, 118, 120–21, 161
Timberg, Robert, 108
Tocqueville, Alexis de, 101
Top Gun (1986), 24–25
Transition Assistance Program, 91
traumatic brain injury (TBI), 5, 62, 71, 110, 162

Troops to Teachers program, 91
Troubled Assets Relief Plan (TARP), 82
Truman, Harry S., 13, 117
Turner, Brian, 149

Uniformed Services Employment and Reemployment Rights Act (1994), 89
United States Sanitary Commission, 133
University of Chicago, 107
University of Phoenix, 97–98, 106–7

Van Devanter, Lynda, 142
Veterans Administration. *See* Department of Veterans Affairs
Veterans Education Success (VES), 99, 113
Veterans' Employment and Training Service, 89–90
Veterans Job Training Program, 86
Veterans of Foreign Wars (VFW), 12, 14, 15, 63, 64, 74, 114, 141–42, 163
Veterans Overmedication Prevention Act (2017), 73
Veterans' Readjustment Assistance Act (1952), 14, 120, 121
Veterans' Readjustment Benefits Act (1966), 14, 83, 121
Veterans Writing Project, 111–12, 116
Vietnam Veterans Against the War (VVAW), 15, 122, 141
Vietnam Veterans of America (VVA), 142–43
Vietnam War, 33, 35, 38, 56, 69, 76, 77, 81, 93, 94, 114, 134; Agent Orange and, 66; in media, 148–63; politics and, 121–30; psychological casualties of, 61–62, 67, 71–72; public opinion and, 49–50, 53, 58, 102, 119; U.S. military after, 36, 55; veterans' economic prospects and, 79, 82–85, 99–100; veterans' educational opportunities and, 103–4, 108, 115; veterans' medical care and, 63–65; veterans' organizations and, 15, 122, 141–42; veterans of, 3, 14–21, 32, 48, 51–52, 57, 59, 86–88, 90, 91, 147; women and, 133, 135, 137, 139
Viqtory Media, 98–99, 113
Volunteers in Service to America, 83
VOW (Veterans Opportunity to Work) to Hire Heroes Act (2011), 91

INDEX

Waller, Willard, 12
Walter Reed Army Medical Center, 62, 65
War Department, 93, 102
Warlock system, 38
Warrior Ethos, 40–41
War Risk Insurance Act of 1917, 11
Washington, George, 8, 9, 117
Wayne, John, 17, 147–48
Webb, James, 108, 111, 125–26, 129, 162
Weigley, Russell, 5, 33–34
White, John P., 69
Wicker, Tom, 53–54
Wilkins, Roy, 19
Willenz, June A., 142
Williams, Ted, 14
Winkler, Henry, 150
Winter Soldier Investigation (1971), 15, 49
Winter Soldier: Iraq and Afghanistan (2008), 114
Women Marines Association, 142
Women's Armed Services Integration Act (1948), 21, 133
Women's Army Corps Veterans' Association, 142
Women Veterans Interactive, 144
World War I, 11, 12, 13, 18, 46
World War II, 2–3, 4, 12, 14, 18, 21, 23, 31, 37, 45, 59, 75, 93, 151, 160; casualties in, 61; combat in, 40; comparison to subsequent conflicts, 32, 35, 48, 50, 53, 64, 67, 77, 82, 88, 91, 100, 102, 115, 122, 148, 161; corporations and, 37, 78–79, 94–95, 119; economic boom following, 78–79; education and, 102–3, 107, 109–10; federal policy and, 101; immigrants and, 11; and politics, 6, 118–21, 128; training for, 36; Veterans Administration and, 13; veterans' health care and, 63, 65; veterans in society, 58, 60; women and, 85, 97, 133–35, 139
Wounded Warrior Project, 77, 115

Yarborough, Ralph W., 120–21, 161
YouTube, 41, 58, 96